THE ESSENTIAL RUTH BADER GINSBURG

KEY MAJORITY, CONCURRING, AND DISSENTING
SUPREME COURT OPINIONS

Edited by
LAWYER'S REFERENCE GUIDES

The Supreme Court opinions published in this edition are unofficial, unpublished versions, may include minor editorial revisions to the text, and are presented "as is." These opinions are in the public domain as U.S. Government works and are available to the public at www. supremecourt.gov. They should not be relied upon as official versions. This publication is sold with the understanding that the Publisher is not engaged in rendering legal, accounting, or other professional advice. If legal advice or other expert assistance is required, the services of a competent professional should be sought.

This book is not authorized by the Supreme Court of the United States, the Government Printing Office, Justice Ginsburg, or her estate. No endorsement is implied or intended.

Introductions and the collection and selection of the contents © 2020 by Lawyer's Reference Guides.

All rights reserved.

No part of this book may be reproduced in any form or by any electronic or mechanical means, including information storage and retrieval systems, without written permission from the publisher, except for the use of brief quotations in a book review.

CONTENTS

PUBLISHER'S PREFACE

Ruth Bader Ginsburg (1933-2020) was a trail-blazing attorney and an iconic Supreme Court Justice. She has left America a lasting legacy through the example of her life and voluminous paper trail — 483 majority, concurring, or dissenting opinions for the Supreme Court. This volume provides a curated sample of her opinions, allowing the reader to witness in her own words the worldview she embraced and the vision she had for society. Each opinion is introduced with a brief explanation of the case and issues presented.

Like many Supreme Court justices, Ruth Bader Ginsburg's views were not without detractors or controversy. The opinions expressed herein are at times contentious, and some are at odds with accepted precedent or majority views. But they are thoroughly researched and well-written, and always thought-provoking.

For anyone concerned about the rights of women, minorities, employees, the disabled, the accused — for anyone concerned about voting rights, the environment, health care — for anyone concerned about the role of Article III judges within our system of government — Justice Ginsburg's writings are essential reading. Agree or disagree, they should be studied, understood, and respected.

SELECTED MAJORITY
OPINIONS

UNITED STATES V. VIRGINIA

518 U.S. 515 (1996)

This case centers on the Virginia Military Institute — a public university — and its long-standing male-only admissions policy. The plaintiff alleged that VMI, as a public school, was violating the Equal Protection Clause of the Fourteenth Amendment by not admitting female cadets. VMI argued that its sponsorship of a separate academic program for female students at another institution assuaged equal protection concerns. While there has been a long history single-sex colleges, at the time of the decision, VMI was the last remaining male-only public university in America.

In a 7-1 decision authored by Justice Ginsburg, the Court ruled that the male-only policy was a violation the Equal Protection Clause of the Fourteenth Amendment, as there was no "exceedingly persuasive justification" for it.

Justice Ginsburg's opinion was joined by Justices Stevens, O'Connor, Kennedy, Souter, and Breyer. Justice Rehnquist wrote a separate concurrence, and Justice Scalia dissented. Justice Thomas recused himself, as his son was enrolled at VMI.

UNITED STATES V. VIRGINIA

518 U.S. 515 (1996)

Virginia's public institutions of higher learning include an incomparable military college, Virginia Military Institute (VMI). The United States maintains that the Constitution's equal protection guarantee precludes Virginia from reserving exclusively to men the unique educational opportunities VMI affords. We agree.

I

Founded in 1839, VMI is today the sole single-sex school among Virginia's 15 public institutions of higher learning. VMI's distinctive mission is to produce "citizen-soldiers," men prepared for leadership in civilian life and in military service. VMI pursues this mission through pervasive training of a kind not available anywhere else in Virginia. Assigning prime place to character development, VMI uses an "adversative method" modeled on English public schools and once characteristic of military instruction. VMI constantly endeavors to instill physical and mental discipline in its cadets and impart to them a strong moral code. The school's graduates leave VMI with heightened comprehension of their capacity to deal with duress and stress, and a large sense of accomplishment for completing the hazardous course.

VMI has notably succeeded in its mission to produce leaders; among its alumni are military generals, Members of Congress, and business executives. The school's alumni overwhelmingly perceive that their VMI training helped them to realize their personal goals. VMI's endowment reflects the loyalty of its graduates; VMI has the largest per-student endowment of all public under-graduate institutions in the Nation.

Neither the goal of producing citizen-soldiers nor VMI's implementing methodology is inherently unsuitable to women. And the school's impressive record in producing leaders has made admission desirable to some women. Nevertheless, Virginia has elected to preserve exclusively for men the advantages and opportunities a VMI education affords.

II

A

From its establishment in 1839 as one of the Nation's first state military colleges, see 1839 Va. Acts, ch. 20, VMI has remained financially supported by Virginia and "subject to the control of the [Virginia] General Assembly," Va. Code Ann. §23-92 (1993). First southern college to teach engineering and industrial chemistry, see H. Wise, Drawing Out the Man: The VMI Story 13 (1978) (The VMI Story), VMI once provided teachers for the Commonwealth's schools, see 1842 Va. Acts, ch. 24, §2 (requiring every cadet to teach in one of the Commonwealth's schools for a 2-year period).[1] Civil War strife threatened the school's vitality, but a resourceful superintendent regained legislative support by highlighting "VMI's great potential[,] through its technical know-how," to advance Virginia's postwar recovery. The VMI Story 47.

VMI today enrolls about 1,300 men as cadets.[2] Its academic offerings in the liberal arts, sciences, and engineering are also available at other public colleges and universities in Virginia. But VMI's mission is special. It is the mission of the school

"to produce educated and honorable men, prepared for the varied work of civil life, imbued with love of learning, confident in the functions and attitudes of leadership, possessing a high sense of public service, advocates of the American democracy and free enterprise system, and ready as citizen-soldiers to defend their country in time of national peril.'" 766 F. Supp. 1407, 1425 (WD Va. 1991) (quoting Mission Study Committee of the VMI Board of Visitors, Report, May 16, 1986).

In contrast to the federal service academies, institutions maintained "to prepare cadets for career service in the armed forces," VMI's program "is directed at preparation for both military and civilian life"; "[o]nly about 15% of VMI cadets enter career military service." 766 F. Supp., at 1432.

VMI produces its "citizen-soldiers" through "an adversative, or doubting, model of education" which features "[physical rigor, mental stress, absolute equality of treatment, absence of privacy, minute regulation of behavior, and indoctrination in desirable values." at 1421. As one Commandant of Cadets described it, the adversarial method "'dissects the young student,'" and makes him aware of his "'limits and capabilities,'" so that he knows "'how far he can go with his anger, . . . how much he can take under stress, . . . exactly what he can do when he is physically exhausted.'" *Id.*, at 1421-1422 (quoting Col. N. Bissell).

VMI cadets live in spartan barracks where surveillance is constant and privacy nonexistent; they wear uniforms, eat together in the mess hall, and regularly participate in drills. *Id.*, at 1424, 1432. Entering students are incessantly exposed to the rat line, "an extreme form of the adversarial model," comparable in intensity to Marine Corps boot camp. *Id.*, at 1422. Tormenting and punishing, the rat line bonds new cadets to their fellow sufferers and, when they have completed the 7-month experience, to their former tormentors. *Ibid.*

VMI's "adversarial model" is further characterized by a hierarchical "class system" of privileges and responsibilities, a "dyke system" for assigning a senior class mentor to each entering class "rat," and a stringently enforced "honor code," which prescribes that a cadet " 'does not lie, cheat, steal nor tolerate those who do.'" *Id.*, at 1422-1423.

VMI attracts some applicants because of its reputation as an extraordinarily challenging military school, and "because its alumni are exceptionally close to the school." at 1421. "[W]omen have no opportunity anywhere to gain the benefits of [the system of education at VMI]." *Ibid.*

B

In 1990, prompted by a complaint filed with the Attorney General by a female high-school student seeking admission to VMI, the United States sued the Commonwealth of Virginia and VMI, alleging that VMI's exclusively male admission policy violated the Equal Protection Clause of the Fourteenth Amendment. *Id.*, at 1408.[3] Trial of the action consumed six days and involved an array of expert witnesses on each side. *Ibid.*

In the two years preceding the lawsuit, the District Court noted, VMI had received inquiries from 347 women, but had responded to none of them. *Id.*, at 1436. "[S]ome women, at least," the court said, "would want to attend the school if they had the opportunity." *Id.*, at 1414. The court further recognized that, with recruitment, VMI could "achieve at least 10% female enrollment"—"a sufficient 'critical mass' to provide the female cadets with a positive educational experience." *Id.*, at 1437-1438. And it was also established that "some women are capable of all of the individual activities required of VMI cadets." *Id.*, at 1412. In addition, experts agreed that if VMI admitted women, "the VMI ROTC experience would become a better training program from the perspective of the armed forces, because it would provide training in dealing with a mixed-gender army." *Id.,* at 1441.

The District Court ruled in favor of VMI, however, and rejected the equal protection challenge pressed by the United States. That court correctly recognized that *Mississippi Univ. for Women v. Hogan,* 458 U.S. 718 (1982), was the closest guide. 766 F. Supp., at 1410. There, this Court underscored that a party seeking to uphold government action based on sex must establish an "exceedingly persuasive justification" for the classification. *Mississippi Univ. for Women,* 458 U.S., at 724 (internal quotation marks omitted). To succeed, the defender of the challenged action must show "at least that the classification serves important governmental objectives and that the discriminatory means employed are substantially related to the achievement of those objectives." *Ibid,* (internal quotation marks omitted).

The District Court reasoned that education in "a single-gender environment, be it male or female," yields substantial benefits. 766 F. Supp., at 1415. VMI's school for men brought diversity to an otherwise coeducational Virginia system, and that diversity was "enhanced by VMI's unique method of instruction." *Ibid.* If single-gender education for males ranks as an important governmental objective, it becomes obvious, the District Court concluded, that the only means of achieving the objective "is to exclude women from the all-male institution—VMI." *Ibid.*

"Women are [indeed] denied a unique educational opportunity that is available only at VMI," the District Court acknowledged. *Id.,* at 1432. But "[VMI's] single-sex status would be lost, and some aspects of the [school's] distinctive method would be altered," if women were admitted, *id.,* at 1413: "Allowance for personal privacy would have to be made," *id.,* at 1412; "[p]hysical education requirements would have to be altered, at least for the women," *id.,* at 1413; the adversative environment could not survive unmodified, *id.,* at 1412-1413. Thus, "sufficient constitutional justification" had been shown, the District Court held, "for continuing [VMI's] single-sex policy." *Id.,* at 1413.

The Court of Appeals for the Fourth Circuit disagreed and vacated the District Court's judgment. The appellate court held: "The Commonwealth of Virginia has not . . . advanced any state policy by which it can justify its determination, under an announced policy of diversity, to afford VMI's unique type of program to men and not to women." 976 F. 2d 890, 892 (1992).

The appeals court greeted with skepticism Virginia's assertion that it offers single-sex education at VMI as a facet of the Commonwealth's overarching and undisputed policy to advance "autonomy and diversity." The court underscored Virginia's nondiscrimination commitment: " '[I]t is extremely important that [colleges and universities] deal with faculty, staff, and students *without regard to sex, race, or ethnic origin.'* " *Id.,* at 899 (quoting 1990 Report of the Virginia Commission on the University of the 21st Century). "That statement," the Court of Appeals said, "is the only explicit one that we have found in the record in which the Commonwealth has expressed itself with respect to gender distinctions." 976 F. 2d, at 899. Furthermore, the appeals court observed, in urging "diversity" to justify an all-male VMI, the Commonwealth had supplied "no explanation for the movement away from [single-sex education] in Virginia by public colleges and universities." *Ibid.* In short, the court concluded, "[a] policy of diversity which aims to provide an array of educational opportunities, including single-gender institutions, must do more than favor one gender." *Ibid.*

The parties agreed that "some women can meet the physical standards now imposed on men," *id.*, at 896, and the court was satisfied that "neither the goal of producing citizen soldiers nor VMI's implementing methodology is inherently unsuitable to women," *id.*, at 899. The Court of Appeals, however, accepted the District Court's finding that "at least these three aspects of VMI's program—physical training, the absence of privacy, and the adversative approach—would be materially affected by coeducation." *Id.*, at 896-897. Remanding the case, the appeals court assigned to Virginia, in the first instance, responsibility for selecting a remedial course. The court suggested these options for the Commonwealth: Admit women to VMI; establish parallel institutions or programs; or abandon state support, leaving VMI free to pursue its policies as a private institution. at 900. In May 1993, this Court denied certiorari. See 508 U.S. 946; see also *ibid,* (opinion of Scalia, J., noting the interlocutory posture of the litigation).

C

In response to the Fourth Circuit's ruling, Virginia proposed a parallel program for women: Virginia Women's Institute for Leadership (VWIL). The 4-year, state-sponsored undergraduate program would be located at Mary Baldwin College, a private liberal arts school for women, and would be open, initially, to about 25 to 30 students. Although VWIL would share VMI's mission—to produce "citizen- soldiers"—the VWIL program would differ, as does Mary Baldwin College, from VMI in academic offerings, methods of education, and financial resources. See 852 F. Supp. 471, 476-477 (WD Va. 1994).

The average combined SAT score of entrants at Mary Baldwin is about 100 points lower than the score for VMI freshmen. See *id.*, at 501. Mary Baldwin's faculty holds "significantly fewer Ph. D.'s than the faculty at VMI," *id.*, at 502, and receives significantly lower salaries, see Tr. 158 (testimony of James Lott, Dean of Mary Baldwin College), reprinted in 2 App. in Nos. 94-1667 and 94-1717 (CA4) (hereinafter Tr.). While VMI offers degrees in liberal arts, the sciences, and engineering, Mary Baldwin, at the time of trial, offered only bachelor of arts degrees. See 852 F. Supp., at 503. A VWIL student seeking to earn an engineering degree could gain one, without public support, by attending Washington University in St. Louis, Missouri, for two years, paying the required private tuition. See *ibid.*

Experts in educating women at the college level composed the Task Force charged with designing the VWIL program; Task Force members were drawn from Mary Baldwin's own faculty and staff. *Id.*, at 476. Training its attention on methods of instruction appropriate for "most women," the Task Force determined that a military model would be "wholly inappropriate" for VWIL. *Ibid.*; see 44 F. 3d 1229, 1233 (CA4 1995).

VWIL students would participate in ROTC programs and a newly established, "largely ceremonial" Virginia Corps of Cadets, *id.*, at 1234, but the VWIL House would not have a military format, 852 F. Supp., at 477, and VWIL would not require its students to eat meals together or to wear uniforms during the schoolday, *id.*, at 495. In lieu of VMI's adversative method, the VWIL Task Force favored "a cooperative method which reinforces self-esteem." *Id.*, at 476. In addition to the standard bachelor of arts program offered at Mary Baldwin, VWIL students would take courses in leadership, complete an off-campus leadership externship, participate in community service projects, and assist in arranging a speaker series. See 44 F. 3d, at 1234.

Virginia represented that it will provide equal financial support for in-state VWIL students and VMI cadets, 852 F. Supp., at 483, and the VMI Foundation agreed to supply a $5.4625 million endowment for the VWIL program, *id.*, at 499. Mary Baldwin's own endowment is about $19 million; VMI's is $131 million. *Id.*, at 503. Mary Baldwin will add $35 million to its endowment based on future commitments; VMI will add $220 million. *Ibid.* The VMI Alumni Association has developed a network of employers interested in hiring VMI graduates. The Association has agreed to open its network to VWIL graduates, *id.*, at 499, but those graduates will not have the advantage afforded by a VMI degree.

D

Virginia returned to the District Court seeking approval of its proposed remedial plan, and the court decided the plan met the requirements of the Equal Protection Clause. *Id.*, at 473. The District Court again acknowledged evidentiary support for these determinations: "[T]he VMI methodology could be used to educate women and, in fact, some women . . . may prefer the VMI methodology to the VWIL methodology." *Id.*, at 481. But the "controlling legal principles," the District Court decided, "do not require the Commonwealth to provide a mirror image VMI for women." *Ibid.* The court anticipated that the two schools would "achieve substantially similar outcomes." *Ibid.* It concluded: "If VMI marches to the beat of a drum, then Mary Baldwin marches to the melody of a fife and when the march is over, both will have arrived at the same destination." *Id.*, at 484.

A divided Court of Appeals affirmed the District Court's judgment. 44 F. 3d 1229 (CA4 1995). This time, the appellate court determined to give "greater scrutiny to the selection of means than to the [Commonwealth's] proffered objective." *Id.*, at 1236. The official objective or purpose, the court said, should be reviewed deferentially. *Ibid.* Respect for the "legislative will," the court reasoned, meant that the judiciary should take a "cautious approach," inquiring into the "legitima[cy]" of the governmental objective and refusing approval for any purpose revealed to be "pernicious." *Ibid.*

"[Providing the option of a single-gender college education may be considered a legitimate and important aspect of a public system of higher education," the appeals court observed, *id.*, at 1238; that objective, the court added, is "not pernicious," *id.*, at 1239. Moreover, the court continued, the adversative method vital to a VMI education "has never been tolerated in a sexually heterogeneous environment." *Ibid.* The method itself "was not designed to exclude women," the court noted, but women could not be accommodated in the VMI program, the court believed, for female participation in VMI's adversative training "would destroy . . . any sense of decency that still permeates the relationship between the sexes." *Ibid.*

Having determined, deferentially, the legitimacy of Virginia's purpose, the court considered the question of means. Exclusion of "men at Mary Baldwin College and women at VMI," the court said, was essential to Virginia's purpose, for without such exclusion, the Commonwealth could not "accomplish [its] objective of providing single-gender education." *Ibid.*

The court recognized that, as it analyzed the case, means merged into end, and the merger risked "bypassing] any equal protection scrutiny." *Id.*, at 1237. The court therefore added another inquiry, a decisive test it called "substantive comparability." *Ibid.* The key question, the court said, was whether men at VMI and women at VWIL would obtain "substantively comparable benefits at their institution or through other means offered by the [S]tate." *Ibid.* Although the appeals court recognized that the VWIL degree "lacks the historical benefit and prestige" of a VMI degree, it nevertheless found the educational opportunities at the two schools "sufficiently comparable." *Id.*, at 1241.

Senior Circuit Judge Phillips dissented. The court, in his judgment, had not held Virginia to the burden of showing an "'exceedingly persuasive [justification]'" for the Commonwealth's action. *Id.*, at 1247 (quoting *Mississippi Univ. for Women*, 458 U.S., at 724). In Judge Phillips' view, the court had accepted "rationalizations compelled by the exigencies of this litigation," and had not confronted the Commonwealth's "actual overriding purpose." 44 F. 3d, at 1247. That purpose, Judge Phillips said, was clear from the historical record; it was "not to create a new type of educational opportunity for women, . . . nor to further diversify the Commonwealth's higher education system[,] . . . but [was] simply . . . to allow VMI to continue to exclude women in order to preserve its historic character and mission." *Ibid.*

Judge Phillips suggested that the Commonwealth would satisfy the Constitution's equal protection requirement if it "simultaneously opened single-gender undergraduate institutions having substantially comparable curricular and extra-curricular programs, funding, physical plant, administration and support services, and faculty and library resources." *Id.,* at 1250. But he thought it evident that the proposed VWIL program, in comparison to VMI, fell "far short . . . from providing substantially equal tangible and intangible educational benefits to men and women." *Ibid.*

The Fourth Circuit denied rehearing en banc. 52 F. 3d 90 (1995). Circuit Judge Motz, joined by Circuit Judges Hall, Murnaghan, and Michael, filed a dissenting opinion.[4] Judge Motz agreed with Judge Phillips that Virginia had not shown an "'exceedingly persuasive justification'" for the disparate opportunities the Commonwealth supported. *Id.,* at 92 (quoting *Mississippi Univ. for Women,* 458 U.S., at 724). She asked: "[H]ow can a degree from a yet to be implemented supplemental program at Mary Baldwin be held 'substantively comparable' to a degree from a venerable Virginia military institution that was established more than 150 years ago?" 52 F. 3d, at 93. "Women need not be guaranteed equal 'results,' " Judge Motz said, "but the Equal Protection Clause does require equal opportunity . . . [and] that opportunity is being denied here." *Ibid.*

III

The cross-petitions in this suit present two ultimate issues. First, does Virginia's exclusion of women from the educational opportunities provided by VMI—extraordinary opportunities for military training and civilian leadership development—deny to women "capable of all of the individual activities required of VMI cadets," 766 F. Supp., at 1412, the equal protection of the laws guaranteed by the Fourteenth Amendment? Second, if VMI's "unique" situation, *id.,* at 1413—as Virginia's sole single-sex public institution of higher education—offends the Constitution's equal protection principle, what is the remedial requirement?

IV

We note, once again, the core instruction of this Court's pathmarking decisions in J E. B. v. Alabama ex rel. T. B., 511 U.S. 127,136-137, and n. 6 (1994), and *Mississippi Univ. for Women,* 458 U.S., at 724 (internal quotation marks omitted):

Parties who seek to defend gender-based government action must demonstrate an "exceedingly persuasive justification" for that action.

Today's skeptical scrutiny of official action denying rights or opportunities based on sex responds to volumes of history. As a plurality of this Court acknowledged a generation ago, "our Nation has had a long and unfortunate history of sex discrimination." *Frontiero v. Richardson*, 411 U.S. 677, 684 (1973). Through a century plus three decades and more of that history, women did not count among voters composing "We the People";[5] not until 1920 did women gain a constitutional right to the franchise. at 685. And for a half century thereafter, it remained the prevailing doctrine that government, both federal and state, could withhold from women opportunities accorded men so long as any "basis in reason" could be conceived for the discrimination. *See, e.g., Goesaert v. Cleary*, 335 U.S. 464, 467 (1948) (rejecting challenge of female tavern owner and her daughter to Michigan law denying bartender licenses to females—except for wives and daughters of male tavern owners; Court would not "give ear" to the contention that "an unchivalrous desire of male bartenders to . . . monopolize the calling" prompted the legislation).

In 1971, for the first time in our Nation's history, this Court ruled in favor of a woman who complained that her State had denied her the equal protection of its laws. *Reed v. Reed*, 404 U.S. 71, 73 (holding unconstitutional Idaho Code prescription that, among "'several persons claiming and equally entitled to administer [a decedent's estate], males must be preferred to females' "). Since *Reed*, the Court has repeatedly recognized that neither federal nor state government acts compatibly with the equal protection principle when a law or official policy denies to women, simply because they are women, full citizenship stature—equal opportunity to aspire, achieve, participate in and contribute to society based on their individual talents and capacities. *See, e.g., Kirchberg v. Feenstra*, 450 U.S. 455, 462-463 (1981) (affirming invalidity of Louisiana law that made husband "head and master" of property jointly owned with his wife, giving him unilateral right to dispose of such property without his wife's consent); *Stanton v. Stanton*, 421 U.S. 7 (1975) (invalidating Utah requirement that parents support boys until age 21, girls only until age 18).

Without equating gender classifications, for all purposes, to classifications based on race or national origin,[6] the Court, in post *Reed* decisions, has carefully inspected official action that closes a door or denies opportunity to women (or to men). See *J. E. B.*, 511 U.S., at 152 (KENNEDY, J., concurring in judgment) (case law evolving since 1971 "reveal[s] a strong presumption that gender classifications are invalid"). To summarize the Court's current directions for cases of official classification based on gender: Focusing on the differential treatment or denial of opportunity for which relief is sought, the reviewing court must determine whether the proffered justification is "exceedingly persuasive." The burden of justification is demanding and it rests entirely on the State. See *Mississippi Univ. for Women*, 458 U.S., at 724. The State must show "at least that the [challenged] classification serves 'important governmental objectives and that the discriminatory means employed' are 'substantially related to the achievement of those objectives.' " *Ibid*, (quoting *Wengler v. Druggists Mut. Ins. Co.*, 446 U.S. 142, 150 (1980)). The justification must be genuine, not hypothesized or invented post hoc in response to litigation. And it must not rely on overbroad generalizations about the different talents, capacities, or preferences of males and females. See *Weinberger v. Wiesenfeld*, 420 U.S. 636, 643, 648 (1975); *Califano v. Goldfarb*, 430 U.S. 199, 223-224 (1977) (STEVENS, J., concurring in judgment).

The heightened review standard our precedent establishes does not make sex a proscribed classification. Supposed "inherent differences" are no longer accepted as a ground for race or national origin classifications. See *Loving v. Virginia*, 388 U.S. 1 (1967). Physical differences between men and women, however, are enduring: "[T]he two sexes are not fungible; a community made up exclusively of one [sex] is different from a community composed of both." *Ballard v. United States*, 329 U.S. 187, 193 (1946).

"Inherent differences" between men and women, we have come to appreciate, remain cause for celebration, but not for denigration of the members of either sex or for artificial constraints on an individual's opportunity. Sex classifications may be used to compensate women "for particular economic disabilities [they have] suffered," *Califano v. Webster*, 430 U.S. 313, 320 (1977) (*per curiam*), to "promot[e] equal employment opportunity," see *California Fed. Sav. & Loan Assn. v. Guerra*, 479 U.S. 272, 289 (1987), to advance full development of the talent and capacities of our Nation's people.[7] But such classifications may not be used, as they once were, see *Goesaert*, 335 U.S., at 467, to create or perpetuate the legal, social, and economic inferiority of women.

Measuring the record in this case against the review standard just described, we conclude that Virginia has shown no "exceedingly persuasive justification" for excluding all women from the citizen-soldier training afforded by VMI. We therefore affirm the Fourth Circuit's initial judgment, which held that Virginia had violated the Fourteenth Amendment's Equal Protection Clause. Because the remedy proffered by Virginia—the Mary Baldwin VWIL program—does not cure the constitutional violation, *i.e.*, it does not provide equal opportunity, we reverse the Fourth Circuit's final judgment in this case.

V

The Fourth Circuit initially held that Virginia had advanced no state policy by which it could justify, under equal protection principles, its determination "to afford VMI's unique type of program to men and not to women." 976 F. 2d, at 892. Virginia challenges that "liability" ruling and asserts two justifications in defense of VMI's exclusion of women. First, the Commonwealth contends, "single-sex education provides important educational benefits," Brief for Cross-Petitioners 20, and the option of single-sex education contributes to "diversity in educational approaches," at 25. Second, the Commonwealth argues, "the unique VMI method of character development and leadership training," the school's adversative approach, would have to be modified were VMI to admit women. *Id.*, at 33-36 (internal quotation marks omitted). We consider these two justifications in turn.

A

Single-sex education affords pedagogical benefits to at least some students, Virginia emphasizes, and that reality is uncontested in this litigation.[8] Similarly, it is not disputed that diversity among public educational institutions can serve the public good. But Virginia has not shown that VMI was established, or has been maintained, with a view to diversifying, by its categorical exclusion of women, educational opportunities within the Commonwealth. In cases of this genre, our precedent instructs that "benign" justifications proffered in defense of categorical exclusions will not be accepted automatically; a tenable justification must describe actual state purposes, not rationalizations for actions in fact differently grounded. See *Wiesenfeld*, 420 U.S., at 648, and n. 16 ("mere recitation of a benign [or] compensatory purpose" does not block "inquiry into the actual purposes" of government-maintained gender-based classifications); *Goldfarb*, 430 U.S., at 212-213 (rejecting government-proffered purposes after "inquiry into the actual purposes" (internal quotation marks omitted)).

Mississippi Univ. for Women is immediately in point. There the State asserted, in justification of its exclusion of men from a nursing school, that it was engaging in "educational affirmative action" by "compensating] for discrimination against women." 458 U.S., at 727. Undertaking a "searching analysis," *id.*, at 728, the Court found no close resemblance between "the alleged objective" and "the actual purpose underlying the discriminatory classification," *id.*, at 730. Pursuing a similar inquiry here, we reach the same conclusion.

Neither recent nor distant history bears out Virginia's alleged pursuit of diversity through single-sex educational options. In 1839, when the Commonwealth established VMI, a range of educational opportunities for men and women was scarcely contemplated. Higher education at the time was considered dangerous for women;[9] reflecting widely held views about women's proper place, the Nation's first universities and colleges—for example, Harvard in Massachusetts, William and Mary in Virginia—admitted only men.

See E. Farello, A History of the Education of Women in the United States 163 (1970). VMI was not at all novel in this respect: In admitting no women, VMI followed the lead of the Commonwealth's flagship school, the University of Virginia, founded in 1819.

"[N]o struggle for the admission of women to a state university," a historian has recounted, "was longer drawn out, or developed more bitterness, than that at the University of Virginia." 2 T. Woody, A History of Women's Education in the United States 254 (1929) (History of Women's Education). In 1879, the State Senate resolved to look into the possibility of higher education for women, recognizing that Virginia " 'has never, at any period of her history,' " provided for the higher education of her daughters, though she " 'has liberally provided for the higher education of her sons.'" Ibid, (quoting 10 Educ. J. Va. 212 (1879)). Despite this recognition, no new opportunities were instantly open to women.[10]

Virginia eventually provided for several women's seminaries and colleges. Farmville Female Seminary became a public institution in 1884. See supra, at 521, n. 2. Two women's schools, Mary Washington College and James Madison University, were founded in 1908; another, Radford University, was founded in 1910. 766 F. Supp., at 1418-1419. By the mid-1970's, all four schools had become coeducational.

Debate concerning women's admission as undergraduates at the main university continued well past the century's midpoint. Familiar arguments were rehearsed. If women were admitted, it was feared, they "would encroach on the rights of men; there would be new problems of government, perhaps scandals; the old honor system would have to be changed; standards would be lowered to those of other coeducational schools; and the glorious reputation of the university, as a school for men, would be trailed in the dust." 2 History of Women's Education 255.

Ultimately, in 1970, "the most prestigious institution of higher education in Virginia," the University of Virginia, introduced coeducation and, in 1972, began to admit women on an equal basis with men. See Kirstein v. Rector and Visitors of Univ. of Virginia, 309 F. Supp. 184, 186 (ED Va. 1970). A three-judge Federal District Court confirmed: "Virginia may not now deny to women, on the basis of sex, educational opportunities at the Charlottesville campus that are not afforded in other institutions operated by the [S]tate." Id., at 187.

Virginia describes the current absence of public single-sex higher education for women as "an historical anomaly." Brief for Cross-Petitioners 30. But the historical record indicates action more deliberate than anomalous: First, protection of women against higher education; next, schools for women far from equal in resources and stature to schools for men; finally, conversion of the separate schools to coeducation. The state legislature, prior to the advent of this controversy, had repealed "[a]ll Virginia statutes requiring individual institutions to admit only men or women." 766 F. Supp., at 1419. And in 1990, an official commission, "legislatively established to chart the future goals of higher education in Virginia," reaffirmed the policy " 'of affording broad access" while maintaining "autonomy and diversity.'" 976 F. 2d, at 898-899 (quoting Report of the Virginia Commission on the University of the 21st Century). Significantly, the commission reported:

> "'Because colleges and universities provide opportunities for students to develop values and learn from role models, it is extremely important that they deal with faculty, staff, and students without regard to sex, race, or ethnic origin.'" *Id.*, at 899 (emphasis supplied by Court of Appeals deleted).

This statement, the Court of Appeals observed, "is the only explicit one that we have found in the record in which the Commonwealth has expressed itself with respect to gender distinctions." *Ibid.*

Our 1982 decision in *Mississippi Univ. Women* prompted VMI to reexamine its male-only admission policy. See 766 F. Supp., at 1427-1428. Virginia relies on that reexamination as a legitimate basis for maintaining VMI's single-sex character. See Reply Brief for Cross-Petitioners 6. A Mission Study Committee, appointed by the VMI Board of Visitors, studied the problem from October 1983 until May 1986, and in that month counseled against "change of VMI status as a single-sex college." See 766 F. Supp., at 1429 (internal quotation marks omitted). Whatever internal purpose the Mission Study Committee served—and however well-meaning the framers of the report—we can hardly extract from that effort any commonwealth policy even- handedly to advance diverse educational options. As the District Court observed, the Committee's analysis "primarily focuse[d] on anticipated difficulties in attracting females to VMI," and the report, overall, supplied "very little indication of how th[e] conclusion was reached." *Ibid.*

In sum, we find no persuasive evidence in this record that VMI's male-only admission policy "is in furtherance of a state policy of 'diversity.'" See 976 F. 2d, at 899. No such policy, the Fourth Circuit observed, can be discerned from the movement of all other public colleges and universities in Virginia away from single-sex education. See *ibid.* That court also questioned "how one institution with autonomy, but with no authority over any other state institution, can give effect to a state policy of diversity among institutions." *Ibid.* A purpose genuinely to advance an array of educational options, as the Court of Appeals recognized, is not served by VMI's historic and constant plan—a plan to "affor[d] a unique educational benefit only to males." *Ibid.* However "liberally" this plan serves the Commonwealth's sons, it makes no provision whatever for her daughters. That is not equal protection.

B

Virginia next argues that VMTs adversative method of training provides educational benefits that cannot be made available, unmodified, to women. Alterations to accommodate women would necessarily be "radical," so "drastic," Virginia asserts, as to transform, indeed "destroy," VMI's program. See Brief for Cross-Petitioners 34-36. Neither sex would be favored by the transformation, Virginia maintains: Men would be deprived of the unique opportunity currently available to them; women would not gain that opportunity because their participation would "eliminat[e] the very aspects of [the] program that distinguish [VMI] from . . . other institutions of higher education in Virginia." *Id.*, at 34.

The District Court forecast from expert witness testimony, and the Court of Appeals accepted, that coeducation would materially affect "at least these three aspects of VMI's program—physical training, the absence of privacy, and the adversative approach." 976 F. 2d, at 896-897. And it is uncontested that women's admission would require accommodations, primarily in arranging housing assignments and physical training programs for female cadets. See Brief for Cross-Respondent 11, 29-30. It is also undisputed, however, that "the VMI methodology could be used to educate women." 852 F. Supp., at 481. The District Court even allowed that some women may prefer it to the methodology a women's college might pursue. See *ibid.* "[S]ome women, at least, would want to attend [VMI] if they had the opportunity," the District Court recognized, 766 F. Supp., at 1414, and "some women," the expert testimony established, "are capable of all of the individual activities required of VMI cadets," *id.*, at 1412. The parties, furthermore, agree that " some women can meet the physical standards [VMI] now impose[s] on men." 976 F. 2d, at 896. In sum, as the Court of Appeals stated, "neither the goal of producing citizen soldiers," VMI's raison d'etre, "nor VMI's implementing methodology is inherently unsuitable to women." *Id.*, at 899.

In support of its initial judgment for Virginia, a judgment rejecting all equal protection objections presented by the United States, the District Court made "findings" on "gender-based developmental differences." 766 F. Supp., at 1434-1435. These "findings" restate the opinions of Virginia's expert witnesses, opinions about typically male or typically female "tendencies." *Id.*, at 1434. For example, "[m]ales tend to need an atmosphere of adversativeness," while "[f]emales tend to thrive in a cooperative atmosphere." *Ibid.* "I'm not saying that some women don't do well under [the] adversative model," VMI's expert on educational institutions testified, "undoubtedly there are some [women] who do"; but educational experiences must be designed "around the rule," this expert maintained, and not "around the exception." *Ibid*, (internal quotation marks omitted).

The United States does not challenge any expert witness estimation on average capacities or preferences of men and women. Instead, the United States emphasizes that time and again since this Court's turning point decision in *Reed v. Reed*, 404 U.S. 71 (1971), we have cautioned reviewing courts to take a "hard look" at generalizations or "tendencies" of the kind pressed by Virginia, and relied upon by the District Court. See O'Connor, Portia's Progress, 66 N. Y. U. L. Rev. 1546,1551 (1991). State actors controlling gates to opportunity, we have instructed, may not exclude qualified individuals based on "fixed notions concerning the roles and abilities of males and females." *Mississippi Univ. for Women*, 458 U.S., at 725; see *J. E. B.*, 511 U.S., at 139, n. 11 (equal protection principles, as applied to gender classifications, mean state actors may not rely on "overbroad" generalizations to make "judgments about people that are likely to . . . perpetuate historical patterns of discrimination").

It may be assumed, for purposes of this decision, that most women would not choose VMI's adversative method. As Fourth Circuit Judge Motz observed, however, in her dissent from the Court of Appeals' denial of rehearing en banc, it is also probable that "many men would not want to be educated in such an environment." 52 F. 3d, at 93. (On that point, even our dissenting colleague might agree.) Education, to be sure, is not a "one size fits all" business. The issue, however, is not whether "women—or men—should be forced to attend VMI"; rather, the question is whether the Commonwealth can constitutionally deny to women who have the will and capacity, the training and attendant opportunities that VMI uniquely affords. *Ibid.*

The notion that admission of women would downgrade VMI's stature, destroy the adversative system and, with it, even the school,[11] is a judgment hardly proved,[12] a prediction hardly different from other "self-fulfilling prophecies]," see *Mississippi Univ. for Women*, 458 U.S., at 730, once routinely used to deny rights or opportunities. When women first sought admission to the bar and access to legal education, concerns of the same order were expressed. For example, in 1876, the Court of Common Pleas of Hennepin County, Minnesota, explained why women were thought ineligible for the practice of law. Women train and educate the young, the court said, which

> "forbids that they shall bestow that time (early and late) and labor, so essential in attaining to the eminence to which the true lawyer should ever aspire. It cannot therefore be said that the opposition of courts to the admission of females to practice . . . is to any extent the outgrowth of . . . 'old fogyism[.]' . . . [I]t arises rather from a comprehension of the magnitude of the responsibilities connected with the successful practice of law, and a desire to grade up the profession." In re Application of Martha Angle Dorsett to Be Admitted to Practice as Attorney and Counselor at Law (Minn. C. P. Hennepin Cty., 1876), in The Syllabi, Oct. 21,1876, pp. 5, 6 (emphasis added).

A like fear, according to a 1925 report, accounted for Columbia Law School's resistance to women's admission, although

> "[t]he faculty . . . never maintained that women could not master legal learning . . . . No, its argument has been . . . more practical. If women were admitted to the Columbia Law School, [the faculty] said, then the choicer, more manly and red-blooded graduates of our great universities would go to the Harvard Law School!" The Nation, Feb. 18, 1925, p. 173.

Medical faculties similarly resisted men and women as partners in the study of medicine. See R. Morantz-Sanchez, Sympathy and Science: Women Physicians in American Medicine 51-54, 250 (1985); see also M. Walsh, "Doctors Wanted: No Women Need Apply" 121-122 (1977) (quoting E. Clarke, Medical Education of Women, 4 Boston Med. & Surg. J. 345, 346 (1869) ("'God forbid that I should ever see men and women aiding each other to display with the scalpel the secrets of the reproductive system . . . .' ")); cf. supra, at 536- 537, n. 9. More recently, women seeking careers in policing encountered resistance based on fears that their presence would "undermine male solidarity," see F. Heidensohn, Women in Control? 201 (1992); deprive male partners of adequate assistance, see id., at 184-185; and lead to sexual misconduct, see C. Milton et al., Women in Policing 32-33 (1974). Field studies did not confirm these fears. See Heidensohn, supra, at 92-93; P. Bloch & D. Anderson, Policewomen on Patrol: Final Report (1974).

Women's successful entry into the federal military academies,[13] and their participation in the Nation's military forces,[14] indicate that Virginia's fears for the future of VMI may not be solidly grounded.[15] The Commonwealth's justification for excluding all women from "citizen-soldier" training for which some are qualified, in any event, cannot rank as "exceedingly persuasive," as we have explained and applied that standard.

Virginia and VMI trained their argument on "means" rather than "end," and thus misperceived our precedent. Single-sex education at VMI serves an "important governmental objective," they maintained, and exclusion of women is not only "substantially related," it is essential to that objective. By this notably circular argument, the "straightforward" test Mississippi Univ. for Women described, see 458 U.S., at 724-725, was bent and bowed.

The Commonwealth's misunderstanding and, in turn, the District Court's, is apparent from VMI's mission: to produce "citizen-soldiers, " individuals

> "'imbued with love of learning, confident in the functions and attitudes of leadership, possessing a high sense of public service, advocates of the American democracy and free enterprise system, and ready . . . to defend their country in

time of national peril.'" 766 F. Supp., at 1425 (quoting Mission Study Committee of the VMI Board of Visitors, Report, May 16, 1986).

Surely that goal is great enough to accommodate women, who today count as citizens in our American democracy equal in stature to men. Just as surely, the Commonwealth's great goal is not substantially advanced by women's categorical exclusion, in total disregard of their individual merit, from the Commonwealth's premier "citizen-soldier" corps.[16] Virginia, in sum, "has fallen far short of establishing the 'exceedingly persuasive justification,'" *Mississippi Univ. for Women*, 458 U.S., at 731, that must be the solid base for any gender-defined classification.

VI

In the second phase of the litigation, Virginia presented its remedial plan—maintain VMI as a male-only college and create VWIL as a separate program for women. The plan met District Court approval. The Fourth Circuit, in turn, deferentially reviewed the Commonwealth's proposal and decided that the two single-sex programs directly served Virginia's reasserted purposes: single-gender education, and "achieving the results of an adversative method in a military environment." See 44 F. 3d, at 1236,1239. Inspecting the VMI and VWIL educational programs to determine whether they "afford[ed] to both genders benefits comparable in substance, [if] not in form and detail," *id.*, at 1240, the Court of Appeals concluded that Virginia had arranged for men and women opportunities "sufficiently comparable" to survive equal protection evaluation, *id.*, at 1240-1241. The United States challenges this "remedial" ruling as pervasively misguided.

A

A remedial decree, this Court has said, must closely fit the constitutional violation; it must be shaped to place persons unconstitutionally denied an opportunity or advantage in "the position they would have occupied in the absence of [discrimination]." See *Milliken v. Bradley*, 433 U.S. 267, 280 (1977) (internal quotation marks omitted). The constitutional violation in this suit is the categorical exclusion of women from an extraordinary educational opportunity afforded men. A proper remedy for an unconstitutional exclusion, we have explained, aims to "eliminate [so far as possible] the discriminatory effects of the past" and to "bar like discrimination in the future." *Louisiana v. United States*, 380 U.S. 145, 154 (1965).

Virginia chose not to eliminate, but to leave untouched, VMI's exclusionary policy. For women only, however, Virginia proposed a separate program, different in kind from VMI and unequal in tangible and intangible facilities.[17] Having violated the Constitution's equal protection requirement, Virginia was obliged to show that its remedial proposal "directly address[ed] and relate[d] to" the violation, see *Milliken*, 433 U.S., at 282, *i.e.*, the equal protection denied to women ready, willing, and able to benefit from educational opportunities of the kind VMI offers. Virginia described VWIL as a "parallel program," and asserted that VWIL shares VMI's mission of producing "citizen-soldiers" and VMI's goals of providing "education, military training, mental and physical discipline, character . . . and leadership development." Brief for Respondents 24 (internal quotation marks omitted). If the VWIL program could not "elimi-nate the discriminatory effects of the past," could it at least "bar like discrimi-nation in the future"? See *Louisiana*, 380 U.S., at 154. A comparison of the programs said to be "parallel" informs our answer. In exposing the character of, and differences in, the VMI and VWIL programs, we recapitulate facts earlier presented. See *supra*, at 520-523,526-527.

VWIL affords women no opportunity to experience the rigorous military training for which VMI is famed. See 766 F. Supp., at 1413-1414 ("No other school in Virginia or in the United States, public or private, offers the same kind of rigorous military training as is available at VMI."); *id.*, at 1421 (VMI "is known to be the most challenging military school in the United States"). Instead, the VWIL program "deemphasize[s]" military education, 44 F. 3d, at 1234, and uses a "cooperative method" of education "which reinforces self-esteem," 852 F. Supp., at 476.

VWIL students participate in ROTC and a "largely ceremonial" Virginia Corps of Cadets, see 44 F. 3d, at 1234, but Virginia deliberately did not make VWIL a military institute. The VWIL House is not a military-style residence and VWIL students need not live together throughout the 4-year program, eat meals together, or wear uniforms during the schoolday. See 852 F. Supp., at 477, 495. VWIL students thus do not experience the "barracks" life "crucial to the VMI experience," the spartan living arrangements designed to foster an "egalitarian ethic." See 766 F. Supp., at 1423- 1424. "[T]he most important aspects of the VMI educational experience occur in the barracks," the District Court found, *id.*, at 1423, yet Virginia deemed that core experience nonessen-tial, indeed inappropriate, for training its female citizen-soldiers.

VWIL students receive their "leadership training" in seminars, externships, and speaker series, see 852 F. Supp., at 477, episodes and encounters lacking the "[p]hysical rigor, mental stress, . . . minute regulation of behavior, and indoctrination in desirable values" made hallmarks of VMI's citizen-soldier training, see 766 F. Supp., at 1421.[18] Kept away from the pressures, hazards, and psychological bonding characteristic of VMI's adversative training, see *id.*, at 1422, VWIL students will not know the "feeling of tremendous accomplish-ment" commonly experienced by VMI's successful cadets, *id.*, at 1426.

Virginia maintains that these methodological differences are "justified pedagogically," based on "important differences between men and women in learning and developmental needs," "psychological and sociological differences" Virginia describes as "real" and "not stereotypes." Brief for Respondents 28 (internal quotation marks omitted). The Task Force charged with developing the leadership program for women, drawn from the staff and faculty at Mary Baldwin College, "determined that a military model and, especially VMI's adversative method, would be wholly inappropriate for educating and training *most women*." 852 F. Supp., at 476 (emphasis added). See also 44 F. 3d, at 1233-1234 (noting Task Force conclusion that, while "some women would be suited to and interested in [a VMI-style experience]," VMI's adversative method "would not be effective for *women as a group*" (emphasis added)). The Commonwealth embraced the Task Force view, as did expert witnesses who testified for Virginia. See 852 F. Supp., at 480-481.

As earlier stated, see *supra*, at 541-542, generalizations about "the way women are," estimates of what is appropriate for *most women*, no longer justify denying opportunity to women whose talent and capacity place them outside the average description. Notably, Virginia never asserted that VMFs method of education suits most men. It is also revealing that Virginia accounted for its failure to make the VWIL experience "the entirely militaristic experience of VMI" on the ground that VWIL "is planned for women who do not necessarily expect to pursue military careers." 852 F. Supp., at 478. By that reasoning, VMI's "entirely militaristic" program would be inappropriate for men in general or *as a group*, for "[o]nly about 15% of VMI cadets enter career military service." See 766 F. Supp., at 1432.

In contrast to the generalizations about women on which Virginia rests, we note again these dispositive realities: VMFs "implementing methodology" is not "inherently unsuitable to women," 976 F. 2d, at 899; "some women . . . do well under [the] adversative model," 766 F. Supp., at 1434 (internal quotation marks omitted); "some women, at least, would want to attend [VMI] if they had the opportunity," *id.*, at 1414; "some women are capable of all of the individual activities required of VMI cadets," *id.*, at 1412, and "can meet the physical standards [VMI] now impose[s] on men," 976 F. 2d, at 896. It is on behalf of these women that the United States has instituted this suit, and it is for them that a remedy must be crafted,[19] a remedy that will end their exclusion from a state-supplied educational opportunity for which they are fit, a decree that will "bar like discrimination in the future." *Louisiana*, 380 U.S., at 154.

B

In myriad respects other than military training, VWIL does not qualify as VMI's equal. VWIL's student body, faculty, course offerings, and facilities hardly match VMI's. Nor can the VWIL graduate anticipate the benefits associated with VMI's 157-year history, the school's prestige, and its influential alumni network.

Mary Baldwin College, whose degree VWIL students will gain, enrolls first-year women with an average combined SAT score about 100 points lower than the average score for VMI freshmen. 852 F. Supp., at 501. The Mary Baldwin faculty holds "significantly fewer Ph. D.'s," *id.*, at 502, and receives substantially lower salaries, see Tr. 158 (testimony of James Lott, Dean of Mary Baldwin College), than the faculty at VMI.

Mary Baldwin does not offer a VWIL student the range of curricular choices available to a VMI cadet. VMI awards baccalaureate degrees in liberal arts, biology, chemistry, civil engineering, electrical and computer engineering, and mechanical engineering. See 852 F. Supp., at 503; Virginia Military Institute: More than an Education 11 (Govt. exh. 75, lodged with Clerk of this Court). VWIL students attend a school that "does not have a math and science focus," 852 F. Supp., at 503; they cannot take at Mary Baldwin any courses in engineering or the advanced math and physics courses VMI offers, see *id.*, at 477.

For physical training, Mary Baldwin has "two multipurpose fields" and "[o]ne gymnasium." *Id.*, at 503. VMI has "an NCAA competition level indoor track and field facility; a number of multi-purpose fields; baseball, soccer and lacrosse fields; an obstacle course; large boxing, wrestling and martial arts facilities; an 11-laps-to-the-mile indoor running course; an indoor pool; indoor and outdoor rifle ranges; and a football stadium that also contains a practice field and outdoor track." *Ibid.*

Although Virginia has represented that it will provide equal financial support for in-state VWIL students and VMI cadets, *id.*, at 483, and the VMI Foundation has agreed to endow VWIL with $5.4625 million, *id.*, at 499, the difference between the two schools' financial reserves is pronounced. Mary Baldwin's endowment, currently about $19 million, will gain an additional $35 million based on future commitments; VMI's current endowment, $131 million —the largest public college per-student endowment in the Nation—will gain $220 million. *Id.*, at 503.

The VWIL student does not graduate with the advantage of a VMI degree. Her diploma does not unite her with the legions of VMI "graduates [who] have distinguished themselves" in military and civilian life. See 976 F. 2d, at 892- 893. "[VMI] alumni are exceptionally close to the school," and that closeness accounts, in part, for VMI's success in attracting applicants. See 766 F. Supp., at 1421. A VWIL graduate cannot assume that the "network of business owners, corporations, VMI graduates and non-graduate employers .. . interested in hiring VMI graduates," 852 F. Supp., at 499, will be equally responsive to her search for employment, see 44 F. 3d, at 1250 (Phillips, J., dissenting) ("the powerful political and economic ties of the VMI alumni network cannot be expected to open" for graduates of the fledgling VWIL program).

Virginia, in sum, while maintaining VMI for men only, has failed to provide any "comparable single-gender women's institution." *Id.*, at 1241. Instead, the Commonwealth has created a VWIL program fairly appraised as a "pale shadow" of VMI in terms of the range of curricular choices and faculty stature, funding, prestige, alumni support and influence. See *id.*, at 1250 (Phillips, J., dissenting).

Virginia's VWIL solution is reminiscent of the remedy Texas proposed 50 years ago, in response to a state trial court's 1946 ruling that, given the equal protection guarantee, African-Americans could not be denied a legal education at a state facility. See *Sweatt v. Painter*, 339 U.S. 629 (1950). Reluctant to admit African-Americans to its flagship University of Texas Law School, the State set up a separate school for Heman Sweatt and other black law students. *Id.*, at 632. As originally opened, the new school had no independent faculty or library, and it lacked accreditation. *Id.*, at 633. Nevertheless, the state trial and appellate courts were satisfied that the new school offered Sweatt opportunities for the study of law "substantially equivalent to those offered by the State to white students at the University of Texas." *Id.*, at 632 (internal quotation marks omitted).

Before this Court considered the case, the new school had gained "a faculty of five full-time professors; a student body of 23; a library of some 16,500 volumes serviced by a full-time staff; a practice court and legal aid association; and one alumnus who ha[d] become a member of the Texas Bar." *Id.*, at 633. This Court contrasted resources at the new school with those at the school from which Sweatt had been excluded. The University of Texas Law School had a full-time faculty of 16, a student body of 850, a library containing over 65,000 volumes, scholarship funds, a law review, and moot court facilities. *Id.*, at 632-633.

More important than the tangible features, the Court emphasized, are "those qualities which are incapable of objective measurement but which make for greatness" in a school, including "reputation of the faculty, experience of the administration, position and influence of the alumni, standing in the community, traditions and prestige." at 634. Facing the marked differences reported in the *Sweatt* opinion, the Court unanimously ruled that Texas had not shown "substantial equality in the [separate] educational opportunities" the State offered. *Id.*, at 633. Accordingly, the Court held, the Equal Protection Clause required Texas to admit African-Americans to the University of Texas Law School. at 636. In line with *Sweatt*, we rule here that Virginia has not shown substantial equality in the separate educational opportunities the Commonwealth supports at VWIL and

When Virginia tendered its VWIL plan, the Fourth Circuit did not inquire whether the proposed remedy, approved by the District Court, placed women denied the VMI advantage in "the position they would have occupied in the absence of [discrimination]." *Milliken*, 433 U.S., at 280 (internal quotation marks omitted). Instead, the Court of Appeals considered whether the Commonwealth could provide, with fidelity to the equal protection principle, separate and unequal educational programs for men and women.

The Fourth Circuit acknowledged that "the VWIL degree from Mary Baldwin College lacks the historical benefit and prestige of a degree from VMI." 44 F. 3d, at 1241. The Court of Appeals further observed that VMI is "an ongoing and successful institution with a long history," and there remains no "comparable single-gender women's institution." *Ibid*. Nevertheless, the appeals court declared the substantially different and significantly unequal VWIL program satisfactory. The court reached that result by revising the applicable standard of review. The Fourth Circuit displaced the standard developed in our precedent, see supra, at 532- 534, and substituted a standard of its own invention.

We have earlier described the deferential review in which the Court of Appeals engaged, see *supra*, at 528-529, a brand of review inconsistent with the more exacting standard our precedent requires, see *supra*, at 532-534. Quoting in part from *Mississippi Univ. for Women*, the Court of Appeals candidly described its own analysis as one capable of checking a legislative purpose ranked as "pernicious," but generally according "deference to [the] legislative will." 44 F. 3d, at 1235, 1236. Recognizing that it had extracted from our decisions a test yielding "little or no scrutiny of the effect of a classification directed at [single-gender education]," the Court of Appeals devised another test, a "substantive comparability" inquiry, *id.*, at 1237, and proceeded to find that new test satisfied, *id.*, at 1241.

The Fourth Circuit plainly erred in exposing Virginia's VWIL plan to a deferential analysis, for "all gender-based classifications today" warrant "heightened scrutiny." See *J. E. B.*, 511 U.S., at 136. Valuable as VWIL may prove for students who seek the program offered, Virginia's remedy affords no cure at all for the opportunities and advantages withheld from women who want a VMI education and can make the grade. See *supra*, at 549-554.[20] In sum, Virginia's remedy does not match the constitutional violation; the Commonwealth has shown no "exceedingly persuasive justification" for withholding from women qualified for the experience premier training of the kind VMI affords.

VII

A generation ago, "the authorities controlling Virginia higher education," despite long established tradition, agreed "to innovate and favorably entertain[ed] the [then] relatively new idea that there must be no discrimination by sex in offering educational opportunity." *Kirstein*, 309 F. Supp., at 186. Commencing in 1970, Virginia opened to women "educational opportunities at the Charlottesville campus that [were] not afforded in other [state-operated] institutions." *Id.*, at 187; see *supra*, at 538. A federal court approved the Commonwealth's innovation, emphasizing that the University of Virginia "offer[ed] courses of instruction . . . not available elsewhere." 309 F. Supp., at 187. The court further noted: "[T]here exists at Charlottesville a 'prestige' factor [not paralleled in] other Virginia educational institutions." *Ibid.*

VMI, too, offers an educational opportunity no other Virginia institution provides, and the school's "prestige"—associated with its success in developing "citizen-soldiers"—is unequaled. Virginia has closed this facility to its daughters and, instead, has devised for them a "parallel program," with a faculty less impressively credentialed and less well paid, more limited course offerings, fewer opportunities for military training and for scientific specialization. *Cf. Sweatt*, 339 U.S., at 633. VMI, beyond question, "possesses to a far greater degree" than the VWIL program "those qualities which are incapable of objective measurement but which make for greatness in a . . . school," including "position and influence of the alumni, standing in the community, traditions and prestige." *Id.*, at 634. Women seeking and fit for a VMI-quality education cannot be offered anything less, under the Commonwealth's obligation to afford them genuinely equal protection.

A prime part of the history of our Constitution, historian Richard Morris recounted, is the story of the extension of constitutional rights and protections to people once ignored or excluded.[21] VMI's story continued as our comprehension of "We the People" expanded. See *supra*, at 532, n. 6. There is no reason to believe that the admission of women capable of all the activities required of VMI cadets would destroy the Institute rather than enhance its capacity to serve the "more perfect Union."

* * *

For the reasons stated, the initial judgment of the Court of Appeals, 976 F. 2d 890 (CA4 1992), is affirmed, the final judgment of the Court of Appeals, 44 F. 3d 1229 (CA4 1995), is reversed, and the case is remanded for further proceedings consistent with this opinion.

It is so ordered.

---

1. During the Civil War, school teaching became a field dominated by women. See A. Scott, The Southern Lady: From Pedestal to Politics, 1830-1930, p. 82 (1970).

2. Historically, most of Virginia's public colleges and universities were single sex; by the mid-1970's, however, all except VMI had become coeducational. 766 F. Supp. 1407, 1418-1419 (WD Va. 1991). For example, Virginia's legislature incorporated Farmville Female Seminary Association in 1839, the year VMI opened. 1839 Va. Acts, ch. 167. Originally providing instruction in "English, Latin, Greek, French, and piano" in a "home atmosphere," R. Sprague, Longwood College: A History 7-8, 15 (1989) (Longwood College), Farmville Female Seminary became a public institution in 1884 with a mission to train "white female teachers for public schools," 1884 Va. Acts, ch. 311. The school became Longwood College in 1949, Longwood College 136, and introduced coeducation in 1976, id., at 133.

3. The District Court allowed the VMI Foundation and the VMI Alumni Association to intervene as defendants. 766 F. Supp., at 1408.

4. Six judges voted to rehear the case en banc, four voted against rehearing, and three were recused. The Fourth Circuit's local Rule permits rehearing en banc only on the vote of a majority of the Circuit's judges in regular active service (currently 13) without regard to recusals. See 52 F. 3d, at 91, and n. 1.

5. As Thomas Jefferson stated the view prevailing when the Constitution was new:

"Were our State a pure democracy . . . there would yet be excluded from their deliberations . . . [w]omen, who, to prevent depravation of morals and ambiguity of issue, could not mix promiscuously in the public meetings of men." Letter from Thomas Jefferson to Samuel Kercheval (Sept. 5,1816), in 10 Writings of Thomas Jefferson 45-46, n. 1 (P. Ford ed. 1899).

6. The Court has thus far reserved most stringent judicial scrutiny for classifications based on race or national origin, but last Term observed that strict scrutiny of such classifications is not inevitably "fatal in fact." *Adarand Constructors, Inc. v. Pena*, 515 U.S. 200, 237 (1995) (internal quotation marks omitted).

7. Several amici have urged that diversity in educational opportunities is an altogether appropriate governmental pursuit and that single-sex schools can contribute importantly to such diversity. Indeed, it is the mission of some single-sex schools "to dissipate, rather than perpetuate, traditional gender classifications." See Brief for Twenty-six Private Women's Colleges as *Amici curiae* 5. We do not question the Commonwealth's prerogative evenhandedly to support diverse educational opportunities. We address specifically and only an educational opportunity recognized by the District Court and the Court of Appeals as "unique," see 766 F. Supp., at 1413, 1432; 976 F. 2d, at 892, an opportunity available only at Virginia's premier military institute, the Commonwealth's sole single-sex public university or college. Cf. *Mississippi Univ. for Women v. Hogan*, 458 U.S. 718, 720, n. 1 (1982) ("Mississippi maintains no other single-sex public university or college. Thus, we are not faced with the question of whether States can provide 'separate but equal' undergraduate institutions for males and females.").

8. On this point, the dissent sees fire where there is no flame. See post, at 596-598, 598-600. "Both men and women can benefit from a single-sex education," the District Court recognized, although "the beneficial effects" of such education, the court added, apparently "are stronger among women than among men." 766 F. Supp., at 1414. The United States does not challenge that recognition. Cf. C. Jencks & D. Riesman, The Academic Revolution 297-298 (1968):

"The pluralistic argument for preserving all-male colleges is uncomfortably similar to the pluralistic argument for preserving all-white colleges . . . . The all-male college would be relatively easy to defend if it emerged from a world in which women were established as fully equal to men. But it does not. It is therefore likely to be a witting or unwitting device for preserving tacit assumptions of male superiority—assumptions for which women must eventually pay."

9. Dr. Edward H. Clarke of Harvard Medical School, whose influential book, Sex in Education, went through 17 editions, was perhaps the most well-known speaker from the medical community opposing higher education for women. He maintained that the physiological effects of hard study and academic competition with boys would interfere with the development of girls' reproductive organs. See E. Clarke, Sex in Education 38-39, 62-63 (1873); id., at 127 ("identical education of the two sexes is a crime before God and humanity, that physiology protests against, and that experience weeps over"); see also H. Maudsley, Sex in Mind and in Education 17 (1874) ("It is not that girls have not ambition, nor that they fail generally to rim the intellectual race [in coeducational settings], but it is asserted that they do it at a cost to their strength and health which entails life-long suffering, and even incapacitates them for the adequate performance of the natural functions of their sex."); C. Meigs, Females and Their Diseases 350 (1848) (after five or six weeks of "mental and educational discipline," a healthy woman would

"lose . . . the habit of menstruation" and suffer numerous ills as a result of depriving her body for the sake of her mind).

10. Virginia's Superintendent of Public Instruction dismissed the coeducational idea as "'repugnant to the prejudices of the people'" and proposed a female college similar in quality to Girton, Smith, or Vassar. 2 History of Women's Education 254 (quoting Dept. of Interior, 1 Report of Commissioner of Education, H. R. Doc. No. 5, 58th Cong., 2d Sess., 438 (1904)).

11. See post, at 566,598-599, 603. Forecasts of the same kind were made regarding admission of women to the federal military academies. See, *e.g.*, Hearings on H. R. 9832 et al. before Subcommittee No. 2 of the House Committee on Armed Services, 93d Cong., 2d Sess., 137 (1975) (statement of Lt. Gen. A. P. Clark, Superintendent of U.S. Air Force Academy) ("It is my considered judgment that the introduction of female cadets will inevitably erode this vital atmosphere."); *id.*, at 165 (statement of Hon. H. H. Callaway, Secretary of the Army) ("Admitting women to West Point would irrevocably change the Academy. . . . The Spartan atmosphere— which is so important to producing the final product—would surely be diluted, and would in all probability disappear.").

12. See 766 F. Supp., at 1413 (describing testimony of expert witness David Riesman: "[I]f VMI were to admit women, it would eventually find it necessary to drop the adversative system altogether, and adopt a system that provides more nurturing and support for the students."). Such judgments have attended, and impeded, women's progress toward full citizenship stature throughout our Nation's history. Speaking in 1879 in support of higher education for females, for example, Virginia State Senator C. T. Smith of Nelson recounted that legislation proposed to protect the property rights of women had encountered resistance. 10 Educ. J. Va. 213 (1879). A Senator opposing the measures objected that "there [was] no formal call for the [legislation]," and "depicted in burning eloquence the terrible consequences such laws would produce." *Ibid.* The legislation passed, and a year or so later, its sponsor, C. T. Smith, reported that "not one of [the forecast "terrible consequences"] has or ever will happen, even unto the sounding of Gabriel's trumpet." *Ibid.* See also *supra*, at 537-538.

13. Women cadets have graduated at the top of their class at every federal military academy. See Brief for Lieutenant Colonel Rhonda Cornum et al. as *Amici curiae* 11, n. 25; *cf.* Defense Advisory Committee on Women in the Services, Report on the Integration and Performance of Women at West Point 64 (1992).

14. Brief for Lieutenant Colonel Rhonda Cornum, *supra*, at 5-9 (reporting the vital contributions and courageous performance of women in the military); see Mintz, President Nominates 1st Woman to Rank of Three-Star General, Washington Post, Mar. 27, 1996, p. A19, col. 1 (announcing President's nomination of Marine Corps Major General Carol Mutter to rank of Lieutenant General; Mutter will head corps manpower and planning); Tousignant, A New Era for the Old Guard, Washington Post, Mar. 23, 1996, p. Cl, col. 2 (reporting admission of Sergeant Heather Johnsen to elite Infantry unit that keeps round-the-clock vigil at Tomb of the Unknowns in Arlington National Cemetery).

15. Inclusion of women in settings where, traditionally, they were not w``d inevitably entails a period of adjustment. As one West Point cadet squad leader recounted: "[T]he classes of '78 and '79 see the women as women, but the classes of '80 and '81 see them as classmates." U.S. Military Academy, A. Vitters, Report of Admission of Women (Project Athena II) 84 (1978) (internal quotation marks omitted).

16. VMI has successfully managed another notable change. The school admitted its first African-American cadets in 1968. See The VMI Story 347-349 (students no longer sing "Dixie," salute the Confederate flag or the tomb of General Robert E. Lee at ceremonies and sports events). As the District Court noted, VMI established a program on "retention of black cadets" designed to offer academic and social-cultural support to "minority members of a dominantly white and tradition-oriented student body." 766 F. Supp., at 1436-1437. The school maintains a "special recruitment program for blacks" which, the District Court found, "has had little, if any, effect on VMI's method of accomplishing its mission." *Id.*, at 1437.

17. As earlier observed, see *supra*, at 529, Judge Phillips, in dissent, measured Virginia's plan against a paradigm arrangement, one that "could survive equal protection scrutiny": single-sex schools with "substantially comparable curricular and extra-curricular programs, funding, physical plant, administration and support services, . . . faculty[,] and library resources." 44 F. 3d 1229, 1250 (CA4 1995). *Cf. Bray v. Lee*, 337 F. Supp. 934 (Mass. 1972) (holding inconsistent with the Equal Protection Clause admission of males to Boston's Boys Latin School with a test score of 120 or higher (up to a top score of 200) while requiring a score, on the same test, of at

least 133 for admission of females to Girls Latin School, but not ordering coeducation). Measuring VMI/VWIL against the paradigm, Judge Phillips said, "reveals how far short the [Virginia] plan falls from providing substantially equal tangible and intangible educational benefits to men and women." 44 F. 3d, at 1250.

18. Both programs include an honor system. Students at VMI are expelled forthwith for honor code violations, see 766 F. Supp., at 1423; the system for VWIL students, see 852 F. Supp., at 496-497, is less severe, see Tr. 414-415 (testimony of Mary Baldwin College President Cynthia Tyson).

19. Admitting women to VMI would undoubtedly require alterations necessary to afford members of each sex privacy from the other sex in living arrangements, and to adjust aspects of the physical training programs. See Brief for Petitioner 27-29; *cf.* note following 10 U.S.C. §4342 (academic and other standards for women admitted to the Military, Naval, and Air Force Academies "shall be the same as those required for male individuals, except for those minimum essential adjustments in such standards required because of physiological differences between male and female individuals")- Experience shows such adjustments are manageable. See U.S. Military Academy, A. Vitters, N. Kinzer, & J. Adams, Report of Admission of Women (Project Athena I-IV) (1977-1980) (4-year longitudinal study of the admission of women to West Point); Defense Advisory Committee on Women in the Services, Report on the Integration and Performance of Women at West Point 17-18 (1992).

20. Virginia's prime concern, it appears, is that "placing] men and women into the adversarial relationship inherent in the VMI program . . . would destroy, at least for that period of the adversative training, any sense of decency that still permeates the relationship between the sexes." 44 F. 3d, at 1239; see *supra*, at 540-546. It is an ancient and familiar fear. Compare In re Lavinia Goodell, 39 Wis. 232, 246 (1875) (denying female applicant's motion for admission to the bar of its court, Wisconsin Supreme Court explained: "Discussions are habitually necessary in courts of justice, which are unfit for female ears. The habitual presence of women at these would tend to relax the public sense of decency and propriety."), with Levine, Closing Comments, 6 Law & Inequality 41 (1988) (presentation at Eighth Circuit Judicial Conference, Colorado Springs, Colo., July 17, 1987) (footnotes omitted):

"Plato questioned whether women should be afforded equal opportunity to become guardians, those elite Rulers of Platonic society. Ironically, in that most undemocratic system of government, the Republic, women's native ability to serve as guardians was not seriously questioned. The concern was over the wrestling and exercise class in which all candidates for guardianship had to participate, for rigorous physical and mental training were prerequisites to attain the exalted status of guardian. And in accord with Greek custom, those exercise classes were conducted in the nude. Plato concluded that their virtue would clothe the women's nakedness and that Platonic society would not thereby be deprived of the talent of qualified citizens for reasons of mere gender."

For Plato's full text on the equality of women, see 2 The Dialogues of Plato 302-312 (B. Jowett transl., 4th ed. 1953). Virginia, not bound to ancient Greek custom in its "rigorous physical and mental training" programs, could more readily make the accommodations necessary to draw on "the talent of [all] qualified citizens." *Cf. supra*, at 550-551, n. 19.

21. R. Morris, The Forging of the Union, 1781-1789, p. 193 (1987); see *id.*, at 191, setting out letter to a friend from Massachusetts patriot (later second President) John Adams, on the subject of qualifications for voting in his home State:

"[I]t is dangerous to open so fruitful a source of controversy and altercation as would be opened by attempting to alter the qualifications of voters; there will be no end of it. New claims will arise; women will demand a vote; lads from twelve to twenty-one will think their rights not enough attended to; and every man who has not a farthing, will demand an equal voice with any other, in all acts of state. It tends to confound and destroy all distinctions, and prostrate all ranks to one common level." Letter from John Adams to James Sullivan (May 26, 1776), in 9 Works of John Adams 378 (C. Adams ed. 1854).

OLMSTEAD V. L. C.

527 U.S. 581 (1999)

This case centers on the rights of the mentally ill under the Americans with Disabilities Act. The plaintiffs were two women who had been diagnosed with schizophrenia and other various mental and intellectual impairments and had been confined to institutions. They sued Georgia health authorities, alleging that their mental illnesses were a form of disability and that they were entitled to certain protections under the American with Disabilities Act, including the right to live and be treated in a community rather than in isolation in an institution.

Justice Ginsburg delivered the majority opinion for the Court, siding with the plaintiffs and declaring that mental illness was a form of disability and that the plaintiffs' "unjustified isolation . . . is properly regarded as discrimination based on disability."

Justices O'Connor, Souter, and Breyer joined her opinion in full. Justice Stevens joined her opinion except for part III-B. Justices Stevens and Kennedy also wrote separate concurring opinions. Justice Thomas, joined by Justices Rehnquist and Scalia, dissented.

OLMSTEAD V. L. C.

527 U.S. 581 (1999)

This case concerns the proper construction of the anti- discrimination provision contained in the public services portion (Title II) of the Americans with Disabilities Act of 1990 (ADA), 104 Stat. 337,42 U.S. C. § 12132. Specifically, we confront the question whether the proscription of discrimination may require placement of persons with mental disabilities in community settings rather than in institutions. The answer, we hold, is a qualified yes. Such action is in order when the State's treatment professionals have determined that community placement is appropriate, the transfer from institutional care to a less restrictive setting is not opposed by the affected individual, and the placement can be reasonably accommodated, taking into account the re-sources available to the State and the needs of others with mental disabilities. In so ruling, we affirm the decision of the Eleventh Circuit in substantial part. We remand the case, however, for further consideration of the appropriate relief, given the range of facilities the State maintains for the care and treatment of persons with diverse mental dis-abilities, and its obligation to administer services with an even hand.

I

This case, as it comes to us, presents no constitutional question. The complaints filed by plaintiffs-respondents L. C. and E. W. did include such an issue; L. C. and E. W. alleged that defendants-petitioners, Georgia health care officials, failed to afford them minimally adequate care and freedom from undue restraint, in violation of their rights under the Due Process Clause of the

Fourteenth Amendment. See Complaint If 87-91; Intervenor's Complaint ff 30-34. But neither the District Court nor the Court of Appeals reached those Fourteenth Amendment claims. See Civ. No. 1:95-cv-1210-MHS (ND Ga., Mar. 26,1997), pp. 5-6, 11-13, App. to Pet. for Cert. 34a-35a, 40a-41a; 138 F. 3d 893, 895, and n. 3 (CA11 1998). Instead, the courts below resolved the case solely on statutory grounds. Our review is similarly confined. *Cf. Cleburne v. Cleburne Living Center, Inc.*, 473 U.S. 432, 450 (1985) (Texas city's requirement of special use permit for operation of group home for mentally retarded, when other care and multiple-dwelling facilities were freely permitted, lacked rational basis and therefore violated Equal Protection Clause of Fourteenth Amendment). Mindful that it is a statute we are construing, we set out first the legislative and regulatory prescriptions on which the case turns.

In the opening provisions of the ADA, Congress stated findings applicable to the statute in all its parts. Most relevant to this case, Congress determined that

"(2) historically, society has tended to isolate and segregate individuals with disabilities, and, despite some improvements, such forms of discrimination against individuals with disabilities continue to be a serious and pervasive social problem;

"(3) discrimination against individuals with disabilities persists in such critical areas as . .. institutionalization . . . ;

. . .

"(5) individuals with disabilities continually encounter various forms of discrimination, including outright intentional exclusion, . . . failure to make modifications to existing facilities and practices, . . . [and] segregation "42U.S.C.§§12101(a)(2),(3),(5).[1]

Congress then set forth prohibitions against discrimination in employment (Title I, §§12111-12117), public services furnished by governmental entities (Title II, §§12131-12165), and public accommodations provided by private entities (Title III, §§12181-12189). The statute as a whole is intended "to provide a clear and comprehensive national mandate for the elimination of discrimination against individuals with disabilities." § 12101(b)(1).[2]

This case concerns Title II, the public services portion of the ADA.[3] The provision of Title II centrally at issue reads:

"Subject to the provisions of this subchapter, no qualified individual with a disability shall, by reason of such disability, be excluded from participation in or be denied the benefits of the services, programs, or activities of a public entity, or be subjected to discrimination by any such entity." §201, as set forth in 42 U.S. C. §12132.

Title II's definition section states that "public entity" includes "any State or local government," and "any department, agency, [or] special purpose district." §§ 12131(1)(A), (B). The same section defines "qualified individual with a disability" as

"an individual with a disability who, with or without reasonable modifications to rules, policies, or practices, the removal of architectural, communication, or transportation barriers, or the provision of auxiliary aids and services, meets the essential eligibility requirements for the receipt of services or the participation in programs or activities provided by a public entity." § 12131(2).

On redress for violations of § 12132's discrimination prohibition, Congress referred to remedies available under § 505 of the Rehabilitation Act of 1973, 92 Stat. 2982, 29 U. S. C. § 794a. See §203, as set forth in 42 U. S. C. §12133 ("The remedies, procedures, and rights set forth in [§505 of the Rehabilitation Act] shall be the remedies, procedures, and rights this subchapter provides to any person alleging discrimination on the basis of disability in violation of section 12132 of this title.").[4]

Congress instructed the Attorney General to issue regulations implementing provisions of Title II, including § 12132's discrimination proscription. See §204, as set forth in § 12134(a) ("[T]he Attorney General shall promulgate regulations in an accessible format that implement this part.")[5] The Attorney General's regulations, Congress further directed, "shall be consistent with this chapter and with the coordination regulations . . . applicable to recipients of Federal financial assistance under [§504 of the Rehabilitation Act]." §204, as set forth in 42 U. S. C. § 12134(b). One of the § 504 regulations requires recipients of federal funds to "administer programs and activities in the most integrated setting appropriate to the needs of qualified handicapped persons." 28 CFR § 41.51(d) (1998).

As Congress instructed, the Attorney General issued Title II regulations, see 28 CFR pt. 35 (1998), including one modeled on the § 504 regulation just quoted; called the "integration regulation," it reads:

"A public entity shall administer services, programs, and activities in the most integrated setting appropriate to the needs of qualified individuals with disabilities." 28 CFR § 35.130(d) (1998).

The preamble to the Attorney General's Title II regulations defines "the most integrated setting appropriate to the needs of qualified individuals with disabilities" to mean "a setting that enables individuals with disabilities to interact with non-disabled persons to the fullest extent possible." 28 CFR pt. 35, App. A, p. 450 (1998). Another regulation requires public entities to "make reasonable modifications" to avoid "discrimination on the basis of disability," unless those modifications would entail a "fundamenta[l] alter[ation] "; called here the "reasonable-modifications regulation," it provides:

> "A public entity shall make reasonable modifications in policies, practices, or procedures when the modifications are necessary to avoid discrimination on the basis of disability, unless the public entity can demonstrate that making the modifications would fundamentally alter the nature of the service, program, or activity." 28 CFR § 35.130(b)(7) (1998).

We recite these regulations with the caveat that we do not here determine their validity. While the parties differ on the proper construction and enforcement of the regulations, we do not understand petitioners to challenge the regulatory formulations themselves as outside the congressional authorization. See Brief for Petitioners 16-17, 36, 40-41; Reply Brief 15-16 (challenging the Attorney General's interpretation of the integration regulation).

II

With the key legislative provisions in full view, we summarize the facts underlying this dispute. Respondents L. C. and E. W. are mentally retarded women; L. C. has also been diagnosed with schizophrenia, and E. W. with a personality disorder. Both women have a history of treatment in institutional settings. In May 1992, L. C. was voluntarily admitted to Georgia Regional Hospital at Atlanta (GRH), where she was confined for treatment in a psychiatric unit. By May 1993, her psychiatric condition had stabilized, and L. C.'s treatment team at GRH agreed that her needs could be met appropriately in one of the community-based programs the State supported. Despite this evaluation, L. C. remained institutionalized until February 1996, when the State placed her in a community-based treatment program.

E. W. was voluntarily admitted to GRH in February 1995; like L. C., E. W. was confined for treatment in a psychiatric unit. In March 1995, GRH sought to discharge E. W. to a homeless shelter, but abandoned that plan after her attorney filed an administrative complaint. By 1996, E. W.'s treating psychiatrist concluded that she could be treated appropriately in a community-based setting. She nonetheless remained institutionalized until a few months after the District Court issued its judgment in this case in 1997.

In May 1995, when she was still institutionalized at GRH, L. C. filed suit in the United States District Court for the Northern District of Georgia, challenging her continued confinement in a segregated environment. Her complaint invoked 42 U. S. C. § 1983 and provisions of the ADA, §§ 12131-12134, and named as defendants, now petitioners, the Commissioner of the

Georgia Department of Human Resources, the Superintendent of GRH, and the Executive Director of the Fulton County Regional Board (collectively, the State). L. C. alleged that the State's failure to place her in a community-based program, once her treating professionals determined that such placement was appropriate, violated, inter alia, Title II of the ADA. L. C.'s pleading requested, among other things, that the State place her in a community care residential program, and that she receive treatment with the ultimate goal of integrating her into the mainstream of society. E. W. intervened in the action, stating an identical claim.[6]

The District Court granted partial summary judgment in favor of L. C. and E. W. See App. to Pet. for Cert. 31a-42a. The court held that the State's failure to place L. C. and E. W. in an appropriate community-based treatment program violated Title II of the ADA. See *id.*, at 39a, 41a. In so ruling, the court rejected the State's argument that inadequate funding, not discrimination against L. C. and E. W. "by reason of" their disabilities, accounted for their retention at GRH. Under Title II, the court concluded, "unnecessary institutional segregation of the disabled constitutes discrimination per se, which cannot be justified by a lack of funding." *Id.*, at 37a.

In addition to contending that L. C. and E. W. had not shown discrimination "by reason of [their] disabilities]," the State resisted court intervention on the ground that requiring immediate transfers in cases of this order would "fundamentally alter" the State's activity. The State reasserted that it was already using all available funds to provide services to other persons with disabilities. See *id.*, at 38a. Rejecting the State's "fundamental alteration" defense, the court observed that existing state programs provided community-based treatment of the kind for which L. C. and E. W. qualified, and that the State could "provide services to plaintiffs in the community at considerably cost than is required to maintain them in an institution." *Id.*, at 39a.

The Court of Appeals for the Eleventh Circuit affirmed the judgment of the District Court, but remanded for reassessment of the State's cost-based defense. See 138 F. 3d, at 905. As the appeals court read the statute and regulations: When "a disabled individual's treating professionals find that a community-based placement is appropriate for that individual, the ADA imposes a duty to provide treatment in a community setting—the most integrated setting appropriate to that patient's needs"; "[w]here there is no such finding [by the treating professionals], nothing in the ADA requires the deinstitutionalization of th[e] patient." *Id.*, at 902.

The Court of Appeals recognized that the State's duty to provide integrated services "is not absolute"; under the Attorney General's Title II regulation, "reasonable modifications" were required of the State, but fundamental alterations were not demanded. *Id.*, at 904. The appeals court thought it clear, however, that "Congress wanted to permit a cost defense only in the most limited of circumstances." *Id.*, at 902. In conclusion, the court stated that a cost justification would fail "[u]nless the State can prove that requiring it to [expend additional funds in order to provide L. C. and E. W. with integrated services] would be so unreasonable given the demands of the State's mental health budget that it would fundamentally alter the service [the State] provides." *Id.*, at 905. Because it appeared that the District Court had entirely ruled out a "lack of funding" justification, see App. to Pet. for Cert. 37a, the appeals court remanded, repeating that the District Court should consider, among other things, "whether the additional expenditures necessary to treat L. C. and E. W. in community-based care would be unreasonable given the demands of the State's mental health budget." 138 F. 3d, at 905.[7]

We granted certiorari in view of the importance of the question presented to the States and affected individuals. See 525 U.S. 1054 (1998).[8]

III

Endeavoring to carry out Congress' instruction to issue regulations implementing Title II, the Attorney General, in the integration and reasonable-modifications regulations, see *supra*, at 591-592, made two key determinations. The first concerned the scope of the ADA's discrimination proscription, 42 U.S. C. § 12132; the second concerned the obligation of the States to counter discrimination. As to the first, the Attorney General concluded that unjustified placement or retention of persons in institutions, severely limiting their exposure to the outside community, constitutes a form of discrimination based on disability prohibited by Title II. See 28 CFR § 35.130(d) (1998) ("A public entity shall administer services . . . in the most integrated setting appropriate to the needs of qualified individuals with disabilities."); Brief for United States as *Amicus Curiae* in *Helen L. v. DiDario*, No. 94-1243 (CA3 1994), pp. 8, 15-16 (unnecessary segregation of persons with disabilities constitutes a form of discrimination prohibited by the ADA and the integration regulation). Regarding the States' obligation to avoid unjustified isolation of individuals with disabilities, the Attorney General provided that States could resist modifications that "would fundamentally alter the nature of the service, program, or activity." 28 CFR § 35.130(b)(7) (1998).

The Court of Appeals essentially upheld the Attorney General's construction of the ADA. As just recounted, see *supra*, at 595-596, the appeals court ruled that the unjustified institutionalization of persons with mental disabilities violated Title II; the court then remanded with instructions to measure the cost of caring for L. C. and E. W. in a community-based facility against the State's mental health budget.

We affirm the Court of Appeals' decision in substantial part. Unjustified isolation, we hold, is properly regarded as discrimination based on disability.

But we recognize, as well, the States' need to maintain a range of facilities for the care and treatment of persons with diverse mental disabilities, and the States' obligation to administer services with an even hand. Accordingly, we further hold that the Court of Appeals' remand instruction was unduly restrictive. In evaluating a State's fundamental-alteration defense, the District Court must consider, in view of the resources available to the State, not only the cost of providing community-based care to the litigants, but also the range of services the State provides others with mental disabilities, and the State's obligation to mete out those services equitably.

A

We examine first whether, as the Eleventh Circuit held, undue institutionalization qualifies as discrimination "by reason of . . . disability." The Department of Justice has consistently advocated that it does.[9] Because the Department is the agency directed by Congress to issue regulations implementing Title II, see *supra*, at 591-592, its views warrant respect. We need not inquire whether the degree of deference described in *Chevron U.S. Inc. v. Natural Resources Defense Council, Inc.,* 467 U.S. 837, 844 (1984), is in order; "[i]t is enough to observe that the well-reasoned views of the agencies implementing a statute 'constitute a body of experience and informed judgment to which courts and litigants may properly resort for guidance.'" *Bragdon v. Abbott,* 524 U.S. 624, 642 (1998) (quoting Skidmore v. Swift & Co., 323 U.S. 134, 139-140 (1944)).

The State argues that L. C. and E. W. encountered no discrimination "by reason of" their disabilities because they were not denied community placement on account of those disabilities. See Brief for Petitioners 20. Nor were they subjected to "discrimination," the State contends, because "'discrimination' necessarily requires uneven treatment of similarly situated individuals," and L. C. and E. W. had identified no comparison class, *i.e.*, no similarly situated individuals given preferential treatment. *Id.*, at 21. We are satisfied that Congress had a more comprehensive view of the concept of discrimination advanced in the ADA.[10]

The ADA stepped up earlier measures to secure opportunities for people with developmental disabilities to enjoy the benefits of community living. The Developmentally Disabled Assistance and Bill of Rights Act, a 1975 measure, stated in aspirational terms that "[t]he treatment, services, and habilitation for a person with developmental disabilities . . . should be provided in the setting that is least restrictive of the person's personal liberty." 89 Stat. 502, 42 U.S. C. §6010(2) (1976 ed.) (emphasis added); see also *Pennhurst State School and Hospital v. Halderman,* 451 U.S. 1, 24 (1981) (concluding that the § 6010 provisions "were intended to be hortatory, not mandatory"). In a related legislative endeavor, the Rehabilitation Act of 1973, Congress used mandatory language to proscribe discrimination against persons with disabilities. See 87 Stat. 394, as amended, 29 U.S. C. § 794 (1976 ed.) ("No otherwise qualified individual with a disability in the United States . . . *shall*, solely by reason of her or his disability, be excluded from the participation in, be denied the benefits of, or be subjected to discrimination under any program or activity receiving Federal financial assistance." (Emphasis added.)) Ultimately, in the ADA, enacted in 1990, Congress not only required all public entities to refrain from discrimination, see 42 U.S. C. § 12132; additionally, in findings applicable to the entire statute, Congress explicitly identified unjustified "segregation" of persons with disabilities as a "for[m] of discrimination." See § 12101(a)(2) ("historically, society has tended to isolate and segregate individuals with disabilities, and, despite some improvements, such forms of discrimination against individuals with disabilities continue to be a serious and pervasive social problem"); § 12101(a)(5) ("individuals with disabilities continually encounter various forms of discrimination, including . ... segregation").[11]

Recognition that unjustified institutional isolation of persons with disabilities is a form of discrimination reflects two evident judgments. First, institutional placement of persons who can handle and benefit from community settings perpetuates unwarranted assumptions that persons so isolated are incapable or unworthy of participating in community life. Cf. *Allen v. Wright*, 468 U.S. 737, 755 (1984) ("There can be no doubt that [stigmatizing injury often caused by racial discrimination] is one of the most serious consequences of discriminatory government action."); *Los Angeles Dept, of Water and Power v. Manhart*, 435 U.S. 702, 707, n. 13 (1978) ("In forbidding employers to discriminate against individuals because of their sex, Congress intended to strike at the entire spectrum of disparate treatment of men and women resulting from sex stereotypes.'" (quoting *Sprogis v. United Air Lines, Inc.*, 444 F. 2d 1194, 1198 (CA7 1971)). Second, confinement in an institution severely diminishes the everyday life activities of individuals, including family relations, social contacts, work options, economic independence, educational advancement, and cultural enrichment. See Brief for American Psychiatric Association et al. as *Amici curiae* 20-22. Dissimilar treatment correspondingly exists in this key respect: In order to receive needed medical services, persons with mental disabilities must, because of those disabilities, relinquish participation in community life they could enjoy given reasonable accommodations, while persons without mental disabilities can receive the medical services they need without similar sacrifice. See Brief for United States as Amicus Curiae 6-7, 17.

The State urges that, whatever Congress may have stated as its findings in the ADA, the Medicaid statute "reflected a congressional policy preference for treatment in the institution over treatment in the community." Brief for Petitioners 31. The State correctly used the past tense. Since 1981, Medicaid has provided funding for state-run home and community-based care through a waiver program. See 95 Stat. 812-813, as amended, 42 U.S. C. § 1396n(c); Brief for United States as Amicus Curiae 20-21.[12] Indeed, the United States points out that the Department of Health and Human Services (HHS) "has a policy of encouraging States to take advantage of the waiver program, and often approves more waiver slots than a State ultimately uses." *Id.,* at 25-26 (further observing that, by 1996, "HHS approved up to 2109 waiver slots for Georgia, but Georgia used only 700").

We emphasize that nothing in the ADA or its implementing regulations condones termination of institutional settings for persons unable to handle or benefit from community settings. Title II provides only that "qualified individuals] with a disability" may not "be subjected to discrimination." 42 U.S. C. § 12132. "Qualified individuals," the ADA further explains, are persons with disabilities who, "with or without reasonable modifications to rules, policies, or practices, . . . mee[t] the essential eligibility requirements for the receipt of services or the participation in programs or activities provided by a public entity." § 12131(2).

Consistent with these provisions, the State generally may rely on the reasonable assessments of its own professionals in determining whether an individual "meets the essential eligibility requirements" for habilitation in a community- based program. Absent such qualification, it would be inappropriate to remove a patient from the more restrictive setting. See 28 CFR § 35.130(d) (1998) (public entity shall administer services and programs in "the most integrated setting appropriate to the needs of qualified individuals with disabilities" (emphasis added)); *cf. School Bd. of Nassau Cty. v. Arline* 480 U.S. 273, 288 (1987) ("[C]ourts normally should defer to the reasonable medical judgments of public health officials.").[13] Nor is there any federal requirement that community-based treatment be imposed on patients who do not desire it. See 28 CFR § 35.130(e)(1) (1998) ("Nothing in this part shall be construed to require an individual with a disability to accept an accommodation . . . which such individual chooses not to accept."); 28 CFR pt. 35, App. A, p. 450 (1998) ("[P]ersons with disabilities must be provided the option of declining to accept a particular accommodation."). In this case, however, there is no genuine dispute concerning the status of L. C. and E. W. as individuals "qualified" for noninstitutional care: The State's own professionals determined that community-based treatment would be appropriate for L. C. and E. W., and neither woman opposed such treatment. See *supra,* at 593.[14]

B

The State's responsibility, once it provides community- based treatment to qualified persons with disabilities, is not boundless. The reasonable-modifications regulation speaks of "reasonable modifications" to avoid discrimination, and allows States to resist modifications that entail a "fundamenta[l] alter[ation]" of the States' services and programs. 28 CFR § 35.130(b)(7) (1998). The Court of Appeals construed this regulation to permit a cost-based defense "only in the most limited of circumstances," 138 F. 3d, at 902, and remanded to the District Court to consider, among other things, "whether the additional expenditures necessary to treat L. C. and E. W. in community-based care would be unreasonable given the demands of the State's mental health budget,"*id.,* at 905.

The Court of Appeals' construction of the reasonable- modifications regulation is unacceptable for it would leave the State virtually defenseless once it is shown that the plaintiff is qualified for the service or program she seeks. If the expense entailed in placing one or two people in a community- based treatment program is properly measured for reasonableness against the State's entire mental health budget, it is unlikely that a State, relying on the fundamental-alteration defense, could ever prevail. See Tr. of Oral Arg. 27 (State's attorney argues that Court of Appeals' understanding of the fundamental-alteration defense, as expressed in its order to the District Court, "will always preclude the State from a meaningful defense"); *cf.* Brief for Petitioners 37-38 (Court of Appeals' remand order "mistakenly asks the district court to examine [the fundamental-alteration] defense based on the cost of providing community care to just two individuals, not all Georgia citizens who desire community care"); 1:95- cv-1210-MHS (ND Ga., Oct. 20, 1998), p. 3, App. 177 (District Court, on remand, declares the impact of its decision beyond L. C. and E. W. "irrelevant"). Sensibly construed, the fundamental-alteration component of the reasonable- modifications regulation would allow the State to show that, in the allocation of available resources, immediate relief for the plaintiffs would be inequitable, given the responsibility the State has undertaken for the care and treatment of a large and diverse population of persons with mental disabilities.

When it granted summary judgment for plaintiffs in this case, the District Court compared the cost of caring for the plaintiffs in a community-based setting with the cost of caring for them in an institution. That simple comparison showed that community placements cost less than institutional confinements. See App. to Pet. for Cert. 39a. As the United States recognizes, however, a comparison so simple overlooks costs the State cannot avoid; most notably, a "State . . . may experience increased overall expenses by funding community placements without being able to take advantage of the savings associated with the closure of institutions." Brief for United States as Amicus Curiae 21.[15]

As already observed, see *supra*, at 601-602, the ADA is not reasonably read to impel States to phase out institutions, placing patients in need of close care at risk. *Cf.* post, at 610 (KENNEDY, J., concurring in judgment). Nor is it the ADA's mission to drive States to move institutionalized patients into an inappropriate setting, such as a homeless shelter, a placement the State proposed, then retracted, for E. W. See *supra,* at 593. Some individuals, like L. C. and E. W. in prior years, may need institutional care from time to time "to stabilize acute psychiatric symptoms." App. 98 (affidavit of Dr. Richard L. Elliott); see 138 F. 3d, at 903 ("[T]here may be times [when] a patient can be treated in the community, and others whe[n] an institutional placement is necessary."); Reply Brief 19 (placement in a community- based treatment program does not mean the State will no longer need to retain hospital accommodations for the person so placed). For other individuals, no placement outside the institution may ever be appropriate. See Brief for American Psychiatric Association et al. as *Amici curiae* 22-23 ("Some individuals, whether mentally retarded or mentally ill, are not prepared at particular times—perhaps in the short run, perhaps in the long run—for the risks and exposure of the less protective environment of community settings"; for these persons, "institutional settings are needed and must remain available."); Brief for Voice of the Retarded et al. as *Amici curiae* 11 ("Each disabled person is entitled to treatment in the most integrated setting possible for that person—recognizing that, on a case-by-case basis, that setting may be in an institution."); *Youngberg v. Romeo,* 457 U.S. 307, 327 (1982) (Blackmun, J., concurring) ("For many mentally retarded people, the difference between the capacity to do things for themselves within an institution and total dependence on the institution for all of their needs is as much liberty as they ever will know.").

To maintain a range of facilities and to administer services with an even hand, the State must have more leeway than the courts below understood the fundamental-alteration defense to allow. If, for example, the State were to demonstrate that it had a comprehensive, effectively working plan for placing qualified persons with mental disabilities in less restrictive settings, and a waiting list that moved at a reasonable pace not controlled by the State's endeavors to keep its institutions fully populated, the reasonable-modifications standard would be met. See Tr. of Oral Arg. 5 (State's attorney urges that, "by asking [a] person to wait a short time until a community bed is available, Georgia does not exclude [that] person by reason of disability, neither does Georgia discriminate against her by reason of disability"); see also *id.,* at 25 ("[I]t is reasonable for the State to ask someone to wait until a community placement is available."). In such circumstances, a court would have no warrant effectively to order displacement of persons at the top of the community- based treatment waiting list by individuals lower down who commenced civil actions.[16]

* * *

For the reasons stated, we conclude that, under Title II of the ADA, States are required to provide community-based treatment for persons with mental disabilities when the State's treatment professionals determine that such placement is appropriate, the affected persons do not oppose such treatment, and the placement can be reasonably accommodated, taking into account the resources available to the State and the needs of others with mental disabilities. The judgment of the Eleventh Circuit is therefore affirmed in part and vacated in part, and the case is remanded for further proceedings.

It is so ordered.

---

1. The ADA, enacted in 1990, is the Federal Government's most recent and extensive endeavor to address discrimination against persons with disabilities. Earlier legislative efforts included the Rehabilitation Act of 1973, 87 Stat. 355, 29 U.S. C. § 701 et seq. (1976 ed.), and the Developmentally Disabled Assistance and Bill of Rights Act, 89 Stat. 486, 42 U.S. C. § 6001 et seq. (1976 ed.), enacted in 1975. In the ADA, Congress for the first time referred expressly to "segregation" of persons with disabilities as a "for[m] of discrimination," and to discrimination that persists in the area of "institutionalization." §§ 12101(a)(2), (3), (5).
2. The ADA defines "disability," "with respect to an individual," as
   "(A) a physical or mental impairment that substantially limits one or more of the major life activities of such individual;
   "(B) a record of such an impairment; or
   "(C) being regarded as having such an impairment." § 12102(2).
   There is no dispute that L. C. and E. W. are disabled within the meaning of the ADA.
3. In addition to the provisions set out in Part A governing public services generally, see §§ 12131-12134, Title II contains in Part B a host of provisions governing public transportation services, see §§12141-12165.
4. Section 505 of the Rehabilitation Act incorporates the remedies, rights, and procedures set forth in Title VI of the Civil Rights Act of 1964 for violations of § 504 of the Rehabilitation Act. See 29 U.S. C. § 794a(a)(2). Title VI, in turn, directs each federal department authorized to extend financial assistance to any department or agency of a State to issue rules and regulations consistent with achievement of the objectives of the statute authorizing financial assistance. See 78 Stat. 252, 42 U.S. C. § 2000d-1. Compliance with such requirements may be effected by the termination or denial of federal funds, or "by any other means authorized by law." *Ibid.* Remedies both at law and in equity are available for violations of the statute. See §2000d-7(a)(2).
5. Congress directed the Secretary of Transportation to issue regulations implementing the portion of Title II concerning public transportation.
   See 42 U.S. C. §§ 12143(b), 12149, 12164. As stated in the regulations, a person alleging discrimination on the basis of disability in violation of Title II may seek to enforce its provisions by commencing a private lawsuit, or by filing a complaint with (a) a federal agency that provides funding to the public entity that is the subject of the complaint, (b) the Department of Justice for referral to an appropriate agency, or (c) one of eight federal agencies responsible for investigating complaints arising under Title II: the Department of Agriculture, the Department of Education, the Department of Health and Human Services, the Department of Housing and Urban Development, the Department of the Interior, the Department of Justice, the Department of Labor, and the Department of Transportation. See 28 CFR §§ 35.170(c), 35.172(b), 35.190(b) (1998).
   The ADA contains several other provisions allocating regulatory and enforcement responsibility. Congress instructed the Equal Employment Opportunity Commission (EEOC) to issue regulations implementing Title I, see 42 U.S. C. § 12116; the EEOC, the Attorney General, and persons alleging discrimination on the basis of disability in violation of Title I may enforce its provisions, see § 12117(a). Congress similarly instructed the Secretary of Transportation and the Attorney General to issue regulations implementing provisions of Title III, see §§ 12186(a)(1),

(b); the Attorney General and persons alleging discrimination on the basis of disability in violation of Title III may enforce its provisions, see §§ 12188(a)(1), (b). Each federal agency responsible for ADA implementation may render technical assistance to affected individuals and institutions with respect to provisions of the ADA for which the agency has responsibility. See § 12206(c)(1).

6. L. C. and E. W. are currently receiving treatment in community-based programs. Nevertheless, the case is not moot. As the District Court and Court of Appeals explained, in view of the multiple institutional placements L. C. and E. W. have experienced, the controversy they brought to court is "capable of repetition, yet evading review." No. 1:95-cv-1210- MHS (ND Ga., Mar. 26, 1997), p. 6, App. to Pet. for Cert. 35a (internal quotation marks omitted); see 138 F. 3d 893, 895, n. 2 (CA11 1998) (citing *Honig v. Doe*, 484 U.S. 305, 318-323 (1988), and *Vitek v. Jones*, 445 U.S. 480, 486-487 (1980)).

7. After this Court granted certiorari, the District Court issued a decision on remand rejecting the State's fundamental-alteration defense. See 1:95-cv-1210-MHS (ND Ga., Jan. 29,1999), p. 1. The court concluded that the annual cost to the State of providing community-based treatment to L. C. and E. W. was not unreasonable in relation to the State's overall mental health budget. See *id.*, at 5. In reaching that judgment, the District Court first declared "irrelevant" the potential impact of its decision beyond L. C. and E. W. 1:95-cv-1210-MHS (ND Ga., Oct. 20, 1998), p. 3, App. 177. The District Court's decision on remand is now pending appeal before the Eleventh Circuit.

8. Twenty-two States and the Territory of Guam joined a brief urging that certiorari be granted. Ten of those States joined a brief in support of petitioners on the merits.

9. See Brief for United States in *Halderman v. Pennhurst State School and Hospital*, Nos. 78-1490, 78-1564, 78-1602 (CA3 1978), p. 45 ("[Institutionalization resulting] in separation of mentally retarded persons for no permissible reason . . . is 'discrimination' and a violation of Section 504 [of the Rehabilitation Act] if it is supported by federal funds."); Brief for United States in *Halderman v. Pennhurst State School and Hospital*, Nos. 78-1490, 78-1564, 78-1602 (CA3 1981), p. 27 ("Pennsylvania violates Section 504 by indiscriminately subjecting handicapped persons to [an institution] without first making an individual reasoned professional judgment as to the appropriate placement for each such person among all available alternatives."); Brief for United States as *Amicus Curiae* in *Helen L. v. DiDario*, No. 94-1243 (CA3 1994), p. 7 ("Both the Section 504 coordination regulations and the rest of the ADA make clear that the unnecessary segregation of individuals with disabilities in the provision of public services is itself a form of discrimination within the meaning of those statutes."); *id.*, at 8-16.

10. The dissent is driven by the notion that "this Court has never endorsed an interpretation of the term 'discrimination' that encompassed disparate treatment among members of the same protected class," post, at 616 (opinion of Thomas, J.), that "[o]ur decisions construing various statutory prohibitions against 'discrimination' have not wavered from this path," post, at 616, and that "a plaintiff cannot prove 'discrimination' by demonstrating that one member of a particular protected group has been favored over another member of that same group," post, at 618. The dissent is incorrect as a matter of precedent and logic. See *O'Connor v. Consolidated Coin Caterers Corp.*, 517 U.S. 308, 312 (1996) (The Age Discrimination in Employment Act of 1967 "does not ban discrimination against employees because they are aged 40 or older; it bans discrimination against employees because of their age, but limits the protected class to those who are 40 or older. The fact that one person in the protected class has lost out to another person in the protected class is thus irrelevant, so long as he has lost out because of his age.")) *cf. Oncale v. Sundowner Offshore Services, Inc.*, 523 U.S. 75, 76 (1998) ("[Workplace harassment can violate Title VII's prohibition against 'discrimination] . . . because of . . . sex,' 42 U.S. C. § 2000e-2(a)(l), when the harasser and the harassed employee are of the same sex."); *Jefferies v. Harris County Community Action Assn.*, 615 F. 2d 1025, 1032 (CA5 1980) ("[Discrimination against black females can exist even in the absence of discrimination against black men or white women.").

11. Unlike the ADA, § 504 of the Rehabilitation Act contains no express recognition that isolation or segregation of persons with disabilities is a form of discrimination. Section 504's discrimination proscription, a single sentence attached to vocational rehabilitation legislation, has yielded divergent court interpretations. See Brief for United States as Amicus Curiae 23-25.

12. The waiver program provides Medicaid reimbursement to States for the provision of community-based services to individuals who would otherwise require institutional care, upon a showing that the average annual cost of such services is not more than the annual cost of institutional services. See § 1396n(c).

13. Georgia law also expresses a preference for treatment in the most integrated setting appropriate. See Ga. Code Ann. §37-4-121 (1995) ("It is the policy of the state that the least restrictive alternative placement be secured for every client at every stage of his habilitation. It shall be the duty of the facility to assist the client in securing placement in noninstitutional community facilities and programs.").

14. We do not in this opinion hold that the ADA imposes on the States a "standard of care" for whatever medical services they render, or that the ADA requires States to "provide a certain level of benefits to individuals with disabilities." *Cf.* post, at 623, 624 (Thomas, J., dissenting). We do hold, however, that States must adhere to the ADA's nondiscrimination requirement with regard to the services they in fact provide.

15. Even if States eventually were able to close some institutions in response to an increase in the number of community placements, the States would still incur the cost of running partially full institutions in the interim. See Brief for United States as Amicus Curiae 21.

16. We reject the Court of Appeals' construction of the reasonable- modifications regulation for another reason. The Attorney General's Title II regulations, Congress ordered, "shall be consistent with" the regulations in part 41 of Title 28 of the Code of Federal Regulations implementing § 504 of the Rehabilitation Act. 42 U.S.C. § 12134(b). The § 504 regulation upon which the reasonable-modifications regulation is based provides now, as it did at the time the ADA was enacted:

"A recipient shall make reasonable accommodation to the known physical or mental limitations of an otherwise qualified handicapped applicant or employee unless the recipient can demonstrate that the accommodation would impose an undue hardship on the operation of its program." 28 CFR §41.53 (1990 and 1998 eds.).

While the part 41 regulations do not define "undue hardship," other §504 regulations make clear that the "undue hardship" inquiry requires not simply an assessment of the cost of the accommodation in relation to the recipient's overall budget, but a "case-by-case analysis weighing factors that include: (1) [t]he overall size of the recipient's program with respect to number of employees, number and type of facilities, and size of budget; (2) [t]he type of the recipient's operation, including the composition and structure of the recipient's workforce; and (3) [t]he nature and cost of the accommodation needed." 28 CFR § 42.511(c) (1998); see 45 CFR § 84.12(c) (1998) (same).

Under the Court of Appeals' restrictive reading, the reasonable- modifications regulation would impose a standard substantially more difficult for the State to meet than the "undue burden" standard imposed by the corresponding § 504 regulation.

FRIENDS OF EARTH, INC. V. LAIDLAW ENVIRONMENTAL SERVICES (TOC), INC.

528 U.S. 167 (2000)

This case centers on the question of who has the right to bring a lawsuit against the alleged polluter of a body of water under the Clean Water Act. The plaintiffs were residents of the area surrounding the North Tyger River in South Carolina who alleged that a factory owned and operated by Laidlaw was polluting the river. Laidlaw argued the case was moot, because the factory was no longer operating, and that the plaintiffs lacked proper standing to bring a suit as they had not shown that they were personally and actually harmed.

In a 7-2 opinion authored by Justice Ginsburg, the Court sided with the plaintiffs and ruled that they did have standing, as they had been injured by "the aesthetic and recreational values of the area" being lessened by the pollution. Moreover, the matter was not moot, because it was possible that the factory could reopen in the future.

Justice Ginsburg's opinion was joined by Justices Rehnquist, Stevens, O'Connor, Kennedy, Souter, and Breyer. Justices Stevens and Kennedy also filed separate concurrences. Justice Scalia, joined by Justice Thomas, dissented.

FRIENDS OF EARTH, INC. V. LAIDLAW ENVIRONMENTAL SERVICES (TOC), INC.

528 U.S. 167 (2000)

T his case presents an important question concerning the operation of the citizen-suit provisions of the Clean Water Act. Congress authorized the federal district courts to entertain Clean Water Act suits initiated by "a person or persons having an interest which is or may be adversely affected." 33 U.S.C. §§ 1365(a), (g). To impel future compliance with the Act, a district court may prescribe injunctive relief in such a suit; additionally or alternatively, the court may impose civil penalties payable to the United States Treasury. § 1365(a). In the Clean Water Act citizen suit now before us, the District Court determined that injunctive relief was inappropriate because the defendant, after the institution of the litigation, achieved substantial compliance with the terms of its discharge permit. 956 F. Supp. 588, 611 (SC 1997). The court did, however, assess a civil penalty of $405,800. at 610. The "total deterrent effect" of the penalty would be adequate to forestall future violations, the court reasoned, taking into account that the defendant "will be required to reimburse plaintiffs for a significant amount of legal fees and has, itself, incurred significant legal expenses." *Id.*, at 610-611.

The Court of Appeals vacated the District Court's order. 149 F. 3d 303 (CA4 1998). The case became moot, the appellate court declared, once the defendant fully complied with the terms of its permit and the plaintiff failed to appeal the denial of equitable relief. "[C]ivil penalties payable to the government," the Court of Appeals stated, "would not redress any injury Plaintiffs have suffered." *Id.*, at 307. Nor were attorneys' fees in order, the Court of Appeals noted, because absent relief on the merits, plaintiffs could not qualify as prevailing parties. *Id.*, at 307, n. 5.

We reverse the judgment of the Court of Appeals. The appellate court erred in concluding that a citizen suitor's claim for civil penalties must be dismissed as moot when the defendant, albeit after commencement of the litigation, has come into compliance. In directing dismissal of the suit on grounds of mootness, the Court of Appeals incorrectly conflated our case law on initial standing to bring suit, see, g., *Steel Co. v. Citizens for Better Environment*, 523 U.S. 83 (1998), with our case law on post-commencement mootness, *See, e.g., City of Mesquite v. Aladdin's Castle, Inc.*, 455 U.S. 283 (1982). A defendant's voluntary cessation of allegedly unlawful conduct ordinarily does not suffice to moot a case. The Court of Appeals also misperceived the remedial potential of civil penalties. Such penalties may serve, as an alternative to an injunction, to deter future violations and thereby redress the injuries that prompted a citizen suitor to commence litigation.

I

A

In 1972, Congress enacted the Clean Water Act (Act), also known as the Federal Water Pollution Control Act, 86 Stat. 816, as amended, 33 U.S.C. § 1251 et seq. Section 402 of the Act, 33 U.S.C. § 1342, provides for the issuance, by the Administrator of the Environmental Protection Agency (EPA) or by authorized States, of National Pollutant Discharge Elimination System (NPDES) permits. NPDES permits impose limitations on the discharge of pollutants, and establish related monitoring and reporting requirements, in order to improve the cleanliness and safety of the Nation's waters. Noncompliance with a permit constitutes a violation of the Act. § 1342(h).

Under § 505(a) of the Act, a suit to enforce any limitation in an NPDES permit may be brought by any "citizen," defined as "a person or persons having an interest which is or may be adversely affected." 33 U.S.C. §§ 1365(a), (g). Sixty days before initiating a citizen suit, however, the would-be plaintiff must give notice of the alleged violation to the EPA, the State in which the alleged violation occurred, and the alleged violator. § 1365(b)(1)(A). "[T]he purpose of notice to the alleged violator is to give it an opportunity to bring itself into complete compliance with the Act and thus . . . render unnecessary a citizen suit." *Gwaltney of Smithfield, Ltd. v. Chesapeake Bay Foundation, Inc.*, 484 U.S. 49, 60 (1987). Accordingly, we have held that citizens lack statutory standing under § 505(a) to sue for violations that have ceased by the time the complaint is filed. *Id.*, at 56-63. The Act also bars a citizen from suing if the EPA or the State has already commenced, and is "diligently prosecuting," an enforcement action. 33 U.S.C. § 1365(b)(1)(B).

The Act authorizes district courts in citizen-suit proceedings to enter injunctions and to assess civil penalties, which are payable to the United States

Treasury. § 1365(a). In determining the amount of any civil penalty, the district court must take into account "the seriousness of the violation or violations, the economic benefit (if any) resulting from the violation, any history of such violations, any good-faith efforts to comply with the applicable requirements, the economic impact of the penalty on the violator, and such other matters as justice may require." § 1319(d). In addition, the court "may award costs of litigation (including reasonable attorney and expert witness fees) to any prevailing or substantially prevailing party, whenever the court determines such award is appropriate." § 1365(d).

B

In 1986, defendant-respondent Laidlaw Environmental Services (TOC), Inc., bought a hazardous waste incinerator facility in Roebuck, South Carolina, that included a waste- water treatment plant. (The company has since changed its name to Safety-Kleen (Roebuck), Inc., but for simplicity we will refer to it as "Laidlaw" throughout.) Shortly after Laidlaw acquired the facility, the South Carolina Department of Health and Environmental Control (DHEC), acting under 33 U.S.C. § 1342(a)(1), granted Laidlaw an NPDES permit authorizing the company to discharge treated water into the North Tyger River. The permit, which became effective on January 1, 1987, placed limits on Laidlaw's discharge of several pollutants into the river, including—of particular relevance to this case—mercury, an extremely toxic pollutant. The permit also regulated the flow, temperature, toxicity, and pH of the effluent from the facility, and imposed monitoring and reporting obligations.

Once it received its permit, Laidlaw began to discharge various pollutants into the waterway; repeatedly, Laidlaw's discharges exceeded the limits set by the permit. In particular, despite experimenting with several technological fixes, Laidlaw consistently failed to meet the permit's stringent 1.3 ppb (parts per billion) daily average limit on mercury discharges. The District Court later found that Laidlaw had violated the mercury limits on 489 occasions between 1987 and 1995. 956 F. Supp., at 613-621.

On April 10, 1992, plaintiff-petitioners Friends of the Earth (FOE) and Citizens Local Environmental Action Network, Inc. (CLEAN) (referred to collectively in this opinion, together with later joined plaintiff-petitioner Sierra Club, as "FOE") took the preliminary step necessary to the institution of litigation. They sent a letter to Laidlaw notifying the company of their intention to file a citizen suit against it under § 505(a) of the Act after the expiration of the requisite 60-day notice period, *i.e.*, on or after June 10, 1992. Laidlaw's lawyer then contacted DHEC to ask whether DHEC would consider filing a lawsuit against Laidlaw. The District Court later found that Laidlaw's reason for requesting that DHEC file a lawsuit against it was to bar FOE's proposed citizen suit through the operation of 33 U.S.C. § 1365(b)(1)(B). 890 F. Supp. 470, 478 (SC 1995). DHEC agreed to file a lawsuit against Laidlaw; the company's lawyer then drafted the complaint for DHEC and paid the filing fee. On June 9, 1992, the last day before FOE's 60-day notice period expired, DHEC and Laidlaw reached a settlement requiring Laidlaw to pay $100,000 in civil penalties and to make "'every effort'" to comply with its permit obligations. *Id.*, at 479-481.

On June 12, 1992, FOE filed this citizen suit against Laidlaw under § 505(a) of the Act, alleging noncompliance with the NPDES permit and seeking declaratory and injunctive relief and an award of civil penalties. Laidlaw moved for summary judgment on the ground that FOE had failed to present evidence demonstrating injury in fact, and therefore lacked Article III standing to bring the lawsuit. Record, Doc. No. 43. In opposition to this motion, FOE submitted affidavits and deposition testimony from members of the plaintiff organizations. Record, Doc. No. 71 (Exhs. 41-51). The record before the District Court also included affidavits from the organizations' members submitted by FOE in support of an earlier motion for preliminary injunctive relief. Record, Doc. No. 21 (Exhs. 5-10). After examining this evidence, the District Court denied Laidlaw's summary judgment motion, finding—albeit "by the very slimmest of margins"—that FOE had standing to bring the suit. App. in No. 97-1246 (CA4), pp. 207-208 (Tr. of Hearing 39-40 (June 30, 1993)).

Laidlaw also moved to dismiss the action on the ground that the citizen suit was barred under 33 U.S. C § 1365(b)(1)(B) by DHEC's prior action against the company. The United States, appearing as amicus curiae, joined FOE in opposing the motion. After an extensive analysis of the Laidlaw-DHEC settlement and the circumstances under which it was reached, the District Court held that DHEC's action against Laidlaw had not been "diligently prosecuted"; consequently, the court allowed FOE's citizen suit to proceed. 890 F. Supp., at 499.[1] The record indicates that after FOE initiated the suit, but before the District Court rendered judgment, Laidlaw violated the mercury discharge limitation in its permit 13 times. 956 F. Supp., at 621. The District Court also found that Laidlaw had committed 13 monitoring and 10 reporting violations during this period. *Id.*, at 601. The last recorded mercury discharge violation occurred in January 1995, long after the complaint was filed but about two years before judgment was rendered. *Id.*, at 621.

On January 22, 1997, the District Court issued its judgment. 956 F. Supp. 588 (SC). It found that Laidlaw had gained a total economic benefit of $1,092,581 as a result of its extended period of noncompliance with the mercury discharge limit in its permit. *Id.*, at 603. The court concluded, however, that a civil penalty of $405,800 was adequate in light of the guiding factors listed in 33 U.S.C. § 1319(d). 956 F. Supp., at 610. In particular, the District Court stated that the lesser penalty was appropriate taking into account the judgment's "total deterrent effect." In reaching this determination, the court "considered that Laidlaw will be required to reimburse plaintiffs for a significant amount of legal fees." *Id.*,at 610-611. The court declined to grant FOE's request for injunctive relief, stating that an injunction was inappropriate because "Laidlaw has been in substantial compliance with all parameters in its NPDES permit since at least August 1992." *Id.*, at 611.

FOE appealed the District Court's civil penalty judgment, arguing that the penalty was inadequate, but did not appeal the denial of declaratory or injunctive relief. Laid- law cross-appealed, arguing, among other things, that FOE lacked standing to bring the suit and that DHEC's action qualified as a diligent prosecution precluding FOE's litigation. The United States continued to participate as amicus curiae in support of FOE.

On July 16,1998, the Court of Appeals for the Fourth Circuit issued its judgment. 149 F. 3d 303. The Court of Appeals assumed without deciding that FOE initially had standing to bring the action, *id.*, at 306, n. 3, but went on to hold that the case had become moot. The appellate court stated, first, that the elements of Article III standing—injury, causation, and redressability—must persist at every stage of review, or else the action becomes moot. *Id.*, at 306. Citing our decision in *Steel Co.*, the Court of Appeals reasoned that the case had become moot because "the only remedy currently available to [FOE]—civil penalties payable to the government—would not redress any injury [FOE has] suffered." 149 F. 3d, at 306-307. The court therefore vacated the District Court's order and remanded with instructions to dismiss the action. In a footnote, the Court of Appeals added that FOE's "failure to obtain relief on the merits of [its] claims precludes any recovery of attorneys' fees or other litigation costs because such an award is available only to a 'prevailing or substantially prevailing party.'" *Id.*, at 307, n. 5 (quoting 33 U.S.C. § 1365(d)).

According to Laidlaw, after the Court of Appeals issued its decision but before this Court granted certiorari, the entire incinerator facility in Roebuck was permanently closed, dismantled, and put up for sale, and all discharges from the facility permanently ceased. Respondent's Suggestion of Mootness 3.

We granted certiorari, 525 U.S. 1176 (1999), to resolve the inconsistency between the Fourth Circuit's decision in this case and the decisions of several other Courts of Appeals, which have held that a defendant's compliance with its permit after the commencement of litigation does not moot claims for civil penalties under the Act. See, *Atlantic States Legal Foundation, Inc. v. Strok Die Casting Co.*, 116 F. 3d 814, 820 (CA7), cert. denied, 522 U.S. 981 (1997); *Natural Resources Defense Council, Inc. v. Texaco Rfg. and Mktg., Inc.*, 2 F. 3d 493, 503-504 (CA3 1993); *Atlantic States Legal Foundation, Inc. v. Pan American Tanning Corp.*, 993 F. 2d 1017, 1020-1021 (CA2 1993); *Atlantic States Legal Foundation, Inc. v. Tyson Foods, Inc.*, 897 F. 2d 1128, 1135- 1136 (CA11 1990).

II

A

The Constitution's case-or-controversy limitation on federal judicial authority, Art. Ill, §2, underpins both our standing and our mootness jurisprudence, but the two inquiries differ in respects critical to the proper resolution of this case, so we address them separately. Because the Court of Appeals was persuaded that the case had become moot and so held, it simply assumed without deciding that FOE had initial standing. See *Arizonans for Official English v. Arizona*, 520 U.S. 43, 66-67 (1997) (court may assume without deciding that standing exists in order to analyze mootness). But because we hold that the Court of Appeals erred in declaring the case moot, we have an obligation to assure ourselves that FOE had Article III standing at the outset of the litigation. We therefore address the question of standing before turning to mootness.

In *Lujan v. Defenders of Wildlife*, 504 U.S. 555, 560-561 (1992), we held that, to satisfy Article Ill's standing requirements, a plaintiff must show (1) it has suffered an "injury in fact" that is (a) concrete and particularized and (b) actual or imminent, not conjectural or hypothetical; (2) the injury is fairly traceable to the challenged action of the defendant; and

(3) it is likely, as opposed to merely speculative, that the injury will be redressed by a favorable decision. An association has standing to bring suit on behalf of its members when its members would otherwise have standing to sue in their own right, the interests at stake are germane to the organization's purpose, and neither the claim asserted nor the relief requested requires the participation of individual members in the lawsuit. *Hunt v. Washington State Apple Advertising Comm'n*, 432 U.S. 333, 343 (1977).

Laidlaw contends first that FOE lacked standing from the outset even to seek injunctive relief, because the plaintiff organizations failed to show that any of their members had sustained or faced the threat of any "injury in fact" from Laidlaw's activities. In support of this contention Laidlaw points to the District Court's finding, made in the course of setting the penalty amount, that there had been "no demonstrated proof of harm to the environment" from Laidlaw's mercury discharge violations. 956 F. Supp., at 602; see also *ibid.* ("[T]he NPDES permit violations at issue in this citizen suit did not result in any health risk or environmental harm.").

The relevant showing for purposes of Article III standing, however, is not injury to the environment but injury to the plaintiff. To insist upon the former rather than the latter as part of the standing inquiry (as the dissent in essence does, post, at 199-200) is to raise the standing hurdle higher than the necessary showing for success on the merits in an action alleging noncompliance with an NPDES permit. Focusing properly on injury to the plaintiff, the District Court found that FOE had demonstrated sufficient injury to establish standing. App.

in No. 97-1246 (CA4), at 207-208 (Tr. of Hearing 39-40). For example, FOE member Kenneth Lee Curtis averred in affidavits that he lived a half-mile from Laidlaw's facility; that he occasionally drove over the North Tyger River, and that it looked and smelled polluted; and that he would like to fish, camp, swim, and picnic in and near the river between 3 and 15 miles downstream from the facility, as he did when he was a teenager, but would not do so because he was concerned that the water was polluted by Laidlaw's discharges. Record, Doc. No. 71 (Exhs. 41, 42). Curtis reaffirmed these statements in extensive deposition testimony. For example, he testified that he would like to fish in the river at a specific spot he used as a boy, but that he would not do so now because of his concerns about Laidlaw's discharges. *Ibid.* (Exh. 43, at 52-53; Exh. 44, at 33).

Other members presented evidence to similar effect. CLEAN member Angela Patterson attested that she lived two miles from the facility; that before Laidlaw operated the facility, she picnicked, walked, birdwatched, and waded in and along the North Tyger River because of the natural beauty of the area; that she no longer engaged in these activities in or near the river because she was concerned about harmful effects from discharged pollutants; and that she and her husband would like to purchase a home near the river but did not intend to do so, in part because of Laidlaw's discharges. Record, Doc. No. 21 (Exh. 10). CLEAN member Judy Pruitt averred that she lived one-quarter mile from Laidlaw's facility and would like to fish, hike, and picnic along the North Tyger River, but has refrained from those activities because of the discharges. *Ibid.* (Exh. 7). FOE member Linda Moore attested that she lived 20 miles from Roebuck, and would use the North Tyger River south of Roebuck and the land surrounding it for recreational purposes were she not concerned that the water contained harmful pollutants. Record, Doc. No. 71 (Exhs. 45, 46). In her deposition, Moore testified at length that she would hike, picnic, camp, swim, boat, and drive near or in the river were it not for her concerns about illegal discharges. *Ibid.* (Exh. 48, at 29, 36-37, 62-63, 72). CLEAN member Gail Lee attested that her home, which is near Laidlaw's facility, had a lower value than similar homes located farther from the facility, and that she believed the pollutant discharges accounted for some of the discrepancy. Record, Doc. No. 21 (Exh. 9). Sierra Club member Norman Sharp averred that he had canoed approximately 40 miles downstream of the Laidlaw facility and would like to canoe in the North Tyger River closer to Laidlaw's discharge point, but did not do so because he was concerned that the water contained harmful pollutants. *Ibid.* (Exh. 8).

These sworn statements, as the District Court determined, adequately documented injury in fact. We have held that environmental plaintiffs adequately allege injury in fact when they aver that they use the affected area and are persons "for whom the aesthetic and recreational values of the area will be lessened" by the challenged activity. *Sierra Club v. Morton*, 405 U.S. 727, 735 (1972). See also *Defenders of Wildlife*, 504 U.S., at 562-563 ("Of course, the desire to use or observe an animal species, even for purely esthetic purposes, is undeniably a cognizable interest for purposes of standing.").

Our decision in *Lujan v. National Wildlife Federation*, 497 U.S. 871 (1990), is not to the contrary. In that case an environmental organization assailed the Bureau of Land Management's "land withdrawal review program," a program covering millions of acres, alleging that the program illegally opened up public lands to mining activities. The defendants moved for summary judgment, challenging the plaintiff organization's standing to initiate the action under the Administrative Procedure Act, 5 U.S.C. § 702. We held that the plaintiff could not survive the summary judgment motion merely by offering "averments which state only that one of [the organization's] members uses unspecified portions of an immense tract of territory, on some portions of which mining activity has occurred or probably will occur by virtue of the governmental action." 497 U.S., at 889.

In contrast, the affidavits and testimony presented by FOE in this case assert that Laidlaw's discharges, and the affiant members' reasonable concerns about the effects of

those discharges, directly affected those affiants' recreational, aesthetic, and economic interests. These submissions present dispositively more than the mere "general averments" and "conclusory allegations" found inadequate in National Wildlife Federation. *Id.*, at 888. Nor can the affiants' conditional statements—that they would use the nearby North Tyger River for recreation if Laidlaw were not discharging pollutants into it—be equated with the speculative "'some day' intentions" to visit endangered species halfway around the world that we held insufficient to show injury in fact in Defenders of Wildlife. 504 U.S., at 564.

Los Angeles v. Lyons, 461 U.S. 95 (1983), relied on by the dissent, post, at 199, does not weigh against standing in this case. In *Lyons*, we held that a plaintiff lacked standing to seek an injunction against the enforcement of a police choke- hold policy because he could not credibly allege that he faced a realistic threat from the policy. 461 U.S., at 107, n. 7. In the footnote from *Lyons* cited by the dissent, we noted that "[t]he reasonableness of Lyons' fear is dependent upon the likelihood of a recurrence of the allegedly unlawful conduct," and that his "subjective apprehensions" that such a recurrence would even take place were not enough to support standing. *Id.*, at 108, n. 8. Here, in contrast, it is undisputed that Laidlaw's unlawful conduct—discharging pollutants in excess of permit limits—was occurring at the time the complaint was filed. Under *Lyons*, then, the only "subjective" issue here is "[t]he reasonableness of [the] fear" that led the affiants to respond to that concededly ongoing conduct by refraining from use of the North Tyger River and surrounding areas. Unlike the dissent, post, at 200, we see nothing "improbable" about the proposition that a company's continuous and pervasive illegal discharges of pollutants into a river would cause nearby residents to curtail their recreational use of that waterway and would subject them to other economic and aesthetic harms. The proposition is entirely reasonable, the District Court found it was true in this case, and that is enough for injury in fact.

Laidlaw argues next that even if FOE had standing to seek injunctive relief, it lacked standing to seek civil penalties. Here the asserted defect is not injury but redressability. Civil penalties offer no redress to private plaintiffs, Laidlaw argues, because they are paid to the Government, and therefore a citizen plaintiff can never have standing to seek them.

Laidlaw is right to insist that a plaintiff must demonstrate standing separately for each form of relief sought. See, e.g., *Lyons*, 461 U.S., at 109 (notwithstanding the fact that plaintiff had standing to pursue damages, he lacked standing to pursue injunctive relief); see also *Lewis v. Casey*, 518 U.S. 343, 358, n. 6 (1996) ("[Standing is not dispensed in gross."). But it is wrong to maintain that citizen plaintiffs facing ongoing violations never have standing to seek civil penalties.

We have recognized on numerous occasions that "all civil penalties have some deterrent effect." *Hudson v. United States*, 522 U.S. 93, 102 (1997); see also, e.g., *Department of Revenue of Mont. v. Kurth Ranch*, 511 U.S. 767, 778 (1994). More specifically, Congress has found that civil penalties in Clean Water Act cases do more than promote immediate compliance by limiting the defendant's economic incentive to delay its attainment of permit limits; they also deter future violations. This congressional determination warrants judicial attention and respect. "The legislative history of the Act reveals that Congress wanted the district court to consider the need for retribution and deterrence, in addition to restitution, when it imposed civil penalties. . . . [The district court may] seek to deter future violations by basing the penalty on its economic impact." *Tull v. United States*, 481 U.S. 412, 422-423 (1987).

It can scarcely be doubted that, for a plaintiff who is injured or faces the threat of future injury due to illegal conduct ongoing at the time of suit, a sanction that effectively

abates that conduct and prevents its recurrence provides a form of redress. Civil penalties can fit that description. To the extent that they encourage defendants to discontinue current violations and deter them from committing future ones, they afford redress to citizen plaintiffs who are injured or threatened with injury as a consequence of ongoing unlawful conduct.

The dissent argues that it is the availability rather than the imposition of civil penalties that deters any particular polluter from continuing to pollute. Post, at 207-208. This argument misses the mark in two ways. First, it overlooks the interdependence of the availability and the imposition; a threat has no deterrent value unless it is credible that it will be carried out. Second, it is reasonable for Congress to conclude that an actual award of civil penalties does in fact bring with it a significant quantum of deterrence over and above what is achieved by the mere prospect of such penalties. A would-be polluter may or may not be dissuaded by the existence of a remedy on the books, but a defendant once hit in its pocketbook will surely think twice before polluting again.[2]

We recognize that there may be a point at which the deterrent effect of a claim for civil penalties becomes so insubstantial or so remote that it cannot support citizen standing. The fact that this vanishing point is not easy to ascertain does not detract from the deterrent power of such penalties in the ordinary case. Justice Frankfurter's observations for the Court, made in a different context nearly 60 years ago, hold true here as well:

"How to effectuate policy—the adaptation of means to legitimately sought ends —is one of the most intractable of legislative problems. Whether proscribed conduct is to be deterred by qui tam action or triple damages or injunction, or by criminal prosecution, or merely by defense to actions in contract, or by some, or all, of these remedies in combination, is a matter within the legislature's range of choice. Judgment on the deterrent effect of the various weapons in the armory of the law can lay little claim to scientific basis." *Tigner v. Texas*, 310 U.S. 141, 148 (1940).[3]

In this case we need not explore the outer limits of the principle that civil penalties provide sufficient deterrence to support redressability. Here, the civil penalties sought by FOE carried with them a deterrent effect that made it likely, as opposed to merely speculative, that the penalties would redress FOE's injuries by abating current violations and preventing future ones—as the District Court reasonably found when it assessed a penalty of $405,800. 956 F. Supp., at 610-611.

Laidlaw contends that the reasoning of our decision in *Steel Co.* directs the conclusion that citizen plaintiffs have no standing to seek civil penalties under the Act. We disagree. *Steel Co.* established that citizen suitors lack standing to seek civil penalties for violations that have abated by the time of suit. 523 U.S., at 106-107. We specifically noted in that case that there was no allegation in the complaint of any continuing or imminent violation, and that no basis for such an allegation appeared to exist. at 108; see also *Gwaltney*, 484 U.S., at 59 ("the harm sought to be addressed by the citizen suit lies in the present or the future, not in the past"). In short, *Steel Co.* held that private plaintiffs, unlike the Federal Government, may not sue to assess penalties for wholly past violations, but our decision in that case did not reach the issue of standing to seek penalties for violations that are ongoing at the time of the complaint and that could continue into the future if undeterred.[4]

B

Satisfied that FOE had standing under Article III to bring this action, we turn to the question of mootness.

The only conceivable basis for a finding of mootness in this case is Laidlaw's voluntary conduct—either its achievement by August 1992 of substantial compliance with its NPDES permit or its more recent shutdown of the Roebuck facility. It is well settled that "a defendant's voluntary cessation of a challenged practice does not deprive a federal court of its power to determine the legality of the practice." *City of Mesquite*, 455 U.S., at 289. "[I]f it did, the courts would be compelled to leave '[t]he defendant . . . free to return to his old ways.'" *Id.*, at 289, n. 10 (citing *United States v. W. T. Grant Co.*, 345 U.S. 629, 632 (1953)). In accordance with this principle, the standard we have announced for determining whether a case has been mooted by the defendant's voluntary conduct is stringent: "A case might become moot if subsequent events made it absolutely clear that the allegedly wrongful behavior could not reasonably be expected to recur." *United States v. Concentrated Phosphate Export Assn., Inc.*, 393 U.S. 199, 203 (1968). The "heavy burden of persua[ding]" the court that the challenged conduct cannot reasonably be expected to start up again lies with the party asserting mootness. *Ibid.*

The Court of Appeals justified its mootness disposition by reference to *Steel Co.*, which held that citizen plaintiffs lack standing to seek civil penalties for wholly past violations. In relying on *Steel Co.*, the Court of Appeals confused mootness with standing. The confusion is understandable, given this Court's repeated statements that the doctrine of mootness can be described as "the doctrine of standing set in a time frame: The requisite personal interest that must exist at the commencement of the litigation (standing) must continue throughout its existence (mootness)." *Arizonans for Official English*, 520 U.S., at 68, n. 22 (quoting *United States Parole Comm'n v. Geraghty*, 445 U.S. 388, 397 (1980), in turn quoting Monaghan, Constitutional Adjudication: The Who and When, 82 Yale L. J. 1363, 1384 (1973)) (internal quotation marks omitted).

Careful reflection on the long-recognized exceptions to mootness, however, reveals that the description of mootness as "standing set in a time frame" is not comprehensive. As just noted, a defendant claiming that its voluntary compliance moots a case bears the formidable burden of showing that it is absolutely clear the allegedly wrongful behavior could not reasonably be expected to recur. *Concentrated Phosphate Export Assn.*, 393 U.S., at 203. By contrast, in a lawsuit brought to force compliance, it is the plaintiff's burden to establish standing by demonstrating that, if unchecked by the litigation, the defendant's allegedly wrongful behavior will likely occur or continue, and that the "threat-ened injury [is] certainly impending." *Whitmore v. Arkansas*, 495 U.S. 149,158 (1990) (citations and internal quotation marks omitted). Thus, in *Lyons*, as already noted, we held that a plaintiff lacked initial standing to seek an injunc-tion against the enforcement of a police chokehold policy because he could not credibly allege that he faced a realistic threat arising from the policy. 461 U.S., at 105-110. Elsewhere in the opinion, however, we noted that a citywide mora-torium on police chokeholds—an action that surely diminished the already slim likelihood that any particular individual would be choked by police— would not have mooted an otherwise valid claim for injunctive relief, because the moratorium by its terms was not permanent. *Id.*, at 101. The plain lesson of these cases is that there are circumstances in which the prospect that a defen-dant will engage in (or resume) harmful conduct may be too speculative to support standing, but not too speculative to overcome mootness.

Furthermore, if mootness were simply "standing set in a time frame," the exception to mootness that arises when the defendant's allegedly unlawful activity is "capable of repetition, yet evading review," could not exist. When, for example, a mentally disabled patient files a lawsuit challenging her confine-ment in a segregated institution, her post-complaint transfer to a community-based program will not moot the action, *Olmstead v. L. C.*, 527 U.S. 581, 594, n. 6 (1999), despite the fact that she would have lacked initial standing had she filed the complaint after the transfer. Standing admits of no similar exception; if a plaintiff lacks standing at the time the action commences, the fact that the dispute is capable of repetition yet evading review will not entitle the complainant to a federal judicial forum. See *Steel* 523 U.S., at 109 (" 'the moot-ness exception for disputes capable of repetition yet evading review . . . will not revive a dispute which became moot before the action commenced' ") (quoting *Renne v. Geary*, 501 U.S. 312, 320 (1991)).

We acknowledged the distinction between mootness and standing most recently in *Steel Co.*:

> "The United States . . . argues that the injunctive relief does constitute remediation because 'there is a presumption of [future] injury when the defendant has voluntarily ceased its illegal activity in response to litigation,' even if that occurs before a complaint is filed. . . . This makes a sword out of a shield. The 'presumption' the Government refers to has been applied to refute the assertion of mootness by a defendant who, when sued in a complaint that alleges present or threatened injury, ceases the complained-of activity. . . . It is an immense and unacceptable stretch to call the presumption into service as a substitute for the allegation of present or threatened injury upon which initial standing must be based." 523 U.S., at 109.

Standing doctrine functions to ensure, among other things, that the scarce resources of the federal courts are devoted to those disputes in which the parties have a concrete stake. In contrast, by the time mootness is an issue, the case has been brought and litigated, often (as here) for years. To abandon the case at an advanced stage may prove more wasteful than frugal. This argument from sunk costs[5] does not license courts to retain jurisdiction over cases in which one or both of the parties plainly lack a continuing interest, as when the parties have settled or a plaintiff pursuing a non-surviving claim has died. See, *DeFunis v. Odegaard*, 416 U.S. 312 (1974) (p curiam) (non-class-action challenge to constitutionality of law school admissions process mooted when plaintiff, admitted pursuant to preliminary injunction, neared graduation and defendant law school conceded that, as a matter of ordinary school policy, plaintiff would be allowed to finish his final term); Arizonans, 520 U.S., at 67 (non-class-action challenge to state constitutional amendment declaring English the official language of the State became moot when plaintiff, a state employee who sought to use her bilingual skills, left state employment). But the argument surely highlights an important difference between the two doctrines. See generally *Honig v. Doe*, 484 U.S. 305, 329-332 (1988) (Rehnquist, C. J., concurring).

In its brief, Laidlaw appears to argue that, regardless of the effect of Laidlaw's compliance, FOE doomed its own civil penalty claim to mootness by failing to appeal the District Court's denial of injunctive relief. Brief for Respondent 14- 17. This argument misconceives the statutory scheme. Under § 1365(a), the district court has discretion to determine which form of relief is best suited, in the particular case, to abate current violations and deter future ones. "[A] federal judge sitting as chancellor is not mechanically obligated to grant an injunction for every violation of law." *Weinberger v. Romero-Barcelo*, 456 U.S. 305, 313 (1982). Denial of injunctive relief does not necessarily mean that the district court has concluded there is no prospect of future violations for civil penalties to deter. Indeed, it meant no such thing in this case. The District Court denied injunctive relief, but expressly based its award of civil penalties on the need for deterrence. See 956 F. Supp., at 610-611. As the dissent notes, post, at 205, federal courts should aim to ensure " 'the framing of relief no broader than required by the precise facts.'" *Schlesinger v. Reservists Comm, to Stop the War*, 418 U.S. 208, 222 (1974). In accordance with this aim, a district court in a Clean Water Act citizen suit properly may conclude that an injunction would be an excessively intrusive remedy, because it could entail continuing superintendence of the permit holder's activities by a federal court—a process burdensome to court and permit holder alike. See *City of Mesquite*, 455 U.S., at 289 (although the defendant's voluntary cessation of the challenged practice does not moot the case, "[s]uch abandonment is an important factor bearing on the question whether a court should exercise its power to enjoin the defendant from renewing the practice").

Laidlaw also asserts, in a supplemental suggestion of mootness, that the closure of its Roebuck facility, which took place after the Court of Appeals issued its decision, mooted the case. The facility closure, like Laidlaw's earlier achievement of substantial compliance with its permit requirements, might moot the case, but—we once more reiterate—only if one or the other of these events made it absolutely clear that Laidlaw's permit violations could not reasonably be expected to recur. *Concentrated Phosphate Export Assn.*, 393 U.S., at 203. The effect of both Laidlaw's compliance and the facility closure on the prospect of future violations is a disputed factual matter. FOE points out, for example—and Laidlaw does not appear to contest—that Laidlaw retains its NPDES permit. These issues have not been aired in the lower courts; they remain open for consideration on remand.[6]

C

FOE argues that it is entitled to attorneys' fees on the theory that a plaintiff can be a "prevailing party" for purposes of 33 U.S.C. § 1365(d) if it was the "catalyst" that triggered a favorable outcome. In the decision under review, the Court of Appeals noted that its Circuit precedent construed our decision in *Farrar v. Hobby*, 506 U.S. 103 (1992), to require rejection of that theory. 149 F. 3d, at 307, n. 5 (citing *S-1 & S-2 v. State Bd. of Ed. of N. C.*, 21 F. 3d 49, 51 (CA4 1994) (en banc)). *Cf. Foreman v. Dallas County*, 193 F. 3d 314, 320 (CA5 1999) (stating, in dicta, that "[a]fter Farrar . . . the continuing validity of the catalyst theory is in serious doubt").

Farrar acknowledged that a civil rights plaintiff awarded nominal damages may be a "prevailing party" under 42 U.S.C. § 1988. 506 U.S., at 112. The case involved no catalytic effect. Recognizing that the issue was not presented for this Court's decision in Farrar, several Courts of Appeals have expressly concluded that Farrar did not repudiate the catalyst theory. See *Marbley v. Bane*, 57 F. 3d 224, 234 (CA2 1995); *Baumgartner v. Harrisburg Housing Authority*, 21 F. 3d 541, 546-550 (CA3 1994); *Zinn v. Shalala*, 35 F. 3d 273, 276 (CA7 1994); *Little Rock School Dist. v. Pulaski County Special Sch. Dist, #1*, 17 F. 3d 260, 263, n. 2 (CA8 1994); *Kilgour v. Pasadena*, 53 F. 3d 1007, 1010 (CA9 1995); *Beard v. Teska*, 31 F. 3d 942, 951-952 (CA10 1994); *Morris v. West Palm Beach*, 194 F. 3d 1203, 1207 (CA11 1999). Other Courts of Appeals have likewise continued to apply the catalyst theory notwithstanding Farrar. *Paris v. United States Dept, of Housing and Urban Development*, 988 F. 3d 236, 238 (CA1 1993); *Citizens Against Tax Waste v. Westerville City School*, 985 F. 2d 255, 257 (CA6 1993).

It would be premature, however, for us to address the continuing validity of the catalyst theory in the context of this case. The District Court, in an order separate from the one in which it imposed civil penalties against Laidlaw, stayed the time for a petition for attorneys' fees until the time for appeal had expired or, if either party appealed, until the appeal was resolved. See 149 F. 3d, at 305 (describing order staying time for attorneys' fees petition). In the opinion accompanying its order on penalties, the District Court stated only that "this court has considered that Laidlaw will be required to reimburse plaintiffs for a significant amount of legal fees," and referred to "potential fee awards." 956 F. Supp., at 610-611. Thus, when the Court of Appeals addressed the availability of counsel fees in this case, no order was before it either denying or awarding fees. It is for the District Court, not this Court, to address in the first instance any request for reimbursement of costs, including fees.

* * *

For the reasons stated, the judgment of the United States Court of Appeals for the Fourth Circuit is reversed, and the case is remanded for further proceedings consistent with this opinion.

It is so ordered.

---

1. The District Court noted that "Laidlaw drafted the state-court complaint and settlement agreement, filed the lawsuit against itself, and paid the filing fee." 890 F. Supp., at 489. Further, "the settlement agreement between DHEC and Laidlaw was entered into with unusual haste, without giving the Plaintiffs the opportunity to intervene." *Ibid.* The court found "most persuasive" the fact that "in imposing the civil penalty of $100,000 against Laidlaw, DHEC failed to recover, or even to calculate, the economic benefit that Laidlaw received by not complying with its permit." *Id.,* at 491.

2. The dissent suggests that there was little deterrent work for civil penalties to do in this case because the lawsuit brought against Laidlaw by DHEC had already pushed the level of deterrence to "near the top of the graph." Post, at 208. This suggestion ignores the District Court's specific finding that the penalty agreed to by Laidlaw and DHEC was far too low to remove Laidlaw's economic benefit from noncompliance, and thus was inadequate to deter future violations. 890 F. Supp. 470, 491-494,497- 498 (SC 1995). And it begins to look especially farfetched when one recalls that Laidlaw itself prompted the DHEC lawsuit, paid the filing fee, and drafted the complaint. See *supra,* at 176-177, 178, n. 1.

3. In *Tigner* the Court rejected an equal protection challenge to a statutory provision exempting agricultural producers from the reach of the Texas antitrust laws.

4. In insisting that the redressability requirement is not met, the dissent relies heavily on *Linda R. S. v. Richard D.,* 410 U.S. 614 (1973). That reliance is sorely misplaced. In *Linda R. S.,* the mother of an out-of-wedlock child filed suit to force a district attorney to bring a criminal prosecution against the absentee father for failure to pay child support. *Id.,* at 616. In finding that the mother lacked standing to seek this extraordinary remedy, the Court drew attention to "the special status of criminal prosecutions in our system," *id.,* at 619, and carefully limited its holding to the "unique context of a challenge to [the nonenforcement of] a criminal statute," *id.,* at 617. Furthermore, as to redressability, the relief sought in *Linda R. S.*—a prosecution which, if successful, would automatically land the delinquent father in jail for a fixed term, *id.,* at 618, with predictably negative effects on his earning power—would scarcely remedy the plaintiffs lack of child support payments. In this regard, the Court contrasted "the civil contempt model whereby the defendant 'keeps the keys to the jail in his own pocket' and may

be released whenever he complies with his legal obligations." *Ibid.* The dissent's contention, post, at 204, that "precisely the same situation exists here" as in *Linda R. S.* is, to say the least, extravagant.

Putting aside its mistaken reliance on *Linda R. S.*, the dissent's broader charge that citizen suits for civil penalties under the Act carry "grave implications for democratic governance," post, at 202, seems to us overdrawn. Certainly the Federal Executive Branch does not share the dissent's view that such suits dissipate its authority to enforce the law. In fact, the Department of Justice has endorsed this citizen suit from the outset, submitting amicus briefs in support of FOE in the District Court, the Court of Appeals, and this Court. See *supra*, at 177, 179. As we have already noted, *supra*, at 175, the Federal Government retains the power to foreclose a citizen suit by undertaking its own action. 33 U.S.C. § 1365(b)(1)(B). And if the Executive Branch opposes a particular citizen suit, the statute allows the Administrator of the EPA to "intervene as a matter of right" and bring the Government's views to the attention of the court. § 1365(c)(2).

5. Of course we mean sunk costs to the judicial system, not to the litigants. *Lewis v. Continental Bank Corp.*, 494 U.S. 472 (1990) (cited by the dissent, post, at 213), dealt with the latter, noting that courts should use caution to avoid carrying forward a moot case solely to vindicate a plaintiff's interest in recovering attorneys' fees.

6. We note that it is far from clear that vacatur of the District Court's judgment would be the appropriate response to a finding of mootness on appeal brought about by the voluntary conduct of the party that lost in the District Court. See *U.S. Bancorp Mortgage Co. v. Bonner Mall Partnership*, 513 U.S. 18 (1994) (mootness attributable to a voluntary act of a non-prevailing party ordinarily does not justify vacatur of a judgment under review): see also *Wallina v. James V. Reuter, Inc.*, 321 U.S. 671 (1944).

KIMBROUGH V. UNITED STATES

552 U.S. 85 (2007)

This case centered on the Federal Sentencing Guidelines, which is a system that attempts to set forth a uniform policy for how individuals convicted of crimes in the U.S. federal courts system are to be sentenced, and whether it is permissible for federal judges to impose sentences outside the range dictated by the Guidelines.

Derrick Kimbrough had been convicted of multiple drug-related crimes involving both crack and powder cocaine. Under the Federal Sentencing Guidelines at the time, crimes involving crack were sentenced significantly more harshly than those involving just powder cocaine, and consequently the guidelines recommended an extremely lengthy sentence — considerably longer than he would have faced if his crimes had involved only powder cocaine. In light of that disparity, a lower court judge recommended a minimum sentence below the Federal Sentencing Guidelines recommendation. Prosecutors appealed, arguing that the short sentence was per se unreasonable.

In a 7-2 opinion authored by Justice Ginsburg, the Court ruled that federal judges do have the discretion to deviate from the Federal Sentencing Guidelines.

Justice Ginsburg's opinion was joined by Justices Roberts, Stevens, Scalia, Kennedy, Souter, and Breyer. Justice Scalia also wrote a separate concurrence. Justices Thomas and Alito dissented.

KIMBROUGH V. UNITED STATES

552 U.S. 85 (2007)

This Court's remedial opinion in United States v. Booker, 543 U.S. 220, 244 (2005), instructed district courts to read the United States Sentencing Guidelines as "effectively advisory," *id.*, at 245. In accord with 18 U. S. C. § 3553(a), the Guidelines, formerly mandatory, now serve as one factor among several courts must consider in determining an appropriate sentence. Booker further instructed that "reasonableness" is the standard controlling appellate review of the sentences district courts impose.

Under the statute criminalizing the manufacture and distribution of crack cocaine, 21 U. S. C. §841, and the relevant Guidelines prescription, §2D1.1, a drug trafficker dealing in crack cocaine is subject to the same sentence as one dealing in 100 times more powder cocaine. The question here presented is whether, as the Court of Appeals held in this case, "a sentence . . . outside the guidelines range is per se unreasonable when it is based on a disagreement with the sentencing disparity for crack and powder cocaine offenses." 174 Fed. Appx. 798, 799 (CA4 2006) curiam). We hold that, under Booker, the cocaine Guidelines, like all other Guidelines, are advisory only, and that the Court of Appeals erred in holding the crack/powder disparity effectively mandatory. A district judge must include the Guidelines range in the array of factors warranting consideration. The judge may determine, however, that, in the particular case, a within- Guidelines sentence is "greater than necessary" to serve the objectives of sentencing. 18 U. S. C. § 3553(a) (2000 ed. and Supp. V). In making that determination, the judge may consider the disparity between the Guidelines' treatment of crack and powder cocaine offenses.

I

In September 2004, petitioner Derrick Kimbrough was indicted in the United States District Court for the Eastern District of Virginia and charged with four offenses: conspiracy to distribute crack and powder cocaine; possession with intent to distribute more than 50 grams of crack cocaine; possession with intent to distribute powder cocaine; and possession of a firearm in furtherance of a drug-trafficking offense. Kimbrough pleaded guilty to all four charges.

Under the relevant statutes, Kimbrough's plea subjected him to an aggregate sentence of 15 years to life in prison: 10 years to life for the three drug offenses, plus a consecutive term of 5 years to life for the firearm offense.[1] In order to determine the appropriate sentence within this statutory range, the District Court first calculated Kimbrough's sentence under the advisory Sentencing Guidelines.[2] Kimbrough's guilty plea acknowledged that he was accountable for 56 grams of crack cocaine and 92.1 grams of powder cocaine. This quantity of drugs yielded a base offense level of 32 for the three drug charges. See United States Sentencing Commission, Guidelines Manual §2D1.1(c) (Nov. 2004) (USSG). Finding that Kimbrough, by asserting sole culpability for the crime, had testified falsely at his codefendant's trial, the District Court increased his offense level to 34. See §3C1.1. In accord with the presentence report, the court determined that Kimbrough's criminal history category was II. An offense level of 34 and a criminal history category of II yielded a Guidelines range of 168 to 210 months for the three drug charges. See *id.*, ch. 5, pt. A, Sentencing Table. The Guidelines sentence for the firearm offense was the statutory minimum, 60 months. See § 2K2.4(b). Kimbrough's final advisory Guidelines range was thus 228 to 270 months, or 19 to 22.5 years.

A sentence in this range, in the District Court's judgment, would have been "greater than necessary" to accomplish the purposes of sentencing set forth in 18 U. S. C. § 3553(a). App. 72. As required by § 3553(a), the court took into account the "nature and circumstances" of the offense and Kimbrough's "history and characteristics." at 72-73. The court also commented that the case exemplified the "disproportionate and unjust effect that crack cocaine guidelines have in sentencing." *Id.*, at 72. In this regard, the court contrasted Kimbrough's Guidelines range of 228 to 270 months with the range that would have applied had he been accountable for an equivalent amount of powder cocaine: 97 to 106 months, inclusive of the 5-year mandatory minimum for the firearm charge, see USSG §2D1.1(c); *id.*, ch. 5, pt. A, Sentencing Table. Concluding that the statutory minimum sentence was "clearly long enough" to accomplish the objectives listed in § 3553(a), the court sentenced Kimbrough to 15 years, or 180 months, in prison plus 5 years of supervised release. App. 74-75.[3]

In an unpublished per curiam opinion, the Fourth Circuit vacated the sentence. Under Circuit precedent, the Court of Appeals observed, a sentence "outside the guidelines range is per se unreasonable when it is based on a disagreement with the sentencing disparity for crack and powder cocaine offenses." 174 Fed. Appx., at 799 (citing United States v.Eura,440 F. 3d 625, 633-634 (CA4 2006)).

We granted certiorari, 551 U.S. 1113 (2007), to determine whether the crack/powder disparity adopted in the United States Sentencing Guidelines has been rendered "advisory" by our decision Booker.[4]

II

We begin with some background on the different treatment of crack and powder cocaine under the federal sentencing laws. Crack and powder cocaine are two forms of the same drug. Powder cocaine, or cocaine hydrochloride, is generally inhaled through the nose; it may also be mixed with water and injected. See United States Sentencing Commission, Special Report to Congress: Cocaine and Federal Sentencing Policy 5, 12 (Feb. 1995), available at http:// www.ussc.gov/crack/exec.htm (hereinafter 1995 Report). (All Internet materials as visited Dec. 7, 2007, and included in Clerk of Court's case file.) Crack cocaine, a type of cocaine base, is formed by dissolving powder cocaine and baking soda in boiling water. *Id.*, at 14. The resulting solid is divided into single-dose "rocks" that users smoke. *Ibid.* The active ingredient in powder and crack cocaine is the same. *Id.*, at 9. The two forms of the drug also have the same physiological and psychotropic effects, but smoking crack cocaine allows the body to absorb the drug much faster than inhaling powder cocaine, and thus produces a shorter, more intense high. *Id.*, at 15-19.[5]

Although chemically similar, crack and powder cocaine are handled very differently for sentencing purposes. The 100- to-1 ratio yields sentences for crack offenses three to six times longer than those for powder offenses involving equal amounts of drugs. See United States Sentencing Commission, Report to Congress: Cocaine and Federal Sentencing Policy iv (May 2002), available at http://www.ussc.gov/r_congress/02crack/2002crackrpt.pdf (hereinafter 2002 Report).[6] This disparity means that a major supplier of powder cocaine may receive a shorter sentence than a low-level dealer who buys powder from the supplier but then converts it to crack. See 1995 Report 193-194.

A

The crack/powder disparity originated in the Anti-Drug Abuse Act of 1986 (1986 Act), 100 Stat. 3207. The 1986 Act created a two-tiered scheme of five- and ten-year mandatory minimum sentences for drug manufacturing and distribution offenses. Congress sought "to link the ten-year mandatory minimum trafficking prison term to major drug dealers and to link the five-year minimum term to serious traffickers." 1995 Report 119. The 1986 Act uses the weight of the drugs involved in the offense as the sole proxy to identify "major" and "serious" dealers. For example, any defendant responsible for 100 grams of heroin is subject to the five-year mandatory minimum, see 21 U.S. C. § 841(b)(l)(B)(i) (2000 ed. and Supp. V), and any defendant responsible for 1,000 grams of heroin is subject to the ten-year mandatory minimum, see § 841(b)(l)(A)(i).

Crack cocaine was a relatively new drug when the 1986 Act was signed into law, but it was already a matter of great public concern: "Drug abuse in general, and crack cocaine in particular, had become in public opinion and in members' minds a problem of overwhelming dimensions." 1995 Report 121. Congress apparently believed that crack was significantly more dangerous than powder cocaine in that: (1) crack was highly addictive; (2) crack users and dealers were more likely to be violent than users and dealers of other drugs; (3) crack was more harmful to users than powder, particularly for children who had been exposed by their mothers' drug use during pregnancy; (4) crack use was especially prevalent among teenagers; and (5) crack's potency and low cost were making it increasingly popular. See 2002 Report 90.

Based on these assumptions, the 1986 Act adopted a "100- to-1 ratio" that treated every gram of crack cocaine as the equivalent of 100 grams of powder cocaine. The 1986 Act's five-year mandatory minimum applies to any defendant accountable for 5 grams of crack or 500 grams of powder, 21 U.S. C. § 841(b)(l)(B)(ii), (iii); its ten-year mandatory minimum applies to any defendant accountable for 50 grams of crack or 5,000 grams of powder, § 841(b)(l)(A)(ii), (iii).

While Congress was considering adoption of the 1986 Act, the Sentencing Commission was engaged in formulating the Sentencing Guidelines.[7] In the main, the Commission developed Guidelines sentences using an empirical approach based on data about past sentencing practices, including 10,000 presentence investigation reports. See USSG §1A.1, intro, comment, pt. A, 13. The Commission "modified] and adjusted] past practice in the interests of greater rationality, avoiding inconsistency, complying with congressional instructions, and the like." *Rita v. United States*, 551 U.S. 338, 349 (2007).

The Commission did not use this empirical approach in developing the Guidelines sentences for drug-trafficking offenses. Instead, it employed the 1986 Act's weight-driven scheme. The Guidelines use a drug quantity table based on drug type and weight to set base offense levels for drug- trafficking offenses. See USSG §2Dl.l(c). In setting offense levels for crack and powder cocaine, the Commission, in line with the 1986 Act, adopted the 100-to-l ratio. The statute itself specifies only two quantities of each drug, but the Guidelines "go further and set sentences for the full range of possible drug quantities using the same 100-to-1 quantity ratio." 1995 Report 1. The Guidelines' drug quantity table sets base offense levels ranging from 12, for offenses involving less than 250 milligrams of crack (or 25 grams of powder), to 38, for offenses involving more than 1.5 kilograms of crack (or 150 kilograms of powder). USSG §2D1.1(c).[8]

B

Although the Commission immediately used the 100-to-1 ratio to define base offense levels for all crack and powder offenses, it later determined that the crack/powder sentencing disparity is generally unwarranted. Based on additional research and experience with the 100-to-1 ratio, the Commission concluded that the disparity "fails to meet the sentencing objectives set forth by Congress in both the Sentencing Reform Act and the 1986 Act." 2002 Report 91. In a series of reports, the Commission identified three problems with the crack/powder disparity.

First, the Commission reported, the 100-to-1 ratio rested on assumptions about "the relative harmfulness of the two drugs and the relative prevalence of certain harmful conduct associated with their use and distribution that more recent research and data no longer support." *Ibid,.*; see United States Sentencing Commission, Report to Congress: Cocaine and Federal Sentencing Policy 8 (May 2007), available at http://www.ussc.gov/r_congress/cocaine2007.pdf (hereinafter 2007 Report) (ratio Congress embedded in the statute far "overstate[s]" both "the relative harmfulness" of crack cocaine, and the "seriousness of most crack cocaine offenses"). For example, the Commission found that crack is associated with "significantly less trafficking-related violence . . . than previously assumed." 2002 Report 100. It also observed that "the negative effects of prenatal crack cocaine exposure are identical to the negative effects of prenatal powder cocaine exposure." *Id.,* at 94. The Commission furthermore noted that "the epidemic of crack cocaine use by youth never materialized to the extent feared." *Id.,* at 96.

Second, the Commission concluded that the crack/powder disparity is inconsistent with the 1986 Act's goal of punishing major drug traffickers more severely than low-level dealers. Drug importers and major traffickers generally deal in powder cocaine, which is then converted into crack by street- level sellers. See 1995 Report 66-67. But the 100-to-1 ratio can lead to the "anomalous" result that "retail crack dealers get longer sentences than the wholesale drug distributors who supply them the powder cocaine from which their crack is produced." *Id.,* at 174.

Finally, the Commission stated that the crack/powder sentencing differential "fosters disrespect for and lack of confidence in the criminal justice system" because of a "widely- held perception" that it "promotes unwarranted disparity based on race." 2002 Report 103. Approximately 85 percent of defendants convicted of crack offenses in federal court are black; thus the severe sentences required by the 100-to-l ratio are imposed "primarily upon black offenders." *Ibid.*

Despite these observations, the Commission's most recent reports do not urge identical treatment of crack and powder cocaine. In the Commission's view, "some differential in the quantity-based penalties" for the two drugs is warranted, *id.*, at 102, because crack is more addictive than powder, crack offenses are more likely to involve weapons or bodily injury, and crack distribution is associated with higher levels of crime, see *id.*, at 93-94, 101-102. But the 100-to-l crack/powder ratio, the Commission concluded, significantly overstates the differences between the two forms of the drug. Accordingly, the Commission recommended that the ratio be "substantially" reduced. *Id.*, at viii.

C

The Commission has several times sought to achieve a reduction in the crack/powder ratio. In 1995, it proposed amendments to the Guidelines that would have replaced the 100-to-l ratio with a 1-to-l ratio. Complementing that change, the Commission would have installed special enhancements for trafficking offenses involving weapons or bodily injury. See Amendments to the Sentencing Guidelines for United States Courts, 60 Fed. Reg. 25075-25077 (1995). Congress, acting pursuant to 28 U.S. C. § 994(p),[9] rejected the amendments. See Pub. L. 104-38, § 1, 109 Stat. 334. Simultaneously, however, Congress directed the Commission to "propose revision of the drug quantity ratio of crack cocaine to powder cocaine under the relevant statutes and guidelines." § 2(a)(2), *id.*, at 335.

In response to this directive, the Commission issued reports in 1997 and 2002 recommending that Congress change the 100-to-l ratio prescribed in the 1986 Act. The 1997 Report proposed a 5-to-l ratio. See United States Sentencing Commission, Special Report to Congress: Cocaine and Federal Sentencing Policy 2 (Apr. 1997), http://www.ussc.gov/r_congress/newcrack.pdf. The 2002 Report recommended lowering the ratio "at least" to 20 to 1. 2002 Report viii. Neither proposal prompted congressional action.

The Commission's most recent report, issued in 2007, again urged Congress to amend the 1986 Act to reduce the 100-to-l ratio. This time, however, the Commission did not simply await congressional action. Instead, the Commission adopted an ameliorating change in the Guidelines. See 2007 Report 9. The alteration, which became effective on November 1, 2007, reduces the base offense level associated with each quantity of crack by two levels. See Amendments to the Sentencing Guidelines for United States Courts, 72 Fed. Reg.

28571-28572 (2007).[10] This modest amendment yields sentences for crack offenses between two and five times longer than sentences for equal amounts of powder. See *ibid.*[11] Describing the amendment as "only . . . a partial remedy" for the problems generated by the crack/powder disparity, the Commission noted that "[a]ny comprehensive solution requires appropriate legislative action by Congress." 2007 Report 10.

III

With this history of the crack/powder sentencing ratio in mind, we next consider the status of the Guidelines tied to the ratio after our decision in United States v. Booker, 543 U.S. 220 (2005). In Booker, the Court held that the mandatory Sentencing Guidelines system violated the Sixth Amendment. See *id.*, at 226-227. The *Booker* remedial opinion determined that the appropriate cure was to sever and excise the provision of the statute that rendered the Guidelines mandatory, 18 U.S.C. § 3553(b)(1) (2000 ed., Supp. IV).[12] This modification of the federal sentencing statute, we explained, "makes the Guidelines effectively advisory." 543 U.S., at 245.

The statute, as modified by *Booker*, contains an overarching provision instructing district courts to "impose a sentence sufficient, but not greater than necessary," to accomplish the goals of sentencing, including "to reflect the seriousness of the offense," "to promote respect for the law," "to provide just punishment for the offense," "to afford adequate deterrence to criminal conduct," and "to protect the public from further crimes of the defendant." 18 U.S.C. § 3553(a) (2000 ed. and Supp. V). The statute further provides that, in determining the appropriate sentence, the court should consider a number of factors, including "the nature and circumstances of the offense," "the history and characteristics of the defendant," "the sentencing range established" by the Guidelines, "any pertinent policy statement" issued by the Sentencing Commission pursuant to its statutory authority, and "the need to avoid unwarranted sentence disparities among defendants with similar records who have been found guilty of similar conduct." *Ibid.* In sum, while the statute still requires a court to give respectful consideration to the Guidelines, see *Gall v. United States, ante*, at 46, 49, *Booker* "permits the court to tailor the sentence in light of other statutory concerns as well," 543 U.S., at 245-246.

The Government acknowledges that the Guidelines "are now advisory" and that, as a general matter, "courts may vary [from Guidelines ranges] based solely on policy considerations, including disagreements with the Guidelines." Brief for United States 16; *cf. Rita*, 551 U.S., at 351 (a district court may consider arguments that "the Guidelines sentence itself fails properly to reflect § 3553(a) considerations"). But the Government contends that the Guidelines adopting the 100-to-1 ratio are an exception to the "general freedom that sentencing courts have to apply the [§ 3553(a)] factors." Brief for United States 16. That is so, according to the Government, because the ratio is a "specific policy determinatio[n] that Congress has directed sentencing courts to observe." *Id.*, at 25. The Government offers three arguments in support of this position. We consider each in turn.

A

As its first and most heavily pressed argument, the Government urges that the 1986 Act itself prohibits the Sentencing Commission and sentencing courts from disagreeing with the 100-to-1 ratio.[13] The Government acknowledges that the "Congress did not *expressly* direct the Sentencing Commission to incorporate the 100:1 ratio in the Guidelines." Brief for United States 33 (brackets and internal quotation marks omitted). Nevertheless, it asserts that the Act "[i]mplicit[ly]" requires the Commission and sentencing courts to apply the 100-to-1 ratio. *Id.*, at 32. Any deviation, the Government urges, would be "logically incoherent" when combined with mandatory minimum sentences based on the 100-to-1 ratio. *Id.*, at 33.

This argument encounters a formidable obstacle: It lacks grounding in the text of the 1986 Act. The statute, by its terms, mandates only maximum and minimum sentences: A person convicted of possession with intent to distribute five grams or more of crack cocaine must be sentenced to a minimum of 5 years and the maximum term is 40 years. A person with 50 grams or more of crack cocaine must be sentenced to a minimum of ten years and the maximum term is life. The statute says nothing about the appropriate sentences within these brackets, and we decline to read any implicit directive into that congressional silence. See *Jama v. Immigration and Customs Enforcement*, 543 U.S. 335, 341 (2005) ("We do not lightly assume that Congress has omitted from its adopted text requirements that it nonetheless intends to apply . . . ."). Drawing meaning from silence is particularly inappropriate here, for Congress has shown that it knows how to direct sentencing practices in express terms. For example, Congress has specifically required the Sentencing Commission to set Guidelines sentences for serious recidivist offenders "at or near" the statutory maximum. 28 U.S. C. § 994(h). See also § 994(i) ("The Commission shall assure that the guidelines specify a sentence to a substantial term of imprisonment" for specified categories of offenders.).

Our cautious reading of the 1986 Act draws force from *Neal v. United States*, 516 U.S. 284 (1996). That case involved different methods of calculating lysergic acid diethylamide (LSD) weights, one applicable in determining statutory minimum sentences, the other controlling the calculation of Guidelines ranges. The 1986 Act sets mandatory minimum sentences based on the weight of "a mixture or substance containing a detectable amount" of LSD. 21 U.S. C. §

841(b)(1)(A)(v), (B)(v). Prior to *Neal*, we had interpreted that language to include the weight of the carrier medium (usually blotter paper) on which LSD is absorbed even though the carrier is usually far heavier than the LSD itself. See *Chapman v. United States*, 500 U.S. 453, 468 (1991). Until 1993, the Sentencing Commission had interpreted the relevant Guidelines in the same way. That year, however, the Commission changed its approach and "instructed courts to give each dose of LSD on a carrier medium a constructive or presumed weight of 0.4 milligrams." *Neal*, 516 U.S., at 287 (citing USSG §2D1.1(c), n. (H) (Nov. 1995)). The Commission's change significantly lowered the Guidelines range applicable to most LSD offenses, but defendants remained subject to higher statutory minimum sentences based on the combined weight of the pure drug and its carrier medium. The defendant in argued that the revised Guidelines and the statute should be interpreted consistently and that the "presumptive-weight method of the Guidelines should also control the mandatory minimum calculation." 516 U.S., at 287. We rejected that argument, emphasizing that the Commission had not purported to interpret the statute and could not in any event overrule our decision in *Chapman*. See 516 U.S., at 293-295.

If the Government's current position were correct, then the Guidelines involved in *Neal* would be in serious jeopardy. We have just recounted the reasons alleged to justify reading into the 1986 Act an implicit command to the Commission and sentencing courts to apply the 100-to-1 ratio to all quantities of crack cocaine. Those same reasons could be urged in support of an argument that the 1986 Act requires the Commission to include the full weight of the carrier medium in calculating the weight of LSD for Guidelines purposes. Yet our opinion in *Neal* never questioned the validity of the altered Guidelines. To the contrary, we stated: "Entrusted within its sphere to make policy judgments, the Commission may abandon its old methods in favor of what it has deemed a more desirable 'approach' to calculating LSD quantities." Id,., at 295.[14] If the 1986 Act does not require the Commission to adhere to the Act's method for determining LSD weights, it does not require the Commission—or, after *Booker*, sentencing courts—to adhere to the 100-to-1 ratio for crack cocaine quantities other than those that trigger the statutory mandatory minimum sentences.

B

In addition to the 1986 Act, the Government relies on Congress' disapproval of the Guidelines amendment that the Sentencing Commission proposed in 1995. Congress "not only disapproved of the 1:1 ratio," the Government urges; it also made clear "that the 1986 Act required the Commission (and sentencing courts) to take drug quantities into account, and to do so in a manner that respects the 100:1 ratio." Brief for United States 35.

It is true that Congress rejected the Commission's 1995 proposal to place a 1-to-1 ratio in the Guidelines, and that Congress also expressed the view that "the sentence imposed for trafficking in a quantity of crack cocaine should generally exceed the sentence imposed for trafficking in a like quantity of powder cocaine." Pub. L. 104-38, § 2(a)(1)(A), 109 Stat. 334. But nothing in Congress' 1995 reaction to the Commission-proposed 1-to-1 ratio suggested that crack sentences must exceed powder sentences by a ratio of 100 to 1. To the contrary, Congress' 1995 action required the Commission to recommend a "revision of the drug quantity ratio of crack cocaine to powder cocaine." § 2(a) (2), *id.*, at 335.

The Government emphasizes that Congress required the Commission to propose changes to the 100-to-1 ratio in both the 1986 Act and the Guidelines. This requirement, the Government contends, implicitly foreclosed any deviation from the 100-to-1 ratio in the Guidelines (or by sentencing courts) in the absence of a corresponding change in the statute. See Brief for United States 35-36. But it does not follow as the night follows the day that, by calling for recommendations to change the statute, Congress meant to bar any Guidelines alteration in advance of congressional action. The more likely reading is that Congress sought proposals to amend both the statute and the Guidelines because the Commission's criticisms of the 100-to-1 ratio, see Part II-B, *supra*, concerned the exorbitance of the crack/powder disparity in both contexts.

Moreover, as a result of the 2007 amendment, see *supra*, at 99-100, the Guidelines now advance a crack/powder ratio that varies (at different offense levels) between 25 to 1 and 80 to 1. See Amendments to the Sentencing Guidelines for United States Courts, 72 Fed. Reg. 28571-28572. Adopting the Government's analysis, the amended Guidelines would conflict with Congress' 1995 action, and with the 1986 Act, because the current Guidelines ratios deviate from the 100- to-1 statutory ratio. Congress, however, did not disapprove or modify the Commission-initiated 2007 amendment. Ordinarily, we resist reading congressional intent into congressional inaction. See Bob Jones Univ. v. United States, 461 U.S. 574,600 (1983). But in this case, Congress failed to act on a proposed amendment to the Guidelines in a high-profile area in which it had previously exercised its disapproval authority under 28 U.S. C. § 994(p). If nothing else, this tacit acceptance of the 2007 amendment undermines the Government's position, which is itself based on implications drawn from congressional silence.

C

Finally, the Government argues that if district courts are free to deviate from the Guidelines based on disagreements with the crack/powder ratio, unwarranted disparities of two kinds will ensue. See 18 U.S. C. § 3553(a)(6) (sentencing courts shall consider "the need to avoid unwarranted sentence disparities")- First, because sentencing courts remain bound by the mandatory minimum sentences prescribed in the 1986 Act, deviations from the 100-to-l ratio could result in sentencing "cliffs" around quantities that trigger the mandatory minimums. Brief for United States 33 (internal quotation marks omitted). For example, a district court could grant a sizable downward variance to a defendant convicted of distributing 49 grams of crack but would be required by the statutory minimum to impose a much higher sentence on a defendant responsible for only 1 additional gram. Second, the Government maintains that, if district courts are permitted to vary from the Guidelines based on their disagreement with the crack/powder disparity, "defendants with identical real conduct will receive markedly different sentences, depending on nothing more than the particular judge drawn for sentencing." *Id.*, at 40.

Neither of these arguments persuades us to hold the crack/ powder ratio untouchable by sentencing courts. As to the first, the LSD Guidelines we approved in Neal create a similar risk of sentencing "cliffs." An offender who possesses LSD on a carrier medium weighing ten grams is subject to the ten-year mandatory minimum, see 21 U.S.C. § 841(b)(l)(A)(v), but an offender whose carrier medium weighs slightly less may receive a considerably lower sentence based on the Guidelines' presumptive-weight methodology. Concerning the second disparity, it is unquestioned that uniformity remains an important goal of sentencing. As we explained in Booker, however, advisory Guidelines combined with appellate review for reasonableness and ongoing revision of the Guidelines in response to sentencing practices will help to "avoid excessive sentencing disparities." 543 U.S., at 264. These measures will not eliminate variations between district courts, but our opinion in *Booker* recognized that some departures from uniformity were a necessary cost of the remedy we adopted. See at 263 ("We cannot and do not claim that use of a 'reasonableness' standard will provide the uniformity that Congress originally sought to secure [through mandatory Guidelines]."). And as to crack cocaine sentences in particular, we note a congressional control on disparities: possible variations among district courts are constrained by the mandatory minimums Congress prescribed in the 1986 Act.[15]

Moreover, to the extent that the Government correctly identifies risks of "unwarranted sentence disparities" within the meaning of 18 U.S. C. § 3553(a) (6), the proper solution is not to treat the crack/powder ratio as mandatory. Section 3553(a)(6) directs district courts to consider the need to avoid unwarranted disparities—along with other § 3553(a) factors—when imposing sentences. See Gall, *ante*, at 50, n. 6, 54. Under this instruction, district courts must take account of sentencing practices in other courts and the "cliffs" resulting from the statutory mandatory minimum sentences. To reach an appropriate sentence, these disparities must be weighed against the other § 3553(a) factors and any unwarranted disparity created by the crack/powder ratio itself.

IV

While rendering the Sentencing Guidelines advisory, *Booker*, 543 U.S., at 245, we have nevertheless preserved a key role for the Sentencing Commission. As explained in *Rita* and *Gall*, district courts must treat the Guidelines as the "starting point and the initial benchmark," *Gall, ante*, at 49. Congress established the Commission to formulate and constantly refine national sentencing standards. See *Rita*, 551 U.S., at 347-350. Carrying out its charge, the Commission fills an important institutional role: It has the capacity courts lack to "base its determinations on empirical data and national experience, guided by a professional staff with appropriate expertise." United States v. Pruitt, 502 F. 3d 1154, 1171 (CA10 2007) (McConnell, J., concurring); see *supra*, at 96.

We have accordingly recognized that, in the ordinary case, the Commission's recommendation of a sentencing range will "reflect a rough approximation of sentences that might achieve §3553(a)'s objectives." *Rita*, 551 U.S., at 350. The sentencing judge, on the other hand, has "greater familiarity with . . . the individual case and the individual defendant before him than the Commission or the appeals court." *Id.*, at 357-358. He is therefore "in a superior position to find facts and judge their import under § 3553(a)" in each particular case. *Gall, ante*, at 51 (internal quotation marks omitted). In light of these discrete institutional strengths, a district court's decision to vary from the advisory Guidelines may attract greatest respect when the sentencing judge finds a particular case "outside the 'heartland' to which the Commission intends individual Guidelines to apply." Rita, 551 U.S., at 351. On the other hand, while the Guidelines are no longer binding, closer review may be in order when the sentencing judge varies from the Guidelines based solely on the judge's view that the Guidelines range "fails properly to reflect § 3553(a) considerations" even in a mine-run case. *Ibid. Cf.* Tr. of Oral Arg. in *Gall v. United States*, O. T. 2007, No. 06-7949, pp. 38-39.

The crack cocaine Guidelines, however, present no occasion for elaborative discussion of this matter because those Guidelines do not exemplify the Commission's exercise of its characteristic institutional role. In formulating Guidelines ranges for crack cocaine offenses, as we earlier noted, the Commission looked to the mandatory minimum sentences set in the 1986 Act, and did not take account of "empirical data and national experience." See *Pruitt*, 502 F. 3d, at 1171 (McConnell, J., concurring). Indeed, the Commission itself has reported that the crack/powder disparity produces disproportionately harsh sanctions, *i.e.*, sentences for crack cocaine offenses "greater than necessary" in light of the purposes of sentencing set forth in § 3553(a). See *supra*, at 97-98. Given all this, it would not be an abuse of discretion for a district court to conclude when sentencing a particular defendant that the crack/powder disparity yields a sentence "greater than necessary" to achieve § 3553(a)'s purposes, even in a mine-run case.

V

Taking account of the foregoing discussion in appraising the District Court's disposition in this case, we conclude that the 180-month sentence imposed on Kimbrough should survive appellate inspection. The District Court began by properly calculating and considering the advisory Guidelines range. It then addressed the relevant § 3553(a) factors. First, the court considered "the nature and circumstances" of the crime, see § 3553(a)(1), which was an unremarkable drug-trafficking offense. App. 72-73 ("[T]his defendant and another defendant were caught sitting in a car with some crack cocaine and powder by two police officers—that's the sum and substance of it—[and they also had] a firearm."). Second, the court considered Kimbrough's "history and characteristics." § 3553(a)(1). The court noted that Kimbrough had no prior felony convictions, that he had served in combat during Operation Desert Storm and received an honorable discharge from the Marine Corps, and that he had a steady history of employment.

Furthermore, the court alluded to the Sentencing Commission's reports criticizing the 100-to-1 ratio, *cf.* § 3553(a)(5) (2000 ed., Supp. V), noting that the Commission "recognizes that crack cocaine has not caused the damage that the Justice Department alleges it has." App. 72. Comparing the Guidelines range to the range that would have applied if Kimbrough had possessed an equal amount of powder, the court suggested that the 100-to-1 ratio itself created an unwarranted disparity within the meaning of § 3553(a). Finally, the court did not purport to establish a ratio of its own. Rather, it appropriately framed its final determination in line with §3553(a)'s overarching instruction to "impose a sentence sufficient, but not greater than necessary," to accomplish the sentencing goals advanced in § 3553(a)(2). See *supra*, at 101. Concluding that "the crack cocaine guidelines [drove] the offense level to a point higher than is necessary to do justice in this case," App. 72, the District Court thus rested its sentence on the appropriate considerations and "committed no procedural error," *Gall, ante*, at 56.

The ultimate question in Kimbrough's case is "whether the sentence was reasonable—*i.e.*, whether the District Judge abused his discretion in determining that the § 3553(a) factors supported a sentence of [15 years] and justified a substantial deviation from the Guidelines range." *Ibid.* The sentence the District Court imposed on Kimbrough was 4.5 years below the bottom of the Guidelines range. But in determining that 15 years was the appropriate prison term, the District Court properly homed in on the particular circumstances of Kimbrough's case and accorded weight to the Sentencing Commission's consistent and emphatic position that the crack/powder disparity is at odds with § 3553(a). See Part II-B, *supra.* Indeed, aside from its claim that the 100-to-1 ratio is mandatory, the Government did not attack the District Court's downward variance as unsupported by § 3553(a). Giving due respect to the District Court's reasoned appraisal, a reviewing court could not rationally conclude that the 4.5-year sentence reduction Kimbrough received qualified as an abuse of discretion. See *Gall, ante,* at 58-60; *Rita,* 551 U.S., at 358-360.

* * *

For the reasons stated, the judgment of the United States Court of Appeals for the Fourth Circuit is reversed, and the case is remanded for further proceedings consistent with this opinion.

It is so ordered.

---

1. The statutory range for possession with intent to distribute more than 50 grams of crack is ten years to life. See 21 U.S. C. § 841(b)(1)(A)(iii) (2000 ed. and Supp. V). The same range applies to the conspiracy offense. See §846 (2000 ed.). The statutory range for possession with intent to distribute powder cocaine is 0 to 20 years. See § 841(b)(1)(C) (Supp. V). Finally, the statutory range for possession of a firearm in furtherance of a drug-trafficking offense is five years to life. See 18 U.S. C. § 924(c)(1)(A)(i). The sentences for the three drug crimes may run concurrently, see § 3584(a), but the sentence for the firearm offense must be consecutive, see § 924(c)(1)(A).
2. Kimbrough was sentenced in April 2005, three months after our decision in United States v. Booker, 543 U.S. 220 (2005), rendered the Guidelines advisory. The District Court employed the version of the Guidelines effective November 1, 2004.
3. The prison sentence consisted of 120 months on each of the three drug counts, to be served concurrently, plus 60 months on the firearm count, to be served consecutively.
4. This question has divided the Courts of Appeals. Compare *United States v. Pickett,* 475 F. 3d 1347, 1355-1356 (CADC 2007) (District Court erred when it concluded that it had no discretion to consider the crack/ powder disparity in imposing a sentence), and *United States v. Gunter,* 462 F. 3d 237, 248-249 (CA3 2006) (same), with *United States v. Leatch,* 482 F. 3d 790, 791 (CA5 2007) (per curiam) (sentencing court may not impose a sentence outside the Guidelines range based on its disagreement with the crack/powder disparity), *United States v. Johnson,* 474 F. 3d 515, 522 (CA8 2007) (same), *United States v. Castillo,* 460 F. 3d 337, 361 (CA2 2006) (same), *United States v. Williams,* 456 F. 3d 1353, 1369 (CA11 2006) (same), *United States v. Miller,* 450 F. 3d 270, 275-276 (CA7 2006) (same), *United States v. Eura,* 440 F. 3d 625, 633-634 (CA4 2006) (same), and *United States v. Pho,* 433 F. 3d 53, 62-63 (CA1 2006) (same).
5. Injecting powder cocaine produces effects similar to smoking crack cocaine, but very few powder users inject the drug. See 1995 Report 18.
6. As explained in Part II-C, *infra,* the Sentencing Commission amended the Guidelines and reduced sentences for crack offenses effective November 1, 2007. Except as noted, this opinion refers to the 2004 Guidelines in effect at the time of Kimbrough's sentencing.

7. Congress created the Sentencing Commission and charged it with promulgating the Guidelines in the Sentencing Reform Act of 1984, 98 Stat. 1987, 18 U.S. C. § 3551 *et seq.* (2000 ed. and Supp. V), but the first version of the Guidelines did not become operative until November 1987, see 1995 Report iii-iv.

8. An offense level of 12 results in a Guidelines range of 10 to 16 months for a first-time offender; an offense level of 38 results in a range of 235 to 293 months for the same offender. See USSG ch. 5, pt. A, Sentencing Table.

9. Subsection 994(p) requires the Commission to submit Guidelines amendments to Congress and provides that such amendments become effective unless "modified or disapproved by Act of Congress."

10. The amended Guidelines still produce sentencing ranges keyed to the mandatory minimums in the 1986 Act. Under the pre-2007 Guidelines, the 5- and 50-gram quantities that trigger the statutory minimums produced sentencing ranges that slightly exceeded those statutory minimums. Under the amended Guidelines, in contrast, the 5- and 50- gram quantities produce "base offense levels corresponding to guideline ranges that include the statutory mandatory minimum penalties." 2007 Report 9.

11. The Commission has not yet determined whether the amendment will be retroactive to cover defendants like Kimbrough. Even under the amendment, however, Kimbrough's Guidelines range would be 195 to 218 months—well above the 180-month sentence imposed by the District Court. See Amendments to the Sentencing Guidelines for United States Courts, 72 Fed. Reg. 28571-28572 (2007); USSG ch. 5, pt. A, Sentencing Table.

12. The remedial opinion also severed and excised the provision of the statute requiring de novo review of departures from the Guidelines, 18 U.S. C. § 3742(e), because that provision depended on the Guidelines' mandatory status. *Booker,* 543 U.S., at 245.

13. The Government concedes that a district court may vary from the 100-to-1 ratio if it does so "based on the individualized circumstance[s]" of a particular case. Brief for United States 45. But the Government maintains that the 100-to-1 ratio is binding in the sense that a court may not give any weight to its own view that the ratio itself is inconsistent with the § 3553(a) factors.

14. At oral argument, the Government sought to distinguish Neal v. United States, 516 U.S. 284 (1996), on the ground that the validity of the amended Guidelines was not before us in that case. See Tr. of Oral Arg. 25. That is true, but only because the Government did not challenge the amendment. In fact, the Government's brief appeared to acknowledge that the Commission may legitimately deviate from the policies and methods embodied in the 1986 Act, even if the deviation produces some inconsistency. See Brief for United States in *Neal v. United States,* 0. T. 1995, No. 94-9088, p. 26 ("When the Commission's views about sentencing policy depart from those of Congress, it may become difficult to achieve entirely consistent sentencing, but that is a matter for Congress, not the courts, to address."). Moreover, our opinion in Neal assumed that the amendment was a legitimate exercise of the Commission's authority. See 516 U.S., at 294 (noting with apparent approval the Commission's position that "the Guidelines calculation is independent of the statutory calculation").

15. The Sentencing Commission reports that roughly 70 percent of crack offenders are responsible for drug quantities that yield base offense levels at or only two levels above those that correspond to the statutory minimums. See 2007 Report 25.

SELECTED CONCURRING
OPINIONS

GRUTTER V. BOLLIGER

539 U.S. 306 (2003)

This case is about the University of Michigan Law School's use of affirmative action in admissions. An applicant who was denied admission alleged that the law school's policy of giving preference to members of certain racial minority groups was a violation of the Fourteenth Amendment's Equal Protection Clause.

Justice O'Connor delivered the Court's opinion, which held that the Equal Protection Clause does not prohibit the "narrowly tailed use of race in admissions decisions to further a compelling interest in obtaining the educational benefits that flow from a diverse student body." Justice Ginsburg joined this opinion and also offered her own concurrence.

GRUTTER V. BOLLINGER

539 U.S. 306 (2003)

T he Court's observation that race-conscious programs "must have a
logical end point," *ante*, at 342, accords with the international understanding of the office of affirmative action. The International Convention on the Elimination of All Forms of Racial Discrimination, ratified by the
United States in 1994, see State Dept., Treaties in Force 422-423 (June 1996),
endorses "special and concrete measures to ensure the adequate development
and protection of certain racial groups or individuals belonging to them, for
the purpose of guaranteeing them the full and equal enjoyment of human
rights and fundamental freedoms." Annex to G. A. Res. 2106, 20 U. N. GAOR,
20th Sess., Res. Supp. (No. 14), p. 47, U. N. Doc. A/6014, Art. 2(2) (1965). But
such measures, the Convention instructs, "shall in no case entail as a consequence the maintenance of unequal or separate rights for different racial
groups after the objectives for which they were taken have been achieved."
Ibid.; see also Art. 1(4)(similarly providing for temporally limited affirmative
action); Convention on the Elimination of All Forms of Discrimination against
Women, Annex to G. A. Res. 34/180, 34 U. N. GAOR, 34th Sess., Res. Supp.
(No. 46), p. 194, U. N. Doc. A/34/46, Art. 4(1) (1979) (authorizing "temporary
special measures aimed at accelerating de facto equality" that "shall be discontinued when the objectives of equality of opportunity and treatment have been
achieved").

The Court further observes that "[i]t has been 25 years since Justice Powell
[in *Regents of Univ. of Cal. v. Bakke*, 438 U.S. 265 (1978)] first approved the use of
race to further an interest in student body diversity in the context of public
higher education." *Ante*, at 343. For at least part of that time, however, the law

could not fairly be described as "settled," and in some regions of the Nation, overtly race conscious admissions policies have been proscribed. See Hopwood v. Texas, 78 F. 3d 932 (CA5 1996); cf. Wessmann v. Gittens, 160 F. 3d 790 (CA1 1998); Tuttle v. Arlington Cty. School Bd., 195 F. 3d 698 (CA4 1999); Johnson v. Board of Regents of Univ. of Ga., 263 F. 3d 1234 (CA11 2001). Moreover, it was only 25 years before Bakke that this Court declared public school segregation unconstitutional, a declaration that, after prolonged resistance, yielded an end to a law-enforced racial caste system, itself the legacy of centuries of slavery. See Brown v. Board of Education, 347 U.S. 483 (1954); cf. Cooper v. Aaron, 358 U.S. 1 (1958).

It is well documented that conscious and unconscious race bias, even rank discrimination based on race, remain alive in our land, impeding realization of our highest values and ideals. See, e.g., Gratz v. Bollinger, ante, at 298-301 (Ginsburg, J., dissenting); Adarand Constructors, Inc. v. Pena, 515 U.S. 200, 272-274 (1995) (Ginsburg, J., dissenting); Krieger, Civil Rights Perestroika: Intergroup Relations after Affirmative Action, 86 Calif. L. Rev. 1251, 1276-1291, 1303 (1998). As to public education, data for the years 2000- 2001 show that 71.6% of African-American children and 76.3% of Hispanic children attended a school in which minorities made up a majority of the student body. See E. Frankenberg, C. Lee, & G. Orfield, A Multiracial Society with Segregated Schools: Are We Losing the Dream? p. 4 (Jan. 2003), http://www.civilrightsproject.harvard.edu/research/ reseg03/AreWeLosingtheDream.pdf (as visited June 16,2003, and available in Clerk of Court's case file). And schools in predominantly minority communities lag far behind others measured by the educational resources available to them. See id., at 11; Brief for National Urban League et al. as Amici curiae 11-12 (citing General Accounting Office, Per-Pupil Spending Differences Between Selected Inner City and Suburban Schools Varied by Metropolitan Area 17 (2002)).

However strong the public's desire for improved education systems may be, see P. Hart & R. Teeter, A National Priority: Americans Speak on Teacher Quality 2, 11 (2002) (public opinion research conducted for Educational Testing Service); No Child Left Behind Act of 2001, Pub. L. 107-110, 115 Stat. 1806, 20 U.S.C. § 7231 (2000 ed., Supp. I), it remains the current reality that many minority students encounter markedly inadequate and unequal educational opportunities. Despite these inequalities, some minority students are able to meet the high threshold requirements set for admission to the country's finest undergraduate and graduate educational institutions. As lower school education in minority communities improves, an increase in the number of such students may be anticipated. From today's vantage point, one may hope, but not firmly forecast, that over the next generation's span, progress toward nondiscrimination and genuinely equal opportunity will make it safe to sunset affirmative action.[1]

1. As the Court explains, the admissions policy challenged here survives review under the standards stated in *Adarand Constructors, Inc. v. Pena*, 515 U.S. 200 (1995), *Richmond v. J. A. Croson Co.*, 488 U.S. 469 (1989), and Justice Powell's opinion in *Regents of Univ. of Cal. v. Bakke*, 438 U.S. 265 (1978). This case therefore does not require the Court to revisit whether all governmental classifications by race, whether designed to benefit or to burden a historically disadvantaged group, should be subject to the same standard of judicial review. *Cf. Gratz, ante*, at 301-302 (Ginsburg, J., dissenting); *Adarand*, 515 U.S., at 274, n. 8 (Ginsburg, J., dissenting). Nor does this case necessitate reconsideration whether interests other than "student body diversity," *ante*, at 325, rank as sufficiently important to justify a race-conscious government program. *Cf. Gratz, ante*, at 301-302 (Ginsburg, J., dissenting); *Adarand*, 515 U.S., at 273-274 (Ginsburg, J., dissenting).

WHOLE WOMAN'S HEALTH
V. HELLERSTEDT

579 U.S. __ (2016)

This case is about whether certain health and safety requirements imposed on abortion clinics by the state of Texas violated a woman's right to an abortion. Among other things, the Texas law imposed new requirements that abortion providers have admitting privileges at a nearby hospital and that abortion clinics meet the same health and safety standards as ambulatory surgical centers — requirements that, allegedly, would put some abortion doctors and clinics out of business.

In a 5-3 decision, the Court held that these requirements constituted an undue burden for women seeking an abortion and were struck down. Justice Breyer wrote for the majority, which Justice Ginsburg joined. Justice Ginsburg also wrote a separate concurring opinion.

WHOLE WOMAN'S HEALTH V. HELLERSTEDT (CONCURRING)

579 U.S. __ (2016)

The Texas law called H. B. 2 inevitably will reduce the number of clinics and doctors allowed to provide abortion services. Texas argues that H. B. 2's restrictions are constitutional because they protect the health of women who experience complications from abortions. In truth, "complications from an abortion are both rare and rarely dangerous." *Planned Parenthood of Wis., Inc. v. Schimel*, 806 F. 3d 908, 912 (CA7 2015). See Brief for American College of Obstetricians and Gynecologists et al. as *Amici curiae* 6—10 (collecting studies and concluding "[a]bortion is one of the safest medical procedures performed in the United States"); Brief for Social Science Researchers as *Amici curiae* 5-9 (compiling studies that show "[c]omplication rates from abortion are very low"). Many medical procedures, including childbirth, are far more dangerous to patients, yet are not subject to ambulatory- surgical-center or hospital admitting-privileges requirements. See *ante*, at 31; *Planned Parenthood of Wis.*, 806 F. 3d, at 921—922. See also Brief for Social Science Researchers 9—11 (comparing statistics on risks for abortion with tonsillectomy, colonoscopy, and in-office dental surgery); Brief for American Civil Liberties Union et al. as *Amici curiae* 7 (all District Courts to consider admitting-privileges requirements found abortion "is at least as safe as other medical procedures routinely performed in outpatient settings"). Given those realities, it is beyond rational belief that H. B. 2 could genuinely protect the health of women, and certain that the law "would simply make it more difficult for them to obtain abortions." Planned Parenthood of Wis., 806 F. 3d, at 910. When a State severely limits access to safe and legal procedures, women in desperate circumstances may resort to unlicensed rogue practitioners, faute de mieux, at great risk to their health and safety. See Brief for Ten Pennsylvania Abortion Care Providers as *Amici curiae* 17-22. So long as this Court adheres to *Roe v. Wade*, 410 U.S. 113 (1973), and *Planned Parenthood of Southeastern Pa. v. Casey*, 505 U.S. 833 (1992), Targeted Regulation of Abortion Providers laws like H. B. 2 that "do little or nothing for health, but rather strew impediments to abortion," *Planned Parenthood of Wis.*, 806 F. 3d, at 921, cannot survive judicial inspection.

SELECTED DISSENTING
OPINIONS

BUSH V. GORE

531 U.S. 98(2000)

This landmark case decided the disputed recount in Florida that held up the resolution of the 2000 presidential election between George Bush and Al Gore. In conducting their recount of the presidential vote, different counties in Florida applied different standards for reviewing and counting rejected ballots. In a 7-2 ruling, which Justice Ginsburg joined, the Court held that this use of different standards was a violation of the Equal Protection Clause.

The Court also ruled 5-4 that there was insufficient time left before Florida's constitutionally-required appointment of electors for an alternative method of counting to be adopted and ordered an end to the recounts.

Justice Ginsburg dissented from this portion of the opinion, joined in part by Justices Stevens, Souter, and Breyer.

BUSH V. GORE

I

The Chief Justice acknowledges that provisions of Florida's Election Code "may well admit of more than one interpretation." *Ante*, at 114 (concurring opinion). But instead of respecting the state high court's province to say what the State's Election Code means, The Chief Justice maintains that Florida's Supreme Court has veered so far from the ordinary practice of judicial review that what it did cannot properly be called judging. My colleagues have offered a reasonable construction of Florida's law. Their construction coincides with the view of one of Florida's seven Supreme Court justices. *Gore v. Harris*, 772 So. 2d 1243, 1264-1270 (Fla. 2000) (Wells, C. J., dissenting); *Palm Beach County Canvassing Bd. v. Harris*, 772 So. 2d 1273, 1291-1292 (Fla. 2000) (on remand) (confirming, 6 to 1, the construction of Florida law advanced in Gore). I might join The Chief Justice were it my commission to interpret Florida law. But disagreement with the Florida court's interpretation of its own State's law does not warrant the conclusion that the justices of that court have legislated. There is no cause here to believe that the members of Florida's high court have done less than "their mortal best to discharge their oath of office," *Sumner v. Mata*, 449 U.S. 539, 549 (1981), and no cause to upset their reasoned interpretation of Florida law.

This Court more than occasionally affirms statutory, and even constitutional, interpretations with which it disagrees. For example, when reviewing challenges to administrative agencies' interpretations of laws they implement, we defer to the agencies unless their interpretation violates "the unambiguously expressed intent of Congress." *Chevron U.S.A. Inc. v. Natural Resources Defense Council, Inc.*, 467 U.S. 837, 843 (1984). We do so in the face of the declaration in Article I of the United States Constitution that "All legislative Powers herein granted shall be vested in a Congress of the United States." Surely the Constitution does not call upon us to pay more respect to a federal administrative agency's construction of federal law than to a state high court's interpretation of its own State's law. And not uncommonly, we let stand state-court interpretations of *federal* law with which we might disagree. Notably, in the habeas context, the Court adheres to the view that "there is 'no intrinsic reason why the fact that a man is a federal judge should make him more competent, or conscientious, or learned with respect to [federal law] than his neighbor in the state courthouse.'" *Stone v. Powell*, 428 U.S. 465,494, n. 35 (1976) (quoting Bator, Finality in Criminal Law and Federal Habeas Corpus for State Prisoners, 76 Harv. L. Rev. 441, 509 (1963)); see *O'Dell v. Netherland*, 521 U.S. 151, 156 (1997) ("[T]he Teague doctrine validates reasonable, good-faith interpretations of existing precedents made by state courts even though they are shown to be contrary to later decisions.") (citing *Butler v. McKellar*, 494 U.S. 407, 414 (1990)); O'Connor, Trends in the Relationship Between the Federal and State Courts from the Perspective of a State Court Judge, 22 Wm. & Mary L. Rev. 801, 813 (1981) ("There is no reason to assume that state court judges cannot and will not provide a 'hospitable forum' in litigating federal constitutional questions.").

No doubt there are cases in which the proper application of federal law may hinge on interpretations of state law. Unavoidably, this Court must sometimes examine state law in order to protect federal rights. But we have dealt with such cases ever mindful of the full measure of respect we owe to interpretations of state law by a State's highest court. In the Contract Clause case, *General Motors v. Romein*, 503 U.S. 181 (1992), for example, we said that although "ultimately we are bound to decide for ourselves whether a contract was made," the Court "accord[s] respectful consideration and great weight to the views of the State's highest court." *Id.*, at 187 (citing *Indiana ex rel. Anderson v. Brand*, 303 U.S. 95, 100 (1938)). And in *Central Union Telephone Co. v. Edwardsville*, 269 U.S. 190 (1925), we upheld the Illinois Supreme Court's interpretation of a state waiver rule, even though that interpretation resulted in the forfeiture of federal constitutional rights. Refusing to supplant Illinois law with a federal definition of waiver, we explained that the state court's declaration "should bind us unless so unfair or unreasonable in its application to those asserting a federal right as to obstruct it." *Id.*, at 195.[1]

In deferring to state courts on matters of state law, we appropriately recognize that this Court acts as an " 'out- side[r]' lacking the common exposure to local law which comes from sitting in the jurisdiction." *Lehman Brothers v.*

Schein, 416 U.S. 386, 391 (1974). That recognition has sometimes prompted us to resolve doubts about the meaning of state law by certifying issues to a State's highest court, even when federal rights are at stake. Cf. *Arizonans for Official English v. Arizona*, 520 U.S. 43, 79 (1997) ("Warnings against premature adjudication of constitutional questions bear heightened attention when a federal court is asked to invalidate a State's law, for the federal tribunal risks friction-generating error when it endeavors to construe a novel state Act not yet reviewed by the State's highest court.") Notwithstanding our authority to decide issues of state law underlying federal claims, we have used the certification device to afford state high courts an opportunity to inform us on matters of their own State's law because such restraint "helps build a cooperative judicial federalism." *Lehman Brothers*, 416 U.S., at 391.

Just last Term, in *Fiore v. White*, 528 U.S. 23 (1999), we took advantage of Pennsylvania's certification procedure. In that case, a state prisoner brought a federal habeas action claiming that the State had failed to prove an essential element of his charged offense in violation of the Due Process Clause. *Id.*, at 25-26. Instead of resolving the state-law question on which the federal claim depended, we certified the question to the Pennsylvania Supreme Court for that court to "help determine the proper state-law predicate for our determination of the federal constitutional questions raised." *Id.*, at 29; *id.*, at 28 (asking the Pennsylvania Supreme Court whether its recent interpretation of the statute under which Fiore was convicted "was always the statute's meaning, even at the time of Fiore's trial"). The Chief Justice's willingness to *reverse* the Florida Supreme Court's interpretation of Florida law in this case is at least in tension with our reluctance in *Fiore* even to interpret Pennsylvania law before seeking instruction from the Pennsylvania Supreme Court. I would have thought the "cautious approach" we counsel when federal courts address matters of state law, *Arizonans*, 520 U.S., at 77, and our commitment to "build[ing] cooperative judicial federalism," *Lehman Brothers*, 416 U.S., at 391, demanded greater restraint.

Rarely has this Court rejected outright an interpretation of state law by a state high court. *Fairfax's Devisee v. Hunter's Lessee*, 7 Cranch 603 (1813), *NAACP v. Alabama ex rel. Patterson*, 357 U.S. 449 (1958), and *Bouie v. City of Columbia*, 378 U.S. 347 (1964), cited by The Chief Justice, are three such rare instances. See *ante*, at 114-115, and n. 1. But those cases are embedded in historical contexts hardly comparable to the situation here. Fairfax's Devisee, which held that the Virginia Court of Appeals had misconstrued its own forfeiture laws to deprive a British subject of lands secured to him by federal treaties, occurred amidst vociferous States' rights attacks on the Marshall Court. G. Gunther & K. Sullivan, Constitutional Law 61-62 (13th ed. 1997). The Virginia court refused to obey this Court's Fairfax's Devisee mandate to enter judgment for the British subject's successor in interest. That refusal led to the Court's pathmarking decision in *Martin v. Hunter's Lessee*, 1 Wheat. 304 (1816). Patterson, a case decided three months after *Cooper v. Aaron*, 358 U.S. 1 (1958), in the face of Southern resistance to the civil rights movement, held that the Alabama Supreme Court had irregularly applied its own procedural rules to deny review of a contempt order against the NAACP arising from its refusal to disclose membership lists. We said that "our jurisdiction is not defeated if the nonfederal ground relied on by the state court is 'without any fair or substantial support.'" 357 U.S., at 455 (quoting *Ward v. Board of Commr's of Love Cty.*, 253 U.S. 17, 22 (1920)). *Bouie*, stemming from a lunch counter "sit-in" at the height of the civil rights movement, held that the South Carolina Supreme Court's construction of its trespass laws—criminalizing conduct not covered by the text of an otherwise clear statute—was "unforeseeable" and thus violated due process when applied retroactively to the petitioners. 378 U.S., at 350, 354.

The Chief Justice's casual citation of these cases might lead one to believe they are part of a larger collection of cases in which we said that the Constitution impelled us to train a skeptical eye on a state court's portrayal of state law. But one would be hard pressed, I think, to find additional cases that fit the mold. As Justice Breyer convincingly explains, see post, at 149-152 (dissenting opinion), this case involves nothing close to the kind of recalcitrance by a state high court that warrants extraordinary action by this Court. The Florida Supreme Court concluded that counting every legal vote was the overriding concern of the Florida Legislature when it enacted the State's Election Code. The court surely should not be bracketed with state high courts of the Jim Crow South.

The Chief Justice says that Article II, by providing that state legislatures shall direct the manner of appointing electors, authorizes federal superintendence over the relationship between state courts and state legislatures, and licenses a departure from the usual deference we give to state-court interpretations of state law. *Ante*, at 115 (concurring opinion) ("To attach definitive weight to the pronouncement of a state court, when the very question at issue is whether the court has actually departed from the statutory meaning, would be to abdicate our responsibility to enforce the explicit requirements of Article II."). The Framers of our Constitution, however, understood that in a republican government, the judiciary would construe the legislature's enactments. See U.S. Const., Art. Ill; The Federalist No. 78 (A. Hamilton). In light of the constitutional guarantee to States of a "Republican Form of Government," U.S. Const., Art. IV, § 4, Article II can hardly be read to invite this Court to disrupt a State's republican regime. Yet The Chief Justice today would reach out to do just that. By holding that Article II requires our revision of a state court's construction of state laws in order to protect one organ of the State from another, The Chief Justice contradicts the basic principle that a State may organize itself as it sees fit. *See, e.g., Gregory v. Ashcroft*, 501 U.S. 452, 460 (1991)

("Through the structure of its government, and the character of those who exercise government authority, a State defines itself as a sovereign."); *Highland Farms Dairy, Inc. v. Agnew*, 300 U.S. 608, 612 (1937) ("How power shall be distributed by a state among its governmental organs is commonly, if not always, a question for the state itself.").[2] Article II does not call for the scrutiny undertaken by this Court.

The extraordinary setting of this case has obscured the ordinary principle that dictates its proper resolution: Federal courts defer to a state high court's interpretations of the State's own law. This principle reflects the core of federalism, on which all agree. "The Framers split the atom of sovereignty. It was the genius of their idea that our citizens would have two political capacities, one state and one federal, each protected from incursion by the other." *Saenz v. Roe*, 526 U.S. 489, 504, n. 17 (1999) (citing *U.S. Term Limits, Inc. v. Thornton*, 514 U.S. 779, 838 (1995) (Kennedy, J., concurring)). The Chief Justice's solicitude for the Florida Legislature comes at the expense of the more fundamental solicitude we owe to the legislature's sovereign. U.S. Const., Art. II, § 1, cl. 2 ("Each State shall appoint, in such Manner as the Legislature thereof may direct," the electors for President and Vice President (emphasis added)); *ante*, at 123-124 (Stevens, J., dissenting).[3] Were the other Members of this Court as mindful as they generally are of our system of dual sovereignty, they would affirm the judgment of the Florida Supreme Court.

II

I agree with Justice Stevens that petitioners have not presented a substantial equal protection claim. Ideally, perfection would be the appropriate standard for judging the recount. But we live in an imperfect world, one in which thousands of votes have not been counted. I cannot agree that the recount adopted by the Florida court, flawed as it may be, would yield a result any less fair or precise than the certification that preceded that recount. See, e. *McDonald v. Board of Election Comm'rs of Chicago*, 394 U.S. 802, 809 (1969) (even in the context of the right to vote, the State is permitted to reform "one step at a time") (citing *Williamson v. Lee Optical of Okla., Inc.*, 348 U.S. 483, 489 (1955)).

Even if there were an equal protection violation, I would agree with Justice Stevens, Justice Souter, and Justice Breyer that the Court's concern about the December 12 date, *ante*, at 110-111, is misplaced. Time is short in part because of the Court's entry of a stay on December 9, several hours after an able circuit judge in Leon County had begun to superintend the recount process. More fundamentally, the Court's reluctance to let the recount go forward—despite its suggestion that "[t]he search for intent can be confined by specific rules designed to ensure uniform treatment," *ante*, at 106—ultimately turns on its own judgment about the practical realities of implementing a recount, not the judgment of those much closer to the process.

Equally important, as Justice Breyer explains, post, at 155 (dissenting opinion), the December 12 date for bringing Florida's electoral votes into 3 U.S.C. § 5's safe harbor lacks the significance the Court assigns it. Were that date to pass, Florida would still be entitled to deliver electoral votes Congress must count unless both Houses find that the votes "ha[d] not been . . . regularly given." 3 U.S.C. § 15. The statute identifies other significant dates. See, e.g., § 7 (specifying December 18 as the date electors "shall meet and give their votes"); § 12 (specifying "the fourth Wednesday in December"—this year, December 27 —as the date on which Congress, if it has not received a State's electoral votes, shall request the state secretary of state to send a certified return immediately). But none of these dates has ultimate significance in light of Congress' detailed provisions for determining, on "the sixth day of January," the validity of electoral votes. § 15.

The Court assumes that time will not permit "orderly judicial review of any disputed matters that might arise." Ante, at 110. But no one has doubted the good faith and diligence with which Florida election officials, attorneys for all sides of this controversy, and the courts of law have performed their duties. Notably, the Florida Supreme Court has produced two substantial opinions within 29 hours of oral argument. In sum, the Court's conclusion that a constitutionally adequate recount is impractical is a prophecy the Court's own judgment will not allow to be tested. Such an untested prophecy should not decide the Presidency of the United States.

I dissent.

---

1. See also *Lucas v. South Carolina Coastal Council*, 505 U.S. 1003,1032, n. 18 (1992) (South Carolina could defend a regulatory taking "if an objectively reasonable application of relevant precedents [by its courts] would exclude . . . beneficial uses in the circumstances in which the land is presently found"); *Bishop v. Wood*, 426 U.S. 341, 344-345 (1976) (deciding whether North Carolina had created a property interest cognizable under the Due Process Clause by reference to state law as interpreted by the North Carolina Supreme Court). Similarly, in *Gurley v. Rhoden*, 421 U.S. 200 (1975), a gasoline retailer claimed that due process entitled him to deduct a state gasoline excise tax in computing the amount of his sales subject to a state sales tax, on the grounds that the legal incidence of the excise tax fell on his customers and that he acted merely as a collector of the tax. The Mississippi Supreme Court held that the legal incidence of the excise tax fell on petitioner. Observing that "a State's highest court is the final judicial arbiter of the meaning of state statutes," we said that "[w]hen a state court has made its own definitive determination as to the operating incidence,. . . [w]e give this finding great weight in determining the natural effect of a statute, and if it is consistent with the statute's reasonable interpretation it will be deemed conclusive." *Id.*, at 208 (citing *American Oil Co. v. Neill*, 380 U.S. 451, 455-456 (1965)).

2. Even in the rare case in which a State's "manner" of making and construing laws might implicate a structural constraint, Congress, not this Court, is likely the proper governmental entity to enforce that constraint. See U.S. Const., Arndt. 12; 3 U.S.C. §§ 1-15; *cf. Ohio ex rel. Davis v. Hildebrant*, 241 U.S. 565, 569 (1916) (treating as a nonjusticiable political question whether use of a

referendum to override a congressional districting plan enacted by the state legislature violates Art. I, §4); *Luther v. Borden,* 7 How. 1, 42 (1849).

3. "[B]ecause the Framers recognized that state power and identity were essential parts of the federal balance, see The Federalist No. 39, the Constitution is solicitous of the prerogatives of the States, even in an otherwise sovereign federal province. The Constitution . . . grants States certain powers over the times, places, and manner of federal elections (subject to congressional revision), Art. I, § 4, cl. 1 . . . , and allows States to appoint electors for the President, Art. II, §1, cl. 2." *US. Term Limits, Inc. v. Thornton,* 514 U.S. 779, 841-842 (1995) (Kennedy, J., concurring).

GRATZ V. BOLLINGER

539 U.S. 244 (2003)

This case is about the University of Michigan's use of a predetermined "points" system in making admissions decisions, where members of certain minority races were granted extra "points" towards admission, in an effort to increase the diversity of the student body. Gratz, a white applicant who was denied admission, sued, alleging this race-based admissions program was racial discrimination and unconstitutional.

In a decision authored by Chief Justice Rehnquist, the Court ruled that the "points" system was unconstitutional, because it did not evaluate students on an individual-by-individual basis. Taking into account race-based diversity when evaluating applicants individually was not ruled unconstitutional.

Justice Ginsburg dissented, joined in part by Justices Breyer and Souter.

GRATZ V. BOLLINGER

I

E ducational institutions, the Court acknowledges, are not barred from any and all consideration of race when making admissions decisions. *Ante*, at 268; see *Grutter v. Bollinger*, post, at 326-333. But the Court once again maintains that the same standard of review controls judicial inspection of all official race classifications. *Ante*, at 270 (quoting *Adarand Constructors, Inc. v. Pena*, 515 U.S. 200, 224 (1995); *Richmond v. J. A. Croson Co.*, 488 U.S. 469, 494 (1989) (plurality opinion)). This insistence on "consistency," *Adarand*, 515 U.S., at 224, would be fitting were our Nation free of the vestiges of rank discrimination long reinforced by law, see *id.*, at 274-276, and n. 8 (Ginsburg, J., dissenting). But we are not far distant from an overtly discriminatory past, and the effects of centuries of law-sanctioned inequality remain painfully evident in our communities and schools.

In the wake "of a system of racial caste only recently ended," *id.*, at 273 (Ginsburg, J., dissenting), large disparities endure. Unemployment,[1] poverty,[2] and access to health care[3] vary disproportionately by race. Neighborhoods and schools remain racially divided.[4] African-American and Hispanic children are all too often educated in poverty-stricken and underperforming institutions.[5] Adult African- Americans and Hispanics generally earn less than whites with equivalent levels of education.[6][[6]] Equally credentialed job applicants receive different receptions depending on their race.[7] Irrational prejudice is still encountered in real estate markets[8] and consumer transactions.[9] "Bias both conscious and unconscious, reflecting traditional and unexamined habits of thought, keeps up barriers that must come down if equal opportunity and nondiscrimination are ever genuinely to become this country's law and practice." at 274 (Ginsburg, J., dissenting); see generally Krieger, Civil Rights Perestroika: Intergroup Relations After Affirmative Action, 86 Calif. L. Rev. 1251, 1276-1291 (1998).

The Constitution instructs all who act for the government that they may not "deny to any person . . . the equal protection of the laws." Amdt. 14, § 1. In implementing this equality instruction, as I see it, government decisionmakers may properly distinguish between policies of exclusion and inclusion. See *Wygant v. Jackson Bd. of Ed.*, 476 U.S. 267, 316 (1986) (Stevens, J., dissenting). Actions designed to burden groups long denied full citizenship stature are not sensibly ranked with measures taken to hasten the day when entrenched discrimination and its aftereffects have been extirpated. See Carter, When Victims Happen To Be Black, 97 Yale L. J. 420, 433-434 (1988) ("[T]o say that two centuries of struggle for the most basic of civil rights have been mostly about freedom from racial categorization rather than freedom from racial oppressio[n] is to trivialize the lives and deaths of those who have suffered under racism. To pretend . . . that the issue presented in *Univ. of Cal. v. Bakke*, 438 U.S. 265 (1978)] was the same as the issue in [*Brown v. Board of Education*, 347 U.S. 483 (1954)] is to pretend that history never happened and that the present doesn't exist.").

Our jurisprudence ranks race a "suspect" category, "not because [race] is inevitably an impermissible classification, but because it is one which usually, to our national shame, has been drawn for the purpose of maintaining racial inequality." *Norwalk Core v. Norwalk Redevelopment Agency*, 395 F. 2d 920, 931-932 (CA2 1968) (footnote omitted). But where race is considered "for the purpose of achieving equality," *id.*, at 932, no automatic proscription is in order. For, as insightfully explained: "The Constitution is both color blind and color conscious. To avoid conflict with the equal protection clause, a classification that denies a benefit, causes harm, or imposes a burden must not be based on race. In that sense, the Constitution is color blind. But the Constitution is color conscious to prevent discrimination being perpetuated and to undo the effects of past discrimination." *United States v. Jefferson County Bd. of Ed.*, 372 F. 2d 836, 876 (CA5 1966) (Wisdom, J.); see Wechsler, The Nationalization of Civil Liberties and Civil Rights, Supp. to 12 Tex. Q. 10, 23 (1968) (*Brown* may be seen as disallowing racial classifications that "impl[y] an invidious assessment" while allowing such classifications when "not invidious in implication" but advanced to "correct inequalities"). Contemporary human rights documents draw just this line; they distinguish between policies of oppression and measures designed to accelerate de facto equality. See *Grutter*, post, at 344 (Ginsburg, J., concurring) (citing the United Nations-initiated Conventions on the Elimination of All Forms of Racial

Discrimination and on the Elimination of All Forms of Discrimination against Women).

The mere assertion of a laudable governmental purpose, of course, should not immunize a race-conscious measure from careful judicial inspection. See *Jefferson County*, 372 F. 2d, at 876 ("The criterion is the relevancy of color to a legitimate governmental purpose."). Close review is needed "to ferret out classifications in reality malign, but masquerading as benign," *Adarand*, 515 U.S., at 275 (Ginsburg, J., dissenting), and to "ensure that preferences are not so large as to trammel unduly upon the opportunities of others or interfere too harshly with legitimate expectations of persons in once- preferred groups," *id.*, at 276.

II

Examining in this light the admissions policy employed by the University of Michigan's College of Literature, Science, and the Arts (College), and for the reasons well stated by Justice Souter, I see no constitutional infirmity. See *ante*, at 293-298 (dissenting opinion). Like other top- ranking institutions, the College has many more applicants for admission than it can accommodate in an entering class. App. to Pet. for Cert. 108a. Every applicant admitted under the current plan, petitioners do not here dispute, is qualified to attend the College. *Id.*, at 111a. The racial and ethnic groups to which the College accords special consideration (African-Americans, Hispanics, and Native-Americans) historically have been relegated to inferior status by law and social practice; their members continue to experience class- based discrimination to this day, see *supra*, at 298-301. There is no suggestion that the College adopted its current policy in order to limit or decrease enrollment by any particular racial or ethnic group, and no seats are reserved on the basis of race. See Brief for Respondent Bollinger et al. 10; Tr. of Oral Arg. 41-42 (in the range between 75 and 100 points, the review committee may look at applications individually and ignore the points). Nor has there been any demonstration that the College's program unduly constricts admissions opportunities for students who do not receive special consideration based on race. *Cf.* Liu, The Causation Fallacy: *Bakke* and the Basic Arithmetic of Selective Admissions, 100 Mich. L. Rev. 1045, 1049 (2002) ("In any admissions process where applicants greatly outnumber admittees, and where white applicants greatly outnumber minority applicants, substantial preferences for minority applicants will not significantly diminish the odds of admission facing white applicants.").[10]

The stain of generations of racial oppression is still visible in our society, see Krieger, 86 Calif. L. Rev., at 1253, and the determination to hasten its removal remains vital. One can reasonably anticipate, therefore, that colleges and universities will seek to maintain their minority enrollment—and the networks and opportunities thereby opened to minority graduates—whether or not they can do so in full candor through adoption of affirmative action plans of the kind here at issue. Without recourse to such plans, institutions of higher education may resort to camouflage. For example, schools may encourage applicants to write of their cultural traditions in the essays they submit, or to indicate whether English is their second language. Seeking to improve their chances for admission, applicants may highlight the minority group associations to which they belong, or the Hispanic surnames of their mothers or grandparents. In turn, teachers' recommendations may emphasize who a student is as much as what he or she has accomplished. *See, e.g.*, Steinberg, Using Synonyms for Race, College Strives for Diversity, N. Y. Times, Dec. 8, 2002, section 1, p. 1, col. 3 (describing admissions process at Rice University); *cf.* Brief for United States as Amicus Curiae 14-15 (suggesting institutions could consider, inter alia, "a history of overcoming disadvantage," "reputation and location of high school," and "individual outlook as reflected by essays"). If honesty is the best policy, surely Michigan's accurately described, fully disclosed College affirmative action program is preferable to achieving similar numbers through winks, nods, and disguises.[11]

* * *

For the reasons stated, I would affirm the judgment of the District Court.

---

1. *See, e.g.*, U.S. Dept, of Commerce, Bureau of Census, Statistical Abstract of the United States: 2002, p. 368 (2002) (Table 562) (hereinafter Statistical Abstract) (unemployment rate among whites was 3.7% in 1999, 3.5% in 2000, and 4.2% in 2001; during those years, the unemployment rate among African-Americans was 8.0%, 7.6%, and 8.7%, respectively; among Hispanics, 6.4%, 5.7%, and 6.6%).
2. *See, e.g.*, U.S. Dept of Commerce, Bureau of Census, Poverty in the United States: 2000, p. 291 (2001) (Table A) (In 2000, 7.5% of non-Hispanic whites, 22.1% of African-Americans, 10.8% of Asian-Americans, and 21.2% of Hispanics were living in poverty.); S. Staveteig & A. Wigton, Racial and Ethnic Disparities: Key Findings from the National Survey of America's Families 1 (Urban Institute Report B-5, Feb. 2000) ("Blacks, Hispanics, and Native Americans . . . each have poverty rates almost twice as high as Asians and almost three times as high as whites.").
3. *See, e.g.*, U.S. Dept, of Commerce, Bureau of Census, Health Insurance Coverage: 2000, p. 391 (2001) (Table A) (In 2000, 9.7% of non-Hispanic whites were without health insurance, as compared to 18.5% of African-Americans, 18.0% of Asian-Americans, and 32.0% of Hispanics.); Waidmann & Raj an, Race and Ethnic Disparities in Health Care Access and Utilization: An Examination of State Variation, 57 Med. Care Res. And Rev. 55, 56 (2000) ("On average, Latinos and African Americans have both worse health and worse access to effective health care than do non-Hispanic whites . . . .").
4. *See, e.g.*, U.S. Dept, of Commerce, Bureau of Census, Racial and Ethnic Residential Segregation in the United States: 1980-2000 (2002) (documenting residential segregation); E. Frankenberg, C. Lee, & G. Orfield, A Multiracial Society with Segregated Schools: Are We Losing the Dream? 4 (Jan. 2003), http://www.civilrightsproject.harvard.edu/research/reseg03/ AreWeLosingthe-Dream.pdf (all Internet materials as visited June 2, 2003, and available in Clerk of Court's case file) ("[W]hites are the most segregated group in the nation's public schools; they attend schools, on average, where eighty percent of the student body is white."); *id.*, at 28 ("[A]lmost three-fourths of black and Latino students attend schools that are predominantly minority . . . .

More than one in six black children attend a school that is 99-100% minority . . . . One in nine Latino students attend virtually all minority schools.")

5. *See, e.g.,* Ryan, Schools, Race, and Money, 109 Yale L. J. 249, 273-274 (1999) ("Urban public schools are attended primarily by African-American and Hispanic students"; students who attend such schools are disproportionately poor, score poorly on standardized tests, and are far more likely to drop out than students who attend nonurban schools.).

6. *See, e.g.,* Statistical Abstract 140 (Table 211).

7. *See, e.g.,* Holzer, Career Advancement Prospects and Strategies for Low-Wage Minority Workers, in Low-Wage Workers in the New Economy 228 (R. Kazis & M. Miller eds. 2001) ("[I]n studies that have sent matched pairs of minority and white applicants with apparently equal credentials to apply for jobs, whites routinely get more interviews and job offers than either black or Hispanic applicants."); M. Bertrand & S. Mullainathan, Are Emily and Brendan More Employable than Lakisha and Jamal?: A Field Experiment on Labor Market Discrimination (Nov. 18, 2002), http:// gsb.uchicago.edu/pdf/bertrand.pdf; Mincy, The Urban Institute Audit Studies: Their Research and Policy Context, in Clear and Convincing Evidence: Measurement of Discrimination in America 165-186 (M. Fix & R. Struyk eds. 1993).

8. *See, e.g.,* M. Turner et al., Discrimination in Metropolitan Housing Markets: National Results from Phase I HDS 2000, pp. i, iii (Nov. 2002), http://www.huduser.org/Publications/pdf/Phase1_Report.pdf (paired testing in which "two individuals—one minority and the other white—pose as otherwise identical homeseekers, and visit real estate or rental agents to inquire about the availability of advertised housing units" revealed that "discrimination still persists in both rental and sales markets of large metropolitan areas nationwide"); M. Turner & F. Skidmore, Mortgage Lending Discrimination: A Review of Existing Evidence 2 (1999) (existing research evidence shows that minority homebuyers in the United States "face discrimination from mortgage lending institutions.").

9. *See, e.g.,* Ayres, Further Evidence of Discrimination in New Car Negotiations and Estimates of its Cause, 94 Mich. L. Rev. 109, 109-110 (1995) (study in which 38 testers negotiated the purchase of more than 400 automobiles confirmed earlier finding "that dealers systematically offer lower prices to white males than to other tester types").

10. The United States points to the "percentage plans" used in California, Florida, and Texas as one example of a "race-neutral alternativ[e]" that would permit the College to enroll meaningful numbers of minority students. Brief for United States as Amicus Curiae 14; see U.S. Commission on Civil Rights, Beyond Percentage Plans: The Challenge of Equal Opportunity in Higher Education 1 (Nov. 2002), http://www.usccr.gov/pubs/ percent2/percent2.pdf (percentage plans guarantee admission to state universities for a fixed percentage of the top students from high schools in the State). Calling such 10% or 20% plans "race-neutral" seems to me disingenuous, for they "unquestionably were adopted with the specific purpose of increasing representation of African-Americans and Hispanics in the public higher education system." Brief for Respondent Bollinger et al. 44; see C. Horn & S. Flores, Percent Plans in College Admissions: A Comparative Analysis of Three States' Experiences 14-19 (2003), http://www.civilrightsproject.harvard.edu/research/affIrmativeaction/tristate.pdf. Percentage plans depend for their effectiveness on continued racial segregation at the secondary school level: They can ensure significant minority enrollment in universities only if the majority-minority high school population is large enough to guarantee that, in many schools, most of the students in the top 10% or 20% are minorities. Moreover, because such plans link college admission to a single criterion—high school class rank—they create perverse incentives. They encourage parents to keep their children in low-performing segregated schools, and discourage students from taking challenging classes that might lower their grade point averages. See Selingo, What States Aren't Saying About the 'X- Percent Solution,' Chronicle of Higher Education, June 2, 2000, p. A31. And even if percentage plans could boost the sheer numbers of minority enrollees at the undergraduate level, they do not touch enrollment in graduate and professional schools.

11. Contrary to the Court's contention, I do not suggest "changing the Constitution so that it conforms to the conduct of the universities." *Ante,* at 275, n. 22. In my view, the Constitution, properly interpreted, permits government officials to respond openly to the continuing importance of race. See *supra,* at 301-302. Among constitutionally permissible options, those that candidly disclose their consideration of race seem to me preferable to those that conceal it.

GONZALES V. CARHART

550 U.S. 124 (2007)

This case involves the federal Partial Birth Abortion Ban Act of 2003, which criminalized a form of late term abortion commonly known as "partial birth abortion" or intact dilation and extraction. This law was unique in that it did not prohibit late term abortions generally but just that specific method of abortion.

In a narrowly-drafted 5-4 decision authored by Justice Kennedy, the Court ruled the Act constitutional and found that it did not impose an undue burden on the due process rights of women to obtain an abortion, as there was diversity of opinion within the medical community on whether the specific prohibited procedure was ever truly necessary to preserve women's health.

Justice Ginsburg dissented, joined by Justices Stevens, Souter, and Breyer.

GONZALES V. CARHART

I n *Planned Parenthood of Southeastern Pa. v. Casey*, 505 U.S. 833, 844 (1992), the Court declared that "[liberty finds no refuge in a jurisprudence of doubt." There was, the Court said, an "imperative" need to dispel doubt as to "the meaning and reach" of the Court's 7-to-2 judgment, rendered nearly two decades earlier in *Roe v. Wade*, 410 U.S. 113 (1973). 505 U.S., at 845. Responsive to that need, the Court endeavored to provide secure guidance to "[s]tate and federal courts as well as legislatures throughout the Union," by defining "the rights of the woman and the legitimate authority of the State respecting the termination of pregnancies by abortion procedures." *Ibid.*

Taking care to speak plainly, the *Casey* Court restated and reaffirmed *Roe's* essential holding. 505 U.S., at 845-846. First, the Court addressed the type of abortion regulation permissible prior to fetal viability. It recognized "the right of the woman to choose to have an abortion before viability and to obtain it without undue interference from the State." *Id.*, at 846. Second, the Court acknowledged "the State's power to restrict abortions *after fetal viability*, if the law contains exceptions for pregnancies which endanger the woman's life or *health.*" *Ibid*, (emphasis added). Third, the Court confirmed that "the State has legitimate interests from the outset of the pregnancy in protecting the health of the woman and the life of the fetus that may become a child." *Ibid*, (emphasis added).

In reaffirming *Roe*, the *Casey* Court described the centrality of "the decision whether to bear . . . a child," *Eisenstadt v. Baird*, 405 U.S. 438, 453 (1972), to a woman's "dignity and autonomy," her "personhood" and "destiny," her "conception of. . . her place in society." 505 U.S., at 851-852. Of signal importance here, the *Casey* Court stated with unmistakable clarity that state regulation of access to abortion procedures, even after viability, must protect "the health of the woman." *Id.*, at 846.

Seven years ago, in *Stenberg v. Carhart*, 530 U.S. 914 (2000), the Court invalidated a Nebraska statute criminalizing the performance of a medical procedure that, in the political arena, has been dubbed "partial-birth abortion."[1] With fidelity to the *Roe-Casey* line of precedent, the Court held the Nebraska statute unconstitutional in part because it lacked the requisite protection for the preservation of a woman's health. *Stenberg*, 530 U.S., at 930; *cf. Ayotte v. Planned Parenthood of Northern New Eng.*, 546 U.S. 320, 327 (2006).

Today's decision is alarming. It refuses to take *Casey* and *Stenberg* seriously. It tolerates, indeed applauds, federal intervention to ban nationwide a procedure found necessary and proper in certain cases by the American College of Obstetricians and Gynecologists (ACOG). It blurs the line, firmly drawn in *Casey*, between previability and postviability abortions. And, for the first time since *Roe*, the Court blesses a prohibition with no exception safeguarding a woman's health.

I dissent from the Court's disposition. Retreating from prior rulings that abortion restrictions cannot be imposed absent an exception safeguarding a woman's health, the Court upholds an Act that surely would not survive under the close scrutiny that previously attended state-decreed limitations on a woman's reproductive choices.

I

A

As *Casey* comprehended, at stake in cases challenging abortion restrictions is a woman's "control over her [own] destiny." 505 U.S., at 869 (plurality opinion). See also at 852 (majority opinion).[2] "There was a time, not so long ago," when women were "regarded as the center of home and family life, with attendant special responsibilities that precluded full and independent legal status under the Constitution." *Id.*, at 896-897 (quoting *Hoyt v. Florida*, 368 U.S. 57, 62 (1961)). Those views, this Court made clear in *Casey*, "are no longer consistent with our understanding of the family, the individual, or the Constitution." 505 U.S., at 897. Women, it is now acknowledged, have the talent, capacity, and right "to participate equally in the economic and social life of the Nation." *Id.*, at 856. Their ability to realize their full potential, the Court recognized, is intimately connected to "their ability to control their reproductive lives." *Ibid.* Thus, legal challenges to undue restrictions on abortion procedures do not seek to vindicate some generalized notion of privacy; rather, they center on a woman's autonomy to determine her life's course, and thus to enjoy equal citizenship stature. *See, e.g.*, Siegel, Reasoning from the Body: A Historical

Perspective on Abortion Regulation and Questions of Equal Protection, 44 Stan. L. Rev. 261 (1992); Law, Rethinking Sex and the Constitution, 132 U. Pa. L. Rev. 955, 1002-1028 (1984).

In keeping with this comprehension of the right to reproductive choice, the Court has consistently required that laws regulating abortion, at any stage of pregnancy and in all cases, safeguard a woman's health. See, *e.g.*, *Ayotte*, 546 U.S., at 327-328 ("[O]ur precedents hold . . . that a State may not restrict access to abortions that are necessary, in appropriate medical judgment, for the preservation of the life or health of the [woman]." (quoting *Casey*, 505 U.S., at 879 (plurality opinion))); *Stenberg*, 530 U.S., at 930 ("Since the law requires a health exception in order to validate even a postviability abortion regulation, it at a minimum requires the same in respect to previability regulation."). See also *Thornburgh v. American College of Obstetricians and Gynecologists*, 476 U.S. 747, 768-769 (1986) (invalidating a postviability abortion regulation for "fail[ure] to require that [a pregnant woman's] health be the physician's paramount consideration").

We have thus ruled that a State must avoid subjecting women to health risks not only where the pregnancy itself creates danger, but also where state regulation forces women to resort to less safe methods of abortion. See *Planned Parenthood of Central Mo. v. Danforth*, 428 U.S. 52, 79 (1976) (holding unconstitutional a ban on a method of abortion that "force[d] a woman . . . to terminate her pregnancy by methods more dangerous to her health"). See also *Stenberg*, 530 U.S., at 931 ("[Our cases] make clear that a risk to . . . women's health is the same whether it happens to arise from regulating a particular method of abortion, or from barring abortion entirely.")- Indeed, we have applied the rule that abortion regulation must safeguard a woman's health to the particular procedure at issue here—intact dilation and evacuation (intact D&E).[3]

In *Stenberg*, we expressly held that a statute banning intact D&E was unconstitutional in part because it lacked a health exception. 530 U.S., at 930, 937. We noted that there existed a division of medical opinion" about the relative safety of intact D&E, *id.*, at 937, but we made clear that as long as "substantial medical authority supports the proposition that banning a particular abortion procedure could endanger women's health," a health exception is required, *id.*, at 938. We explained:

"The word 'necessary' in *Casey's* phrase 'necessary, in appropriate medical judgment, for the preservation of the life or health of the [pregnant woman],' cannot refer to an absolute necessity or to absolute proof. Medical treatments and procedures are often considered appropriate (or inappropriate) in light of estimated comparative health risks (and health benefits) in particular cases. Neither can that phrase require unanimity of medical opinion. Doctors often differ in their estimation of comparative health risks and appropriate treatment.

And *Casey's* words 'appropriate medical judgment' must embody the judicial
need to tolerate responsible differences of medical opinion . . . ." *Id.*, at 937
(citation omitted).

Thus, we reasoned, division in medical opinion "at most means uncertainty,
a factor that signals the presence of risk, not its absence." *Ibid.* "[A] statute that
altogether forbids [intact D&E] . . . consequently must contain a health exception." *Id.*, at 938. See also *id.*, at 948 (O'Connor, J., concurring) ("Th[e] lack of a
health exception necessarily renders the statute unconstitutional.").

B

In 2003, a few years after our ruling in *Stenberg*, Congress passed the
Partial-Birth Abortion Ban Act—without an exception for women's health. See
18 U.S.C. § 1531(a) (2000 ed., Supp. IV).[4] The congressional findings on which
the Partial-Birth Abortion Ban Act rests do not withstand inspection, as the
lower courts have determined and this Court is obliged to concede. *Ante*, at
165-166. See *National Abortion Federation v. Ashcroft*, 330 F. Supp. 2d 436, 482
(SDNY 2004) ("Congress did not . . . carefully consider the evidence before
arriving at its findings."), aff'd sub nom. *National Abortion Federation v.
Gonzales*, 437 F. 3d 278 (CA2 2006). See also *Planned Parenthood Federation of Am.
v. Ashcroft*, 320 F. Supp. 2d 957, 1019 (ND Cal. 2004) ("[N]one of the six physicians who testified before Congress had ever performed an intact D&E. Several
did not provide abortion services at all; and one was not even an obgyn. . . .
[T]he oral testimony before Congress was not only unbalanced, but intention-
ally polemic."), aff'd, 435 F. 3d 1163 (CA9 2006); *Carhart v. Ashcroft*, 331 F. Supp.
2d 805, 1011 (Neb. 2004) ("Congress arbitrarily relied upon the opinions of
doctors who claimed to have no (or very little) recent and relevant experience
with surgical abortions, and disregarded the views of doctors who had significant and relevant experience with those procedures."), aff'd, 413 F. 3d 791 (CA8
2005).

Many of the Act's recitations are incorrect. See *ante*, at 165-166. For example,
Congress determined that no medical schools provide instruction on intact
D&E. §2(14)(B), 117 Stat. 1204, notes following 18 U.S.C. §1531 (2000 ed., Supp.
IV), p. 769,1 (14)(B) (Congressional Findings). But in fact, numerous leading
medical schools teach the procedure. See *Planned Parenthood*, 320 F. Supp. 2d, at
1029; *National Abortion Federation*, 330 F. Supp. 2d, at 479. See also Brief for
ACOG as *Amicus Curiae* 18 ("Among the schools that now teach the intact
variant are Columbia, Cornell, Yale, New York University, Northwestern,
University of Pittsburgh, University of Pennsylvania, University of Rochester,
and University of Chicago.").

More important, Congress claimed there was a medical consensus that the banned procedure is never necessary. Congressional Findings 1 (1). But the evidence "very clearly demonstrate[d] the opposite." *Planned Parenthood*, 320 F. Supp. 2d, at 1025. See also *Carhart*, 331 F. Supp. 2d, at 1008-1009 ("[T]here was no evident consensus in the record that Congress compiled. There was, however, a substantial body of medical opinion presented to Congress in opposition. If anything . . . the congressional record establishes that there was a 'consensus' in favor of the banned procedure."); *National Abortion Federation*, 330 F. Supp. 2d, at 488 ("The congressional record itself undermines [Congress'] finding" that there is a medical consensus that intact D&E "is never medically necessary and should be prohibited." (internal quotation marks omitted)).

Similarly, Congress found that "[t]here is no credible medical evidence that partial-birth abortions are safe or are safer than other abortion procedures." Congressional Findings (14)(B), in notes following 18 U.S.C. § 1531 (2000 ed., Supp. IV), p. 769. But the congressional record includes letters from numerous individual physicians stating that pregnant women's health would be jeopardized under the Act, as well as statements from nine professional associations, including ACOG, the American Public Health Association, and the California Medical Association, attesting that intact D&E carries meaningful safety advantages over other methods. See *National Abortion Federation*, 330 F. Supp. 2d, at 490. See also *Planned Parenthood*, 320 F. Supp. 2d, at 1021 ("Congress in its findings .. . chose to disregard the statements by ACOG and other medical organizations."). No comparable medical groups supported the ban. In fact, "all of the government's own witnesses disagreed with many of the specific congressional findings." *Id.*, at 1024.

C

In contrast to Congress, the District Courts made findings after full trials at which all parties had the opportunity to present their best evidence. The courts had the benefit of "much more extensive medical and scientific evidence . . . concerning the safety and necessity of intact D&Es." *Planned Parenthood*, 320 F. Supp. 2d, at 1014; *cf. National Abortion Federation*, 330 F. Supp. 2d, at 482 (District Court "heard more evidence during its trial than Congress heard over the span of eight years.").

During the District Court trials, "numerous" "extraordinarily accomplished" and "very experienced" medical experts explained that, in certain circumstances and for certain women, intact D&E is safer than alternative procedures and necessary to protect women's health. *Carhart*, 331 F. Supp. 2d, at 1024-1027; see *Planned Parenthood*, 320 F. Supp. 2d, at 1001 ("[A]ll of the doctors who actually perform intact D&Es concluded that in their opinion and clinical judgment, intact D&Es remain the safest option for certain individual women under certain individual health circumstances, and are significantly safer for these women than other abortion techniques, and are thus medically necessary."); *cf. ante*, at 161 ("Respondents presented evidence that intact D&E may be the safest method of abortion, for reasons similar to those adduced in *Stenberg*.").

According to the expert testimony plaintiffs introduced, the safety advantages of intact D&E are marked for women with certain medical conditions, for example, uterine scarring, bleeding disorders, heart disease, or compromised immune systems. See *Carhart*, 331 F. Supp. 2d, at 924-929, 1026-1027; *National Abortion Federation*, 330 F. Supp. 2d, at 472-473; *Planned Parenthood*, 320 F. Supp. 2d, at 992-994, 1001. Further, plaintiffs' experts testified that intact D&E is significantly safer for women with certain pregnancy- related conditions, such as placenta previa and accreta, and for women carrying fetuses with certain abnormalities, such as severe hydrocephalus. See *Carhart*, 331 F. Supp. 2d, at 924, 1026-1027; *National Abortion Federation*, 330 F. Supp. 2d, at 473-474; *Planned Parenthood*, 320 F. Supp. 2d, at 992- 994, 1001. See also *Stenberg*, 530 U.S., at 929; Brief for ACOG as *Amicus Curiae* 2, 13-16.

Intact D&E, plaintiffs' experts explained, provides safety benefits over D&E by dismemberment for several reasons: First, intact D&E minimizes the number of times a physician must insert instruments through the cervix and into the uterus, and thereby reduces the risk of trauma to, and perforation of, the cervix and uterus—the most serious complication associated with nonintact D&E. See *Carhart*, 331 F. Supp. 2d, at 923-928,1025; *National Abortion Federation*, 330 F. Supp. 2d, at 471; *Planned Parenthood*, 320 F. Supp. 2d, at 982, 1001. Second, removing the fetus intact, instead of dismembering it in utero, decreases the likelihood that fetal tissue will be retained in the uterus, a condition that can cause infection, hemorrhage, and infertility. See *Carhart*, 331 F. Supp. 2d, at 923-928, 1025-1026; *National Abortion Federation*, 330 F. Supp. 2d, at 472; *Planned Parenthood*, 320 F. Supp. 2d, at 1001. Third, intact D&E diminishes the chances of exposing the patient's tissues to sharp bony fragments sometimes resulting from dismemberment of the fetus. See *Carhart*, 331 F. Supp. 2d, at 923-928, 1026; *National Abortion Federation*, 330 F. Supp. 2d, at 471; *Planned Parenthood*, 320 F. Supp. 2d, at 1001. Fourth, intact D&E takes less operating time than D&E by dismemberment, and thus may reduce bleeding, the risk of infection, and complications relating to anesthesia. See *Carhart*, 331 F. Supp. 2d, at 923-928,1026; *National Abortion Federation*, 330 F. Supp. 2d, at 472; *Planned Parenthood*, 320 F. Supp. 2d, at 1001. See also *Stenberg*, 530 U.S., at 928-929, 932; Brief for ACOG as *Amicus Curiae* 2, 11-13.

Based on thoroughgoing review of the trial evidence and the congressional record, each of the District Courts to consider the issue rejected Congress' findings as unreasonable and not supported by the evidence. See *Carhart*, 331 F. Supp. 2d, at 1008-1027; *National Abortion Federation*, 330 F. Supp. 2d, at 482, 488-

491; *Planned Parenthood*, 320 F. Supp. 2d, at 1032. The trial courts concluded, in contrast to Congress' findings, that "significant medical authority supports the proposition that in some circumstances, [intact D&E] is the safest procedure." *Id.*, at 1033 (quoting *Stenberg*, 530 U.S., at 932); accord *Carhart*, 331 F. Supp. 2d, at 1008-1009, 1017-1018; *National Abortion Federation*, 330 F. Supp. 2d, at 480-482;[5] *cf. Stenberg*, 530 U.S., at 932 ("[T]he record shows that significant medical authority supports the proposition that in some circumstances, [intact D&E] would be the safest procedure.").

The District Courts' findings merit this Court's respect. *See, e.g.,* Fed. Rule Civ. Proc. 52(a); *Salve Regina College v. Russell*, 499 U.S. 225, 233 (1991). Today's opinion supplies no reason to reject those findings. Nevertheless, despite the District Courts' appraisal of the weight of the evidence, and in undisguised conflict with *Stenberg*, the Court asserts that the Partial-Birth Abortion Ban Act can survive "when . . . medical uncertainty persists." *Ante*, at 163. This assertion is bewildering. Not only does it defy the Court's longstanding precedent affirming the necessity of a health exception, with no carve-out for circumstances of medical uncertainty, see *supra*, at 172-173; it gives short shrift to the records before us, carefully canvassed by the District Courts. Those records indicate that "the majority of highly-qualified experts on the subject believe intact D&E to be the safest, most appropriate procedure under certain circumstances." *Planned Parenthood*, 320 F. Supp. 2d, at 1034. See *supra*, at 177.

The Court acknowledges some of this evidence, *ante*, at 161, but insists that, because some witnesses disagreed with ACOG and other experts' assessment of risk, the Act can stand. *Ante*, at 162, 166-167. In this insistence, the Court brushes under the rug the District Courts' well-supported findings that the physicians who testified that intact D&E is never necessary to preserve the health of a woman had slim authority for their opinions. They had no training for, or personal experience with, the intact D&E procedure, and many performed abortions only on rare occasions. See *Planned Parenthood*, 320 F. Supp. 2d, at 980; *Carhart*, 331 F. Supp. 2d, at 1025; *cf. National Abortion Federation*, 330 F. Supp. 2d, at 462-464. Even indulging the assumption that the Government witnesses were equally qualified to evaluate the relative risks of abortion procedures, their testimony could not erase the "significant medical authority supporting] the proposition that in some circumstances, [intact D&E] would be the safest procedure." *Stenberg*, 530 U.S., at 932.[6]

II

A

The Court offers flimsy and transparent justifications for upholding a nationwide ban on intact D&E any exception to safeguard a woman's health. Today's ruling, the Court declares, advances "a premise central to [*Casey's*] conclusion"—*i.e.*, the Government's "legitimate and substantial interest in preserving and promoting fetal life." *Ante*, at 145. See also *ante*, at 146 ("[W]e must determine whether the Act furthers the legitimate interest of the Government in protecting the life of the fetus that may become a child."). But the Act scarcely furthers that interest: The law saves not a single fetus from destruction, for it targets only a method of performing abortion. See *Stenberg*, 530 U.S., at 930. And surely the statute was not designed to protect the lives or health of pregnant women. *Id.*, at 951 (Ginsburg, J., concurring); *cf. Casey*, 505 U.S., at 846 (recognizing along with the State's legitimate interest in the life of the fetus, its "legitimate interes[t] . . . in protecting the health of the woman" (emphasis added)). In short, the Court upholds a law that, while doing nothing to "preserv[e] . . . fetal life," *ante*, at 145, bars a woman from choosing intact D&E although her doctor "reasonably believes [that procedure] will best protect [her]," *Stenberg*, 530 U.S., at 946 (Stevens, J., concurring).

As another reason for upholding the ban, the Court emphasizes that the Act does not proscribe the nonintact D&E procedure. See *ante*, at 164. But why not, one might ask. Nonintact D&E could equally be characterized as "brutal," *ante*, at 157, involving as it does "tearing] [a fetus] apart" and "ripp[ing] off" its limbs, *ante*, at 135. "[T]he notion that either of these two equally gruesome procedures . . . is more akin to infanticide than the other, or that the State furthers any legitimate interest by banning one but not the other, is simply irrational." *Stenberg*, 530 U.S., at 946-947 (Stevens, J., concurring).

Delivery of an intact, albeit nonviable, fetus warrants special condemnation, the Court maintains, because a fetus that is not dismembered resembles an infant. *Ante*, at 158. But so, too, does a fetus delivered intact after it is terminated by injection a day or two before the surgical evacuation, *ante*, at 136, 164, or a fetus delivered through medical induction or cesarean, *ante*, at 140. Yet, the availability of those procedures—along with D&E by dismemberment—the Court says, saves the ban on intact D&E from a declaration of unconstitutionality. *Ante*, at 164-165. Never mind that the procedures deemed acceptable might put a woman's health at greater risk. See *supra*, at 180, and n. 6; *cf. ante*, at 136, 161-162.

Ultimately, the Court admits that "moral concerns" are at work, concerns that could yield prohibitions on any abortion. See *ante*, at 158 ("Congress could . .. conclude that the type of abortion proscribed by the Act requires specific regulation because it implicates additional ethical and moral concerns that justify a special prohibition."). Notably, the concerns expressed are untethered to any ground genuinely serving the Government's interest in preserving life. By allowing such concerns to carry the day and case, overriding fundamental rights, the Court dishonors our precedent. *See, e.g., Casey*, 505 U.S., at 850 ("Some of us as individuals find abortion offensive to our most basic principles of morality, but that cannot control our decision. Our obligation is to define the liberty of all, not to mandate our own moral code."); *Lawrence v. Texas*, 539 U.S. 558, 571 (2003) (Though "[f]or many persons [objections to homosexual conduct] are not trivial concerns but profound and deep convictions accepted as ethical and moral principles," the power of the State may not be used "to enforce these views on the whole society through operation of the criminal law." (citing *Casey*, 505 U.S., at 850)).

Revealing in this regard, the Court invokes an antiabortion shibboleth for which it concededly has no reliable evidence: Women who have abortions come to regret their choices, and consequently suffer from "[s]evere depression and loss of esteem." *Ante*, at 159.[7] Because of women's fragile emotional state and because of the "bond of love the mother has for her child," the Court worries, doctors may withhold information about the nature of the intact D&E procedure. *Ante*, at 159.[8] The solution the Court approves, then, is not to require doctors to inform women, accurately and adequately, of the different procedures and their attendant risks. *Cf. Casey*, 505 U.S., at 873 (plurality opinion) ("States are free to enact laws to provide a reasonable framework for a woman to make a decision that has such profound and lasting meaning."). Instead, the Court deprives women of the right to make an autonomous choice, even at the expense of their safety.[9]

This way of thinking reflects ancient notions about women's place in the family and under the Constitution— ideas that have long since been discredited. Compare, *Muller v. Oregon*, 208 U.S. 412, 422-423 (1908) ("protective" legislation imposing hours-of-work limitations on women only held permissible in view of women's "physical structure and a proper discharge of her maternal functio[n]"); *Bradwell v. State*, 16 Wall. 130, 141 (1873) (Bradley, J., concurring) ("Man is, or should be, woman's protector and defender. The natural and proper timidity and delicacy which belongs to the female sex evidently unfits it for many of the occupations of civil life. . . . The paramount destiny and mission of woman are to fulfil[l] the noble and benign offices of wife and mother."), with *United States v. Virginia*, 518 U.S. 515, 533, 542, n. 12 (1996) (State may not rely on "overbroad generalizations" about the "talents, capacities, or preferences" of women; "[s]uch judgments have . . . impeded . . . women's progress toward full citizenship stature throughout our Nation's history"); *Califano v. Goldfarb*, 430 U.S. 199, 207 (1977) (gender-based Social Security classification rejected because it rested on "archaic and overbroad generalizations" "such as assumptions as to [women's] dependency" (internal quotation marks omitted)).

Though today's majority may regard women's feelings on the matter as "self-evident," *ante*, at 159, this Court has repeatedly confirmed that "[t]he destiny of the woman must be shaped . . . on her own conception of her spiritual imperatives and her place in society," *Casey*, 505 U.S., at 852. See also *id.*, at 877 (plurality opinion) ("[M]eans chosen by the State to further the interest in potential life must be calculated to inform the woman's free choice, not hinder it."); *supra*, at 171-172.

B

In cases on a "woman's liberty to determine whether to [continue] her pregnancy," this Court has identified viability as a critical consideration. See *Casey*, 505 U.S., at 869-870 (plurality opinion). "[T]here is no line [more workable] than viability," the Court explained in *Casey*, for viability is "the time at which there is a realistic possibility of maintaining and nourishing a life outside the womb, so that the independent existence of the second life can in reason and all fairness be the object of state protection that now overrides the rights of the woman. . . . In some broad sense it might be said that a woman who fails to act before viability has consented to the State's intervention on behalf of the developing child." *Id.*, at 870.

Today, the Court blurs that line, maintaining that "[t]he Act [legitimately] applies] both previability and postviability because . . . a fetus is a living organism while within the womb, whether or not it is viable outside the womb." *Ante*, at 147. Instead of drawing the line at viability, the Court refers to Congress' purpose to differentiate "abortion and infanticide" based not on whether a fetus can survive outside the womb, but on where a fetus is anatomically located when a particular medical procedure is performed. See *ante*, at 158 (quoting Congressional Findings 1 (14)(G)).

One wonders how long a line that saves no fetus from destruction will hold in face of the Court's "moral concerns." See *supra*, at 182; *cf. ante*, at 147 (noting that "[i]n this litigation" the Attorney General "does not dispute that the Act would impose an undue burden if it covered standard D&E"). The Court's hostility to the right *Roe* and *Casey* secured is not concealed. Throughout, the opinion refers to obstetrician-gynecologists and surgeons who perform abortions not by the titles of their medical specialties, but by the pejorative label "abortion doctor." *Ante*, at 144,154,155,161, 163. A fetus is described as an "unborn child," and as a "baby," *ante*, at 134, 138; second-trimester, previability abortions are referred to as "late-term," *ante*, at 156; and the reasoned medical judgments of highly trained doctors are dismissed as "preferences" motivated by "mere convenience," *ante*, at 134, 166. Instead of the heightened scrutiny we have previously applied, the Court determines that a "rational" ground is enough to uphold the Act, *ante*, at 158,166. And, most troubling, *Casey*'s principles, confirming the continuing vitality of "the essential holding of *Roe*," are merely "assume[d]" for the moment, *ante*, at 146, 161, rather than "retained" or "reaffirmed," *Casey*, 505 U.S., at 846.

III

A

The Court further confuses our jurisprudence when it declares that "facial attacks" are not permissible in "these circumstances,"*i.e.,* where medical uncertainty exists. *Ante,* at 167; see *ibid.* ("In an as-applied challenge the nature of the medical risk can be better quantified and balanced than in a facial attack."). This holding is perplexing given that, in materially identical circumstances we held that a statute lacking a health exception was unconstitutional on its face. *Stenberg,* 530 U.S., at 930; see *id.,* at 937 (in facial challenge, law held unconstitutional because "significant body of medical opinion believes [the] procedure may bring with it greater safety for some patients" (emphasis added)). See also *Sabri v. United States,* 541 U.S. 600, 609-610 (2004) (identifying abortion as one setting in which we have recognized the validity of facial challenges); Fallon, Making Sense of Overbreadth, 100 Yale L. J. 853, 859, n. 29 (1991) ("[Virtually all of the abortion cases reaching the Supreme Court since *Roe v. Wade,* 410 U.S. 113 (1973), have involved facial attacks on state statutes, and the Court, whether accepting or rejecting the challenges on the merits, has typically accepted this framing of the question presented.")- Accord Fallon, As-Applied and Facial Challenges and Third-Party Standing, 113 Harv. L. Rev. 1321, 1356 (2000); Dorf, Facial Challenges to State and Federal Statutes, 46 Stan. L. Rev. 235, 271-276 (1994).

Without attempting to distinguish *Stenberg* and earlier decisions, the majority asserts that the Act survives review because respondents have not shown that the ban on intact D&E would be unconstitutional "in a large fraction of [relevant] cases." *Ante,* at 167 (citing *Casey,* 505 U.S., at 895). But *Casey* makes clear that, in determining whether any restriction poses an undue burden on a "large fraction" of women, the relevant class is not "all women," nor "all pregnant women," nor even all women "seeking abortions." *Ibid.* Rather, a provision restricting access to abortion "must be judged by reference to those [women] for whom it is an actual rather than an irrelevant restriction." *Ibid.* Thus the absence of a health exception burdens all women for whom it is relevant—women who, in the judgment of their doctors, require an intact D&E because other procedures would place their health at risk.[10] Cf. *Stenberg,* 530 U.S., at 934 (accepting the "relative rarity" of medically indicated intact D&Es as true but not "highly relevant"— for "the health exception question is whether protecting women's health requires an exception for those infrequent occasions"); *Ayotte,* 546 U.S., at 328 (facial challenge entertained where "[i]n some very small percentage of cases . . . women . . . need immediate abortions to avert serious and often irreversible damage to their health"). It makes no sense to conclude that this facial challenge fails because respondents have not shown that a health exception is necessary for a large fraction of second-

trimester abortions, including those for which a health exception is unnecessary: The very purpose of a health exception is to protect women in exceptional
cases.

B

If there is anything at all redemptive to be said of today's opinion, it is that
the Court is not willing to foreclose entirely a constitutional challenge to the
Act. "The Act is open," the Court states, "to a proper as-applied challenge in a
discrete case." *Ante*, at 168; see *ante*, at 167 ("The Government has acknowledged that preenforcement, as-applied challenges to the Act can be maintained."). But the Court offers no clue on what a "proper" lawsuit might look
like. See *ante*, at 167-168. Nor does the Court explain why the injunctions
ordered by the District Courts should not remain in place, trimmed only to
exclude instances in which another procedure would safeguard a woman's
health at least equally well. Surely the Court cannot mean that no suit may be
brought until a woman's health is immediately jeopardized by the ban on
intact D&E. A woman "suffering] from medical complications," *ante*, at 168,
needs access to the medical procedure at once and cannot wait for the judicial
process to unfold. See *Ayotte*, 546 U.S., at 328.

The Court appears, then, to contemplate another lawsuit by the initiators of
the instant actions. In such a second round, the Court suggests, the challengers
could succeed upon demonstrating that "in discrete and well-defined instances
a particular condition has or is likely to occur in which the procedure prohibited by the Act must be used." *Ante*, at 167. One may anticipate that such a
preenforcement challenge will be mounted swiftly, to ward off serious, sometimes irremediable harm, to women whose health would be endangered by the
intact D&E prohibition.

The Court envisions that in an as-applied challenge, "the nature of the
medical risk can be better quantified and balanced." *Ibid.* But it should not
escape notice that the record already includes hundreds and hundreds of pages
of testimony identifying "discrete and well-defined instances" in which
recourse to an intact D&E would better protect the health of women with
particular conditions. See *supra*, at 177-179. Record evidence also documents
that medical exigencies, unpredictable in advance, may indicate to a well-
trained doctor that intact D&E is the safest procedure. See *ibid.* In light of this
evidence, our unanimous decision just one year ago in *Ayotte* counsels against
reversal. See 546 U.S., at 331 (remanding for reconsideration of the remedy for
the absence of a health exception, suggesting that an injunction prohibiting
unconstitutional applications might suffice).

The Court's allowance only of an "as-applied challenge in a discrete case,"
ante, at 168—jeopardizes women's health and places doctors in an untenable

position. Even if courts were able to carve out exceptions through piecemeal litigation for "discrete and well-defined instances," *ante*, at 167, women whose circumstances have not been anticipated by prior litigation could well be left unprotected. In treating those women, physicians would risk criminal prosecution, conviction, and imprisonment if they exercise their best judgment as to the safest medical procedure for their patients. The Court is thus gravely mistaken to conclude that narrow as-applied challenges are "the proper manner to protect the health of the woman." *Cf. ibid.*

IV

As the Court wrote in *Casey*, "overruling *Roe's* central holding would not only reach an unjustifiable result under principles of stare decisis, but would seriously weaken the Court's capacity to exercise the judicial power and to function as the Supreme Court of a Nation dedicated to the rule of law." 505 U.S., at 865. "[T]he very concept of the rule of law underlying our own Constitution requires such continuity over time that a respect for precedent is, by definition, indispensable." *Id.*, at 854. See also *id.*, at 867 ("[T]o overrule under fire in the absence of the most compelling reason to reexamine a watershed decision would subvert the Court's legitimacy beyond any serious question.").

Though today's opinion does not go so far as to discard or *Casey*, the Court, differently composed than it was when we last considered a restrictive abortion regulation, is hardly faithful to our earlier invocations of "the rule of law" and the "principles of stare decisis." Congress imposed a ban despite our clear prior holdings that the State cannot proscribe an abortion procedure when its use is necessary to protect a woman's health. See *supra*, at 174-175, n. 4. Although Congress' findings could not withstand the crucible of trial, the Court defers to the legislative override of our Constitution-based rulings. See *supra*, at 174-176. A decision so at odds with our jurisprudence should not have staying power.

In sum, the notion that the Partial-Birth Abortion Ban Act furthers any legitimate governmental interest is, quite simply, irrational. The Court's defense of the statute provides no saving explanation. In candor, the Act, and the Court's defense of it, cannot be understood as anything other than an effort to chip away at a right declared again and again by this Court—and with increasing comprehension of its centrality to women's lives. See *supra*, at 171, n. 2; *supra*, at 174-175, n. 4. When "a statute burdens constitutional rights and all that can be said on its behalf is that it is the vehicle that legislators have chosen for expressing their hostility to those rights, the burden is undue." *Stenberg*, 530 U.S., at 952 (Ginsburg, J., concurring) (quoting *Hope Clinic v. Ryan*, 195 F. 3d 857, 881 (CA7 1999) (Posner, C. J., dissenting)).

* * *

For the reasons stated, I dissent from the Court's disposition and would affirm the judgments before us for review.

---

1. The term "partial-birth abortion" is neither recognized in the medical literature nor used by physicians who perform second-trimester abortions. See *Planned Parenthood Federation of Am. v. Ashcroft*, 320 F. Supp. 2d 957, 964 (ND Cal. 2004), aff'd, 435 F. 3d 1163 (CA9 2006). The medical community refers to the procedure as either dilation & extraction (D&X) or intact dilation and evacuation (intact D&E). See, e. *ante*, at 136; *Stenberg v. Carhart*, 530 U.S. 914, 927 (2000).
2. *Planned Parenthood of Southeastern Pa. v. Casey*, 505 U.S. 833, 851- 852 (1992), described more precisely than did *Roe v. Wade*, 410 U.S. 113 (1973), the impact of abortion restrictions on women's liberty. *Roe*'s focus was in considerable measure on "vindicat[ing] the right of the physician to administer medical treatment according to his professional judgment." *Id.*, at 165.
3. Dilation and evacuation (D&E) is the most frequently used abortion procedure during the second trimester of pregnancy; intact D&E is a variant of the D&E procedure. See *ante*, at 135, 137; Stenberg, 530 U.S., at 924, 927; *Planned Parenthood*, 320 F. Supp. 2d, at 966. Second-trimester abortions (*i.e.*, midpregnancy, previability abortions) are, however, relatively uncommon. Between 85 and 90 percent of all abortions performed in the United States take place during the first three months of pregnancy. See *ante*, at 134. See also *Stenberg*, 530 U.S., at 923-927; *National Abortion Federation v. Ashcroft*, 330 F. Supp. 2d 436, 464 (SDNY 2004), aff'd sub nom. *National Abortion Federation v. Gonzales*, 437 F. 3d 278 (CA2 2006); *Planned Parenthood*, 320 F. Supp. 2d, at 960, and n. 4.

   Adolescents and indigent women, research suggests, are more likely than other women to have difficulty obtaining an abortion during the first trimester of pregnancy. Minors may be unaware they are pregnant until relatively late in pregnancy, while poor women's financial constraints are an obstacle to timely receipt of services. See Finer, Frohwirth, Dauphinee, Singh, & Moore, Timing of Steps and Reasons for Delays in Obtaining Abortions in the United States, 74 Contraception 334, 341-343 (2006). See also Drey et al., Risk Factors Associated with Presenting for Abortion in the Second Trimester, 107 Obstetrics & Gynecology 128, 133 (Jan. 2006) (concluding that women who have second-trimester abortions typically discover relatively late that they are pregnant). Severe fetal anomalies and health problems confronting the pregnant woman are also causes of second-trimester abortions; many such conditions cannot be diagnosed or do not develop until the second trimester. See, e.g., Finer, supra, at 344; F. Cunningham et al., Williams Obstetrics 242, 290, 328-329 (22d ed. 2005); cf. Schechtman, Gray, Baty, & Rothman, Decision-Making for Termination of Pregnancies with Fetal Anomalies: Analysis of 53,000 Pregnancies, 99 Obstetrics & Gynecology 216, 220-221 (Feb. 2002) (nearly all women carrying fetuses with the most serious central nervous system anomalies chose to abort their pregnancies).
4. The Act's sponsors left no doubt that their intention was to nullify our ruling in *Stenberg*, 530 U.S. 914. *See, e.g.*, 149 Cong. Rec. 5731 (2003) (statement of Sen. Santorum) ("Why are we here? We are here because the Supreme Court defended the indefensible. . . . We have responded to the Supreme Court."). See also 148 Cong. Rec. 14273 (2002) (statement of Rep. Linder) (rejecting proposition that Congress has "no right to legislate a ban on this horrible practice because the Supreme Court says [it] cannot").
5. Even the District Court for the Southern District of New York, which was more skeptical of the health benefits of intact D&E, see *ante*, at 162, recognized: "[T]he Government's own experts disagreed with almost all of Congress's factual findings"; a "significant body of medical opinion" holds that intact D&E has safety advantages over nonintact D&E; "[professional medical associations have also expressed their view that [intact D&E] may be the safest procedure for some women"; and "[t]he evidence indicates that the same disagreement among experts found by the Supreme Court in *Stenberg* existed throughout the time that Congress was considering the legislation, despite Congress's findings to the contrary." *National Abortion Federation*, 330 F. Supp. 2d, at 480-482.

6. The majority contends that "[i]f the intact D&E procedure is truly necessary in some circumstances, it appears likely an injection that kills the fetus is an alternative under the Act that allows the doctor to perform the procedure." *Ante,* at 164. But a "significant body of medical opinion believes that inducing fetal death by injection is almost always inappropriate to the preservation of the health of women undergoing abortion because it poses tangible risk and provides no benefit to the woman." *Carhart v. Ashcroft,* 331 F. Supp. 2d 805, 1028 (Neb. 2004) (internal quotation marks omitted), aff'd, 413 F. 3d 791 (CA8 2005). In some circumstances, injections are "absolutely [medically] contraindicated." 331 F. Supp. 2d, at 1027. See also *id.,* at 907-912; *National Abortion Federation,* 330 F. Supp. 2d, at 474-475; *Planned Parenthood,* 320 F. Supp. 2d, at 995-997. The Court also identifies medical induction of labor as an alternative. See *ante,* at 140. That procedure, however, requires a hospital stay, *ibid.,* rendering it inaccessible to patients who lack financial resources, and it too is considered less safe for many women, and impermissible for others. See *Carhart,* 331 F. Supp. 2d, at 940-949, 1017; *National Abortion Federation,* 330 F. Supp. 2d, at 468-470; *Planned Parenthood,* 320 F. Supp. 2d, at 961, n. 5, 992-994, 1000-1002.

7. The Court is surely correct that, for most women, abortion is a painfully difficult decision. See *ante,* at 159. But "neither the weight of the scientific evidence to date nor the observable reality of 33 years of legal abortion in the United States comports with the idea that having an abortion is any more dangerous to a woman's long-term mental health than delivering and parenting a child that she did not intend to have . . . ." Cohen, Abortion and Mental Health: Myths and Realities, 9 Guttmacher Policy Rev. 8 (2006); see generally Bazelon, Is There a Post-Abortion Syndrome? N. Y. Times Magazine, Jan. 21, 2007, p. 40. See also, *e.g.,* American Psychological Association, APA Briefing Paper on the Impact of Abortion (2005) (rejecting theory of a postabortion syndrome and stating that "[a]ccess to legal abortion to terminate an unwanted pregnancy is vital to safeguard both the physical and mental health of women"); Schmiege & Russo, Depression and Unwanted First Pregnancy: Longitudinal Cohort Study, 331 British Medical J. 1303 (2005) (finding no credible evidence that choosing to terminate an unwanted first pregnancy contributes to risk of subsequent depression); Gilchrist, Hannaford, Frank, & Kay, Termination of Pregnancy and Psychiatric Morbidity, 167 British J. of Psychiatry 243, 247-248 (1995) (finding, in a cohort of more than 13,000 women, that the rate of psychiatric disorder was no higher among women who terminated pregnancy than among those who carried pregnancy to term); Stotland, The Myth of the Abortion Trauma Syndrome, 268 JAMA 2078, 2079 (1992) ("Scientific studies indicate that legal abortion results in fewer deleterious sequelae for women compared with other possible outcomes of unwanted pregnancy. There is no evidence of an abortion trauma syndrome."); American Psychological Association, Council Policy Manual: (N)(I)(3), Public Interest (1989) (declaring assertions about widespread severe negative psychological effects of abortion to be "without fact"). But see Cougle, Reardon, & Coleman, Generalized Anxiety Following Unintended Pregnancies Resolved Through Childbirth and Abortion: A Cohort Study of the 1995 National Survey of Family Growth, 19 J. Anxiety Disorders 137,142 (2005) (advancing theory of a postabortion syndrome but acknowledging that "no causal relationship between pregnancy outcome and anxiety could be determined" from study); Reardon et al., Psychiatric Admissions of Low-Income Women Following Abortion and Childbirth, 168 Canadian Medical Assn. J. 1253, 1255-1256 (May 13, 2003) (concluding that psychiatric admission rates were higher for women who had an abortion compared with women who delivered); *cf.* Major, Psychological Implications of Abortion—Highly Charged and Rife with Misleading Research, 168 Canadian Medical Assn. J. 1257, 1258 (May 13, 2003) (critiquing Reardon study for failing to control for a host of differences between women in the delivery and abortion samples).

8. Notwithstanding the "bond of love" women often have with their children, see *ante,* at 159, not all pregnancies, this Court has recognized, are wanted, or even the product of consensual activity. See *Casey,* 505 U.S., at 891 ("[O]n an average day in the United States, nearly 11,000 women are severely assaulted by their male partners. Many of these incidents involve sexual assault."). See also Glander, Moore, Michielutte, & Parsons, The Prevalence of Domestic Violence Among Women Seeking Abortion, 91 Obstetrics & Gynecology 1002 (1998); Holmes, Resnick, Kilpatrick, & Best, Rape-Related Pregnancy: Estimates and Descriptive Characteristics from a National Sample of Women, 175 Am. J. Obstetrics & Gynecology 320 (Aug. 1996).

9. Eliminating or reducing women's reproductive choices is manifestly not a means of protecting them. When safe abortion procedures cease to be an option, many women seek other means to end unwanted or coerced pregnancies. *See, e.g.,* World Health Organization, Unsafe Abortion: Global and Regional Estimates of the Incidence of Unsafe Abortion and Associated Mortality in

2000, pp. 3, 16 (4th ed. 2004) ("Restrictive legislation is associated with a high incidence of unsafe abortion" worldwide; unsafe abortion represents 13 percent of all "maternal" deaths); Henshaw, Unintended Pregnancy and Abortion: A Public Health Perspective, in A Clinician's Guide to Medical and Surgical Abortion 11, 19 (M. Paul, E. Lichtenberg, L. Borgatta, D. Grimes, & P. Stubblefield eds. 1999) ("Before legalization, large numbers of women in the United States died from unsafe abortions."); H. Boonstra, R. Gold, C. Richards, & L. Finer, Abortion in Women's Lives 13, and fig. 2.2 (2006) ("as late as 1965, illegal abortion still accounted for an estimated . . . 17% of all officially reported pregnancy-related deaths"; "[d]eaths from abortion declined dramatically after legalization").

10. There is, in short, no fraction because the numerator and denominator are the same: The health exception reaches only those cases where a woman's health is at risk. Perhaps for this reason, in mandating safeguards for women's health, we have never before invoked the "large fraction" test.

LEDBETTER V. GOODYEAR TIRE & RUBBER CO.

550 U.S. 618 (2007)

This case involves the mechanics of making a pay discrimination claim under Title VII of the Civil Rights Act of 1964. Title VII prohibits employers from discriminating against any individual with respect to compensation because of an individual's race, color, religion, sex, or national origin. However, in order to make a claim under the Act, the employee is required to file the claim within 180 days of when the unlawful discriminatory act occurred. Lily Ledbetter was a long-term employee of Goodyear who alleged she had consistently been underpaid during the entire course of her career and, after retiring, filed suit, arguing that the clock on her 180 day time limit to file a claim restarted every time she received an unfairly low paycheck.

In a 5-4 decision authored by Justice Alito, the Court ruled that each paycheck did not constitute a discrete discriminatory act and that Ledbetter's claim consequently fell beyond Title VII's 180-day statutory charging period, as she should have sued after the original pay decision was made.

Justice Ginsburg dissented, joined by Justices Stevens, Souter, and Breyer.

In 2009, Congress passed the Lily Ledbetter Fair Pay Act, which amended this time limit for filing discrimination suits under Title VII, effectively reversing the Court's decision.

LEDBETTER V. GOODYEAR TIRE & RUBBER CO.

L illy Ledbetter was a supervisor at Goodyear Tire & Rubber's plant in Gadsden, Alabama, from 1979 until her retirement in 1998. For most of those years, she worked as an area manager, a position largely occupied by men. Initially, Ledbetter's salary was in line with the salaries of men performing substantially similar work. Over time, however, her pay slipped in comparison to the pay of male area managers with equal or less seniority. By the end of 1997, Ledbetter was the only woman working as an area manager and the pay discrepancy between Ledbetter and her 15 male counterparts was stark: Ledbetter was paid $3,727 per month; the lowest paid male area manager received $4,286 per month, the highest paid, $5,236. See 421 F. 3d 1169, 1174 (CA11 2005); Brief for Petitioner 4.

Ledbetter launched charges of discrimination before the Equal Employment Opportunity Commission (EEOC) in March 1998. Her formal administrative complaint specified that, in violation of Title VII, Goodyear paid her a discriminatorily low salary because of her sex. See 42 U.S.C. §2000e-2(a)(l) (rendering it unlawful for an employer "to discriminate against any individual with respect to [her] compensation . . . because of such individual's . . . sex"). That charge was eventually tried to a jury, which found it "more likely than not that [Goodyear] paid [Ledbetter] a[n] unequal salary because of her sex." App. 102. In accord with the jury's liability determination, the District Court entered judgment for Ledbetter for backpay and damages, plus counsel fees and costs.

The Court of Appeals for the Eleventh Circuit reversed. Relying on Goodyear's system of annual merit-based raises, the court held that Ledbetter's claim, in relevant part, was time barred. 421 F. 3d, at 1171, 1182-1183. Title

YII provides that a charge of discrimination "shall be filed within [180] days after the alleged unlawful employment practice occurred." 42 U.S.C. § 2000e-5(e)(l).[1] Ledbetter charged, and proved at trial, that within the 180-day period, her pay was substantially less than the pay of men doing the same work. Further, she introduced evidence sufficient to establish that discrimination against female managers at the Gadsden plant, not performance inadequacies on her part, accounted for the pay differential. *See, e.g.,* App. 36-47, SI- 68, 82-87, 90-98, 112-113. That evidence was unavailing, the Eleventh Circuit held, and the Court today agrees, because it was incumbent on Ledbetter to file charges year by year, each time Goodyear failed to increase her salary commensurate with the salaries of male peers. Any annual pay decision not contested immediately (within 180 days), the Court affirms, becomes grandfathered, a fait accompli beyond the province of Title VII ever to repair.

The Court's insistence on immediate contest overlooks common characteristics of pay discrimination. Pay disparities often occur, as they did in Ledbetter's case, in small increments; cause to suspect that discrimination is at work develops only over time. Comparative pay information, moreover, is often hidden from the employee's view. Employers may keep under wraps the pay differentials maintained among supervisors, no less the reasons for those differentials. Small initial discrepancies may not be seen as meet for a federal case, particularly when the employee, trying to succeed in a nontraditional environment, is averse to making waves.

Pay disparities are thus significantly different from adverse actions "such as termination, failure to promote,. . . or refusal to hire," all involving fully communicated discrete acts, "easy to identify" as discriminatory. See *National Railroad Passenger Corporation v. Morgan*, 536 U.S. 101, 114 (2002). It is only when the disparity becomes apparent and sizable, *e.g.*, through future raises calculated as a percentage of current salaries, that an employee in Ledbetter's situation is likely to comprehend her plight and, therefore, to complain. Her initial readiness to give her employer the benefit of the doubt should not preclude her from later challenging the then current and continuing payment of a wage depressed on account of her sex.

On questions of time under Title VII, we have identified as the critical inquiries: "What constitutes an 'unlawful employment practice' and when has that practice 'occurred'?" *Id.*, at 110. Our precedent suggests, and lower courts have overwhelmingly held, that the unlawful practice is the current payment of salaries infected by gender-based (or race- based) discrimination—a practice that occurs whenever a paycheck delivers less to a woman than to a similarly situated man. See *Bazemore v. Friday*, 478 U.S. 385,395 (1986) (Brennan, J., joined by all other Members of the Court, concurring in part).

I

Title VII proscribes as an "unlawful employment practice" discrimination "against any individual with respect to his compensation . . . because of such individual's race, color, religion, sex, or national origin." 42 U.S.C. § 2000e-2(a) (1). An individual seeking to challenge an employment practice under this proscription must file a charge with the EEOC within 180 days "after the alleged unlawful employment practice occurred." § 2000e-5(e)(1). See *ante*, at 624; *supra*, at 644, n. 1.

Ledbetter's petition presents a question important to the sound application of Title VII: What activity qualifies as an unlawful employment practice in cases of discrimination with respect to compensation. One answer identifies the paysetting decision, and that decision alone, as the unlawful practice. Under this view, each particular salary-setting decision is discrete from prior and subsequent decisions, and must be challenged within 180 days on pain of forfeiture. Another response counts both the pay-setting decision and the actual payment of a discriminatory wage as unlawful practices. Under this approach, each payment of a wage or salary infected by sex-based discrimination constitutes an unlawful employment practice; prior decisions, outside the 180-day charge-filing period, are not themselves actionable, but they are relevant in determining the lawfulness of conduct within the period. The Court adopts the first view, see *ante*, at 621, 624, 628-629, but the second is more faithful to precedent, more in tune with the realities of the workplace, and more respectful of Title VII's remedial purpose.

A

In *Bazemore*, we unanimously held that an employer, the North Carolina Agricultural Extension Service, committed an unlawful employment practice each time it paid black employees less than similarly situated white employees. 478 U.S., at 395 (opinion of Brennan, J.). Before 1965, the Extension Service was divided into two branches: a white branch and a "Negro branch." at 390. Employees in the "Negro branch" were paid less than their white counterparts. In response to the Civil Rights Act of 1964, which included Title VII, the State merged the two branches into a single organization, made adjustments to reduce the salary disparity, and began giving annual raises based on nondiscriminatory factors. *Id.*, at 390-391, 394-395. Nonetheless, "some pre-existing salary disparities continued to linger on." *Id.*, at 394 (internal quotation marks omitted). We rejected the Court of Appeals' conclusion that the plaintiffs could not prevail because the lingering disparities were simply a continuing effect of a decision lawfully made prior to the effective date of Title VII. See *id.*, at 395-396. Rather, we reasoned, "[e]ach week's paycheck that delivers less to a black than to a similarly situated white is a wrong actionable under Title VII." *Id.*, at 395. Paychecks perpetuating past discrimination, we thus recognized, are actionable not simply because they are "related" to a decision made outside the charge-filing period, *cf. ante*, at 636, but because they discriminate anew each time they issue, see *Bazemore*, 478 U.S., at 395-396, and n. 6; *Morgan*, 536 U.S., at 111-112.

Subsequently, in *Morgan*, we set apart, for purposes of Title VII's timely filing requirement, unlawful employment actions of two kinds: "discrete acts" that are "easy to identify" as discriminatory, and acts that recur and are cumulative in impact. See *id.*, at 110,113-115. "[A] [discrete ac[t] such as termination, failure to promote, denial of transfer, or refusal to hire," *id.*, at 114, we explained, "'occur[s]' on the day that it 'happen[s].' A party, therefore, must file a charge within . . . 180 . . . days of the date of the act or lose the ability to recover for it." *Id.*, at 110; see *id.*, at 113 ("[Discrete discriminatory acts are not actionable if time barred, even when they are related to acts alleged in timely filed charges. Each discrete discriminatory act starts a new clock for filing charges alleging that act.").

"[Different in kind from discrete acts," we made clear, are "claims . . . based on the cumulative effect of individual acts." *Id.*, at 115. The *Morgan* decision placed hostile work environment claims in that category. "Their very nature involves repeated conduct." *Ibid.* "The unlawful employment practice" in hostile work environment claims "cannot be said to occur on any particular day. It occurs over a series of days or perhaps years and, in direct contrast to discrete acts, a single act of harassment may not be actionable on its own." *Ibid*, (internal quotation marks omitted). The persistence of the discriminatory conduct both indicates that management should have known of its existence and produces a cognizable harm. *Ibid.* Because the very nature of the hostile work environment claim involves repeated conduct,

> "[i]t does not matter, for purposes of the statute, that some of the component acts of the hostile work environment fall outside the statutory time period. Provided that an act contributing to the claim occurs within the filing period, the entire time period of the hostile environment may be considered by a court for the purposes of determining liability." *Id.*, at 117.

Consequently, although the unlawful conduct began in the past, "a charge may be filed at a later date and still encompass the whole." *Ibid.*

Pay disparities, of the kind Ledbetter experienced, have a closer kinship to hostile work environment claims than to charges of a single episode of discrimination. Ledbetter's claim, resembling *Morgan's*, rested not on one particular pay- check, but on "the cumulative effect of individual acts." See *id.*, at 115. See also Brief for Petitioner 13, 15-17, and n. 9 (analogizing Ledbetter's claim to the recurring and cumulative harm at issue in *Morgan*)', Reply Brief for Petitioner 13 (distinguishing pay discrimination from "easy to identify" discrete acts (internal quotation marks omitted)).

She charged insidious discrimination building up slowly but steadily. See Brief for Petitioner 5-8. Initially in line with the salaries of men performing substantially the same work, Ledbetter's salary fell 15 to 40 percent behind her male counterparts only after successive evaluations and percentage-based pay adjustments. See *supra*, at 643-644. Over time, she alleged and proved, the repetition of pay decisions undervaluing her work gave rise to the current discrimination of which she complained. Though component acts fell outside the charge-filing period, with each new pay-check, Goodyear contributed incrementally to the accumulating harm. See Morgan, 536 U.S., at 117; *Bazemore*, 478 U.S., at 395-396; *cf. Hanover Shoe, Inc. v. United Shoe Machinery Corp.*, 392 U.S. 481, 502, n. 15 (1968).[2]

B

The realities of the workplace reveal why the discrimination with respect to compensation that Ledbetter suffered does not fit within the category of singular discrete acts "easy to identify." A worker knows immediately if she is denied a promotion or transfer, if she is fired or refused employment. And promotions, transfers, hirings, and firings are generally public events, known to co-workers. When an employer makes a decision of such open and definitive character, an employee can immediately seek out an explanation and evaluate it for pretext. Compensation disparities, in contrast, are often hidden from sight. It is not unusual, decisions in point illustrate, for management to decline to publish employee pay levels, or for employees to keep private their own salaries. *See, e.g., Goodwin v. General Motors Corp.*, 275 F. 3d 1005, 1008-1009 (CA10 2002) (plaintiff did not know what her colleagues earned until a printout listing of salaries appeared on her desk, seven years after her starting salary was set lower than her co-workers' salaries); *McMillan v. Massachusetts Soc. for Prevention of Cruelty to Animals*, 140 F. 3d 288, 296 (CA1 1998) (plaintiff worked for employer for years before learning of salary disparity published in a newspaper).[3] Tellingly, as the record in this case bears out, Goodyear kept salaries confidential; employees had only limited access to information regarding their colleagues' earnings. App. 56-57, 89.

The problem of concealed pay discrimination is particularly acute where the disparity arises not because the female employee is flatly denied a raise but because male counterparts are given larger raises. Having received a pay increase, the female employee is unlikely to discern at once that she has experienced an adverse employment decision. She may have little reason even to suspect discrimination until a pattern develops incrementally and she ultimately becomes aware of the disparity. Even if an employee suspects that the reason for a comparatively low raise is not performance but sex (or another protected ground), the amount involved may seem too small, or the employer's intent too ambiguous, to make the issue immediately actionable—or winnable.

Further separating pay claims from the discrete employment actions identified in *Morgan*, an employer gains from sex-based pay disparities in a way it does not from a discriminatory denial of promotion, hiring, or transfer. When a male employee is selected over a female for a higher level position, someone still gets the promotion and is paid a higher salary; the employer is not enriched. But when a woman is paid less than a similarly situated man, the employer reduces its costs each time the pay differential is implemented. Furthermore, decisions on promotions, like decisions installing seniority systems, often implicate the interests of third-party employees in a way that pay differentials do not. Cf. *Teamsters v. United States*, 431 U.S. 324, 352-353 (1977) (recognizing that seniority systems involve "vested . . . rights of employees" and concluding that Title VII was not intended to "destroy or water down" those rights). Disparate pay, by contrast, can be remedied at any time solely at the expense of the employer who acts in a discriminatory fashion.

C

In light of the significant differences between pay disparities and discrete employment decisions of the type identified in *Morgan*, the cases on which the Court relies hold no sway. See *ante*, at 625-629 (discussing *United Air Lines, Inc. v. Evans*, 431 U.S. 553 (1977), *Delaware State College v. Ricks*, 449 U.S. 250 (1980), and *Lorance v. AT&T Technologies, Inc.*, 490 U.S. 900 (1989)). *Evans* and *Ricks* both involved a single, immediately identifiable act of discrimination: in *Evans*, a constructive discharge, 431 U.S., at 554; in *Ricks*, a denial of tenure, 449 U.S., at 252. In each case, the employee filed charges well after the discrete discriminatory act occurred: When United Airlines forced Evans to resign because of its policy barring married female flight attendants, she filed no charge; only four years later, when *Evans* was rehired, did she allege that the airline's former no-marriage rule was unlawful and therefore should not operate to deny her seniority credit for her prior service. See *Evans*, 431 U.S., at 554- 557. Similarly, when Delaware State College denied Ricks tenure, he did not object until his terminal contract came to an end, one year later. *Ricks*, 449 U.S., at 253-254,257-258. No repetitive, cumulative discriminatory employment practice was at issue in either case. See *Evans*, 431 U.S., at 557-558; *Ricks*, 449 U.S., at 258.[4]

Lorance is also inapposite, for, in this Court's view, it too involved a one-time discrete act: the adoption of a new seniority system that "had its genesis in sex discrimination." See 490 U.S., at 902, 905 (internal quotation marks omitted). The Court's extensive reliance on *Lorance, ante,* at 626-629, 633, 636-637, moreover, is perplexing for that decision is no longer effective: In the 1991 Civil Rights Act, Congress superseded *Lorance's* holding. § 112, 105 Stat. 1079 (codified as amended at 42 U.S.C. § 2000e-5(e)(2)). Repudiating our judgment that a facially neutral seniority system adopted with discriminatory intent must be challenged immediately, Congress provided:

> "For purposes of this section, an unlawful employment practice occurs . . . when the seniority system is adopted, when an individual becomes subject to the seniority system, or when a person aggrieved is injured by the application of the seniority system or provision of the system." *Ibid.*

Congress thus agreed with the dissenters in *Lorance* that "the harsh reality of [that] decision" was "glaringly at odds with the purposes of Title VII." 490 U.S., at 914 (opinion of Marshall, J.). See also §3, 105 Stat. 1071 (1991 Civil Rights Act was designed "to respond to recent decisions of the Supreme Court by expanding the scope of relevant civil rights statutes in order to provide adequate protection to victims of discrimination").

True, § 112 of the 1991 Civil Rights Act directly addressed only seniority systems. See *ante,* at 627, and n. 2. But Congress made clear (1) its view that this Court had unduly contracted the scope of protection afforded by Title VII and other civil rights statutes, and (2) its aim to generalize the ruling in *Bazemore.* As the Senate Report accompanying the proposed Civil Rights Act of 1990, the precursor to the 1991 Act, explained:

> "Where, as was alleged in *Lorance,* an employer adopts a rule or decision with an unlawful discriminatory motive, each application of that rule or decision is a new violation, . . . In *Bazemore* . . . , for example,. . . . the Supreme Court properly held that each application of th[e] racially motivated salary structure, *i.e.,* each new paycheck, constituted a distinct violation of Title VII. Section 7(a) (2) generalizes the result correctly reached in *Bazemore.*" Civil Rights Act of 1990, S. Rep. No. 101-315, p. 54 (1990).[5]

See also 137 Cong. Rec. 29046, 29047 (1991) (Sponsors' Interpretative Memorandum) ("This legislation should be interpreted as disapproving the extension of *[Lorance]* to contexts outside of seniority systems."). But *cf. ante,* at 637 (relying on *Lorance* to conclude that "when an employer issues paychecks pursuant to a system that is facially nondiscriminatory and neutrally applied" a new Title VII violation does not occur (internal quotation marks omitted)).

Until today, in the more than 15 years since Congress amended Title VII, the Court had not once relied upon *Lorance.* It is mistaken to do so now. Just as Congress' "goals in enacting Title VII . . . never included conferring absolute immunity on discriminatorily adopted seniority systems that survive their first [180] days," 490 U.S., at 914 (Marshall, J., dissenting), Congress never intended to immunize forever discriminatory pay differentials unchallenged within 180 days of their adoption. This assessment gains weight when one comprehends that even a relatively minor pay disparity will expand exponentially over an employee's working life if raises are set as a percentage of prior pay.

A clue to congressional intent can be found in Title VII's backpay provision. The statute expressly provides that backpay may be awarded for a period of up to two years before the discrimination charge is filed. 42 U.S.C. § 2000e-5(g) (1) ("Back pay liability shall not accrue from a date more than two years prior to the filing of a charge with the Commission."). This prescription indicates that Congress contemplated challenges to pay discrimination commencing before, but continuing into, the 180-day filing period. See *Morgan*, 536 U.S., at 119 ("If Congress intended to limit liability to conduct occurring in the period within which the party must file the charge, it seems unlikely that Congress would have allowed recovery for two years of backpay."). As we recognized in *Morgan*, "the fact that Congress expressly limited the amount of recoverable damages elsewhere to a particular time period [*i.e.*, two years] indicates that the [180-day] timely filing provision was not meant to serve as a specific limitation . . . [on] the conduct that may be considered." *Ibid.*

D

In tune with the realities of wage discrimination, the Courts of Appeals have overwhelmingly judged as a present violation the payment of wages infected by discrimination: Each paycheck less than the amount payable had the employer adhered to a nondiscriminatory compensation regime, courts have held, constitutes a cognizable harm. *See, e.g., Forsyth v. Federation Employment and Guidance* 409 F. 3d 565, 573 (CA2 2005) ("Any paycheck given within the [charge-filing] period . . . would be actionable, even if based on a discriminatory pay scale set up outside of the statutory period."); *Shea v. Rice*, 409 F. 3d 448, 452-453 (CADC 2005) ("[An] employer commit[s] a separate unlawful employment practice each time he pa[ys] one employee less than another for a discriminatory reason" (citing *Bazemore*, 478 U.S., at 396)); *Goodwin*, 275 F. 3d, at 1009-1010 has taught a crucial distinction with respect to discriminatory disparities in pay, establishing that a discriminatory salary is not merely a lingering effect of past discrimination—instead it is itself a continually recurring violation. . . . [E]ach race-based discriminatory salary payment constitutes a fresh violation of Title VII." (footnote omitted)); *Anderson v. Zubieta*, 180 F. 3d 329, 335 (CADC 1999) ("The Courts of Appeals have repeatedly reached the . . . conclusion" that pay discrimination is "actionable upon receipt of each paycheck."); accord *Hildebrandt v. Illinois Dept, of Natural Resources*, 347 F. 3d 1014,

1025-1029 (CA7 2003); *Cardenas v. Massey*, 269 F. 3d 251, 257 (CA3 2001); *Ashley v. Boyle's Famous Corned Beef Co.*, 66 F. 3d 164, 167-168 (CA8 1995) (en banc); *Brinkley-Obu v. Hughes Training, Inc.*, 36 F. 3d 336, 347-349 (CA4 1994); *Gibbs v. Pierce Cty. Law Enforcement Support Agcy.*, 785 F. 2d 1396, 1399-1400 (CA9 1986).

Similarly in line with the real-world characteristics of pay discrimination, the EEOC—the federal agency responsible for enforcing Title VII, *see, e.g.,* 42 U.S.C. §§2000e-5(f), 2000e-12(a)—has interpreted the Act to permit employees to challenge disparate pay each time it is received. The EEOC's Compliance Manual provides that "[Repeated occurrences of the same discriminatory employment action, such as discriminatory paychecks, can be challenged as long as one discriminatory act occurred within the charge filing period." 2 EEOC Compliance Manual §2-IV-C(l)(a), p. 605:0024, and n. 183 (2006); *cf. id.,* § 10-III, p. 633:0002 (Title VII requires an employer to eliminate pay disparities attributable to a discriminatory system, even if that system has been discontinued).

The EEOC has given effect to its interpretation in a series of administrative decisions. See *Albritton v. Potter*, No. 01A44063, 2004 WL 2983682, *2 (EEOC Office of Fed. Operations, Dec. 17, 2004) (although disparity arose and employee became aware of the disparity outside the charge filing period, claim was not time barred because "[e]ach pay- check that complainant receives which is less than that of similarly situated employees outside of her protected classes could support a claim under Title VII if discrimination is found to be the reason for the pay discrepancy." (citing *Bazemore*, 478 U.S., at 396)). See also *Bynum-Doles v. Winter*, No. 01A53973, 2006 WL 2096290 (EEOC Office of Fed. Operations, July 18, 2006); *Ward v. Potter*, No. 01A60047, 2006 WL 721992 (EEOC Office of Fed. Operations, Mar. 10, 2006). And in this very case, the EEOC urged the Eleventh Circuit to recognize that Ledbetter's failure to challenge any particular pay-setting decision when that decision was made "does not deprive her of the right to seek relief for discriminatory paychecks she received in 1997 and 1998." Brief of EEOC in Support of Petition for Rehearing and Suggestion for Rehearing En Banc, in No. 03-15264-GG (CA11), p. 14 (hereinafter EEOC Brief) (citing *Morgan*, 536 U.S., at 113).[6]

II

The Court asserts that treating pay discrimination as a discrete act, limited to each particular pay-setting decision, is necessary to "protec[t] employers from the burden of defending claims arising from employment decisions that are long past." *Ante*, at 630 (quoting *Ricks*, 449 U.S., at 256- 257). But the discrimination of which Ledbetter complained is not long past. As she alleged, and as the jury found, Goodyear continued to treat Ledbetter differently because of sex each pay period, with mounting harm. Allowing employees to challenge discrimination "that extend[s] over long periods of time," into the charge-filing period, we have previously explained, "does not leave employers defenseless" against unreasonable or prejudicial delay. *Morgan*, 536 U.S., at 121. Employers disadvantaged by such delay may raise various defenses. *Id.*, at 122. Doctrines such as "waiver, estoppel, and equitable tolling" "allow us to honor Title VII's remedial purpose without negating the particular purpose of the filing requirement, to give prompt notice to the employer." *Id.*, at 121 (quoting *Zipes v. Trans World Airlines, Inc.*, 455 U.S. 385, 398 (1982)); see 536 U.S., at 121 (defense of laches may be invoked to block an employee's suit "if he unreasonably delays in filing [charges] and as a result harms the defendant"); EEOC Brief 15 ("[I]f Ledbetter unreasonably delayed challenging an earlier decision, and that delay significantly impaired Goodyear's ability to defend itself . . . Goodyear can raise a defense of laches . . .").[7]

In a last-ditch argument, the Court asserts that this dissent would allow a plaintiff to sue on a single decision made 20 years ago "even if the employee had full knowledge of all the circumstances relating to the . . . decision at the time it was made." *Ante*, at 639. It suffices to point out that the defenses just noted would make such a suit foolhardy. No sensible judge would tolerate such inexcusable neglect. See *Morgan*, 536 U.S., at 121 ("In such cases, the federal courts have the discretionary power . . . to locate a just result in light of the circumstances peculiar to the case." (internal quotation marks omitted)).

Ledbetter, the Court observes, *ante*, at 640-641, n. 9, dropped an alternative remedy she could have pursued: Had she persisted in pressing her claim under the Equal Pay Act of 1963 (EPA), 29 U.S.C. § 206(d), she would not have encountered a time bar.[8] See *ante*, at 640 ("If Ledbetter had pursued her EPA claim, she would not face the Title VII obstacles that she now confronts."); *cf. Corning Glass Works v. Brennan*, 417 U.S. 188,208-210 (1974). Notably, the EPA provides no relief when the pay discrimination charged is based on race, religion, national origin, age, or disability. Thus, in truncating the Title VII rule this Court announced in *Bazemore*, the Court does not disarm female workers from achieving redress for unequal pay, but it does impede racial and other minorities from gaining similar relief.[9]

Furthermore, the difference between the EPA's prohibition against paying unequal wages and Title VII's ban on discrimination with regard to compensation is not as large as the Court's opinion might suggest. See *ante*, at 640. The key distinction is that Title VII requires a showing of intent. In practical effect, "if the trier of fact is in equipoise about whether the wage differential is motivated by gender discrimination," Title VII compels a verdict for the employer, while the EPA compels a verdict for the plaintiff. 2 C. Sullivan, M. Zimmer, & R. White, Employment Discrimination: Law and Practice §7.08[F][3], p. 532 (3d ed. 2002). In this case, Ledbetter carried the burden of persuading the jury that the pay disparity she suffered was attributable to intentional sex discrimination. See *supra,* at 643-644; *infra* this page and 660.

III

To show how far the Court has strayed from interpretation of Title VII with fidelity to the Act's core purpose, I return to the evidence Ledbetter presented at trial. Ledbetter proved to the jury the following: She was a member of a protected class; she performed work substantially equal to work of the dominant class (men); she was compensated less for that work; and the disparity was attributable to gender- based discrimination. See *supra,* at 643-644.

Specifically, Ledbetter's evidence demonstrated that her current pay was discriminatorily low due to a long series of decisions reflecting Goodyear's pervasive discrimination against women managers in general and Ledbetter in particular. Ledbetter's former supervisor, for example, admitted to the jury that Ledbetter's pay, during a particular one-year period, fell below Goodyear's minimum threshold for her position. App. 93-97. Although Goodyear claimed the pay disparity was due to poor performance, the supervisor acknowledged that Ledbetter received a "Top Performance Award" in 1996. *Id.,* at 90-93. The jury also heard testimony that another supervisor—who evaluated Ledbetter in 1997 and whose evaluation led to her most recent raise denial—was openly biased against women. at 46, 77-82. And two women who had previously worked as managers at the plant told the jury they had been subject to pervasive discrimination and were paid less than their male counterparts. One was paid less than the men she supervised. *Id.,* at 51-68. Ledbetter herself testified about the discriminatory animus conveyed to her by plant officials. Toward the end of her career, for instance, the plant manager told Ledbetter that the "plant did not need women, that [women] didn't help it, [and] caused problems." *Id.,* at 36.[10] After weighing all the evidence, the jury found for Ledbetter, concluding that the pay disparity was due to intentional discrimination.

Yet, under the Court's decision, the discrimination Ledbetter proved is not redressable under Title VII. Each and every pay decision she did not immediately challenge wiped the slate clean. Consideration may not be given to the cumulative effect of a series of decisions that, together, set her pay well below that of every male area manager. Knowingly carrying past pay discrimination forward must be treated as lawful conduct. Ledbetter may not be compensated for the lower pay she was in fact receiving when she complained to the EEOC. Nor, were she still employed by Goodyear, could she gain, on the proof she presented at trial, injunctive relief requiring, prospectively, her receipt of the same compensation men receive for substantially similar work. The Court's approbation of these consequences is totally at odds with the robust protection against workplace discrimination Congress intended Title VII to secure. *See, e.g., Teamsters v. United States,* 431 U.S., at 348 ("The primary purpose of Title VII was to assure equality of employment opportunities and to eliminate . . . discriminatory practices and devices . . . (internal quotation marks omitted); *Albemarle Paper Co. v. Moody,* 422 U.S. 405, 418 (1975) ("It is . . . the purpose of Title VII to make persons whole for injuries suffered on account of unlawful employment discrimination.").

This is not the first time the Court has ordered a cramped interpretation of Title VII, incompatible with the statute's broad remedial purpose. See *supra,* at 652-654. See also *Wards Cove Packing Co. v. Atonio,* 490 U.S. 642 (1989) (superseded in part by the Civil Rights Act of 1991); *Price Waterhouse v. Hopkins,* 490 U.S. 228 (1989) (plurality opinion) (same); 1 B. Lindemann & R Grossman, Employment Discrimination Law 2 (3d ed. 1996) ("A spate of Court decisions in the late 1980s drew congressional fire and resulted in demands for legislative change[,]" culminating in the 1991 Civil Rights Act (footnote omitted)). Once again, the ball is in Congress' court. As in 1991, the Legislature may act to correct this Court's parsimonious reading of Title VII.

* * *

For the reasons stated, I would hold that Ledbetter's claim is not time barred and would reverse the Eleventh Circuit's judgment.

---

1. If the complainant has first instituted proceedings with a state or local agency, the filing period is extended to 300 days or 30 days after the denial of relief by the agency. 42 U.S.C. § 2000e-5(e) (l). Because the 180-day period applies to Ledbetter's case, that figure will be used throughout. See *ante,* at 622, 624.
2. *National Railroad Passenger Corporation v. Morgan,* 536 U.S. 101, 117 (2002), the Court emphasizes, required that "an act contributing to the claim occu[r] within the [charge-]filing period." *Ante,* at 638, and n. 7 (emphasis deleted; internal quotation marks omitted). Here, each pay- check within the filing period compounded the discrimination Ledbetter encountered, and thus contributed to the "actionable wrong," *i.e.,* the succession of acts composing the pattern of discriminatory pay, of which she complained.
3. See also Bierman & Gely, "Love, Sex and Politics? Sure. Salary? No Way": Workplace Social Norms and the Law, 25 Berkeley J. Emp. & Lab. L. 167,168,171 (2004) (one-third of private sector employers have adopted specific rules prohibiting employees from discussing their wages with co-workers; only one in ten employers has adopted a pay openness policy).
4. The Court also relies on *Machinists v. NLRB,* 362 U.S. 411 (1960), which like *Evans* and *Ricks,* concerned a discrete act: the execution of a collective-bargaining agreement containing a union security clause. 362 U.S., at 412, 417. In Machinists, it was undisputed that under the National Labor Relations Act (NLRA), a union and an employer may not agree to a union security clause "if at the time of original execution the union does not represent a majority of the employees in the [bargaining] unit." *Id.,* at 412-414, 417. The complainants, however, failed to file a charge within the NLRA's six-month charge-filing period; instead, they filed charges 10 and 12 months after the execution of the agreement, objecting to its subsequent enforcement. See *id.,* at 412, 414. Thus, as in *Evans* and *Ricks,* but in contrast to Ledbetter's case, the employment decision at issue was easily identifiable and occurred on a single day.

5. No Senate Report was submitted with the Civil Rights Act of 1991, which was in all material respects identical to the proposed 1990 Act.

6. The Court dismisses the EEOC's considerable "experience and informed judgment," *Firefighters v. Cleveland*, 478 U.S. 501, 518 (1986) (internal quotation marks omitted), as unworthy of any deference in this case, see *ante*, at 642-643, n. 11. But the EEOC's interpretations mirror workplace realities and merit at least respectful attention. In any event, the level of deference due the EEOC here is an academic question, for the agency's conclusion that Ledbetter's claim is not time barred is the best reading of the statute even if the Court "were interpreting [Title VII] from scratch." See *Edelman v. Lynchburg College*, 535 U.S. 106, 114 (2002); see *supra*, at 646-655 and this page.

7. Further, as the EEOC appropriately recognized in its brief to the Eleventh Circuit, Ledbetter's failure to challenge particular pay raises within the charge-filing period "significantly limit[s] the relief she can seek. By waiting to file a charge, Ledbetter lost her opportunity to seek relief for any discriminatory paychecks she received between 1979 and late 1997." EEOC Brief 14. See also *supra*, at 654-656.

8. Under the EPA, 29 U.S.C. § 206(d), which is subject to the Fair Labor Standards Act's time prescriptions, a claim charging denial of equal pay accrues anew with each paycheck. 1 B. Lindemann & P. Grossman, Employment Discrimination Law 529 (3d ed. 1996); *cf.* 29 U.S.C. § 255(a) (prescribing a two-year statute of limitations for violations generally, but a three-year limitation period for willful violations).

9. For example, under today's decision, if a black supervisor initially received the same salary as his white colleagues, but annually received smaller raises, there would be no right to sue under Title VII outside the 180-day window following each annual salary change, however strong the cumulative evidence of discrimination might be. The Court would thus force plaintiffs, in many cases, to sue too soon to prevail, while cutting them off as time barred once the pay differential is large enough to enable them to mount a winnable case.

10. Given this abundant evidence, the Court cannot tenably maintain that Ledbetter's case "turned principally on the misconduct of a single Goodyear supervisor." See *ante*, at 632, n. 4.

VANCE V. BALL STATE UNIV.

570 U.S. 421 (2013)

This case involves the question of who is a "supervisor" for purposes of a workplace discrimination or harassment claim under Title VII of the Civil Rights Act of 1964. Under that law and related EEOC regulations, an employer is liable for the harassing acts of the "supervisors" it employs. For harassment by non-supervisor employees, an employer is only liable if it was "negligent" in responding to complaints about harassment. In this case, Maetta Vance contended that Saundra Davis, a fellow employee who she alleged was her supervisor — but who her employer, Ball State University, argued was not a supervisor — harassed her and that liability for Davis's alleged misconduct consequently should be imputed to Ball State, regardless of whether or not Ball State was negligent.

In a 5-4 decision authored by Justice Alito, the Court ruled that Davis was not Vance's supervisor, as she did not have the authority to take tangible action against her — that is, she did not have the power to hire or fire or to direct other terms and conditions of her employment.

Justice Ginsburg dissented, joined by Justices Breyer, Sotomayor, and Kagan.

VANCE V. BALL STATE UNIV.

I n *Faragher v. Boca Raton*, 524 U.S. 775 (1998), and *Burlington Industries, Inc. v. Ellerth*, 524 U.S. 742 (1998), this Court held that an employer can be vicariously liable under Title VII of the Civil Rights Act of 1964 for harassment by an employee given supervisory authority over subordinates. In line with those decisions, in 1999, the Equal Employment Opportunity Commission (EEOC) provided enforcement guidance "regarding employer liability for harassment by supervisors based on sex, race, color, religion, national origin, age, disability, or protected activity." EEOC, Guidance on Vicarious Employer Liability for Unlawful Harassment by Supervisors, 8 BNA FEP Manual 405:7651 (Feb. 2003) (hereinafter EEOC Guidance). Addressing who qualifies as a supervisor, the EEOC answered: (1) an individual authorized "to undertake or recommend tangible employment decisions affecting the employee," including "hiring, firing, promoting, demoting, and reassigning the employee"; or (2) an individual authorized "to direct the employee's daily work activities." *Id.*, at 405:7654.

The Court today strikes from the supervisory category employees who control the day-to-day schedules and assignments of others, confining the category to those formally empowered to take tangible employment actions. The limitation the Court decrees diminishes the force of *Faragher* and *Ellerth*, ignores the conditions under which members of the work force labor, and disserves the objective of Title VII to prevent discrimination from infecting the Nation's workplaces. I would follow the EEOC Guidance and hold that the authority to direct an employee's daily activities establishes supervisory status under Title VII.

I

A

Title VII makes it "an unlawful employment practice for an employer" to "discriminate against any individual with respect to" the "terms, conditions, or privileges of employment, because of such individual's race, color, religion, sex, or national origin." 42 U.S.C. §2000e-2(a). The creation of a hostile work environment through harassment, this Court has long recognized, is a form of proscribed discrimination. *Oncale v. Sundowner Offshore Services, Inc.*, 523 U.S. 75, 78 (1998); *Meritor Savings Bank, FSB v. Vinson*, 477 U.S. 57, 64-65 (1986).

What qualifies as harassment? Title VII imposes no "general civility code." *Oncale*, 523 U.S., at 81. It does not reach "the ordinary tribulations of the workplace," for example, "sporadic use of abusive language" or generally boorish conduct. B. Lindemann & D. Kadue, Sexual Harassment in Employment Law 175 (1992). See also 1 B. Lindemann & P. Grossman, Employment Discrimination Law 1335-1343 (4th ed. 2007) (hereinafter Lindemann & Gross- man). To be actionable, charged behavior need not drive the victim from her job, but it must be of such severity or pervasiveness as to pollute the working environment, thereby "altering] the conditions of the victim's employment." *Harris v. Forklift Systems, Inc.*, 510 U.S. 17, 21- 22 (1993).

In *Faragher* and *Ellerth*, this Court established a framework for determining when an employer may be held liable for its employees' creation of a hostile work environment. Recognizing that Title VII's definition of "employer" includes an employer's "agent[s]," 42 U.S.C. §2000e(b), the Court looked to agency law for guidance in formulating liability standards. Faragher, 524 U.S., at 791, 801; *Ellerth*, 524 U.S., at 755-760. In particular, the Court drew upon §219(2)(d) of the Restatement (Second) of Agency (1957), which makes an employer liable for the conduct of an employee, even when that employee acts beyond the scope of her employment, if the employee is "aided in accomplishing" a tort "by the existence of the agency relation." See *Faragher*, 524 U.S., at 801; *Ellerth*, 524 U.S., at 758.

Stemming from that guide, *Faragher* and *Ellerth* distinguished between harassment perpetrated by supervisors, which is often enabled by the supervisor's agency relationship with the employer, and harassment perpetrated by co-workers, which is not similarly facilitated. *Faragher*, 524 U.S., at 801-803; *Ellerth*, 524 U.S., at 763-765. If the harassing employee is a supervisor, the Court held, the employer is vicariously liable whenever the harassment culminates in a tangible employment action. *Faragher*, 524 U.S., at 807-808; *Ellerth*, 524 U.S., at 764-765. The term "tangible employment action," *Ellerth* observed, "constitutes a significant change in employment status, such as hiring, firing, failing to promote, reassignment with significantly different responsibilities, or a decision causing a significant change in benefits." *Id.*, at 761. Such an action, the

Court explained, provides "assurance the injury could not have been inflicted absent the agency relation." *Id.*, at 761-762.

An employer may also be held vicariously liable for a supervisor's harassment that does not culminate in a tangible employment action, the Court next determined. In such a case, however, the employer may avoid liability by showing that (1) it exercised reasonable care to prevent and promptly correct harassing behavior, and (2) the complainant unreasonably failed to take advantage of preventative or corrective measures made available to her. *Faragher*, 524 U.S., at 807; *Ellerth*, 524 U.S., at 765. The employer bears the burden of establishing this affirmative defense by a preponderance of the evidence. *Faragher*, 524 U.S., at 807; *Ellerth*, 524 U.S., at 765.

In contrast, if the harassing employee is a co-worker, a negligence standard applies. To satisfy that standard, the complainant must show that the employer knew or should have known of the offensive conduct but failed to take appropriate corrective action. See *Faragher*, 524 U.S., at 799; *Ellerth*, 524 U.S., at 758-759. See also 29 CFR § 1604.11(d) (2012); EEOC Guidance 405:7652.

B

The distinction *Faragher* and *Ellerth* drew between supervisors and co-workers corresponds to the realities of the workplace. Exposed to a fellow employee's harassment, one can walk away or tell the offender to "buzz off." A supervisor's slings and arrows, however, are not so easily avoided. An employee who confronts her harassing supervisor risks, for example, receiving an undesirable or unsafe work assignment or an unwanted transfer. She may be saddled with an excessive workload or with placement on a shift spanning hours disruptive of her family life. And she may be demoted or fired. Facing such dangers, she may be reluctant to blow the whistle on her superior, whose "power and authority invests his or her harassing conduct with a particular threatening character." *Ellerth*, 524 U.S., at 763. See also *Faragher*, 524 U.S., at 803; Brief for Respondent Ball State University 23 ("The potential threat to one's livelihood or working conditions will make the victim think twice before resisting harassment or fighting back."). In short, as *Faragher* and *Ellerth* recognized, harassment by supervisors is more likely to cause palpable harm and to persist unabated than similar conduct by fellow employees.

II

While *Faragher* and *Ellerth* differentiated harassment by supervisors from harassment by co-workers, neither decision gave a definitive answer to the question: Who qualifies as a supervisor? Two views have emerged. One view, in line with the EEOC Guidance, counts as a supervisor anyone with authority to take tangible employment actions or to direct an employee's daily work activities. *E.g., Mack v. Otis Elevator Co.*, 326 F. 3d 116, 127 (CA2 2003); *Whitten v. Fred's, Inc.*, 601 F. 3d 231, 246 (CA4 2010); EEOC Guidance 405:7654. The other view ranks as supervisors only those authorized to take tangible employment actions. *E. Noviello v. Boston*, 398 F. 3d 76, 96 (CA1 2005); *Parkins v. Civil Constructors of Ill., Inc.*, 163 F. 3d 1027, 1034 (CA7 1998); *Joens v. John Morrell & Co.*, 354 F. 3d 938, 940-941 (CA8 2004).

Notably, respondent Ball State University agreed with petitioner Vance and the United States, as amicus curiae, that the tangible-employment-action-only test "does not necessarily capture all employees who may qualify as supervisors." Brief for Respondent 1. "[Vicarious liability," Ball State acknowledged, "also may be triggered when the harassing employee has the authority to control the victim's daily work activities in a way that materially enables the harassment." *Id.*, at 1-2.

The different view taken by the Court today is out of accord with the agency principles that, *Faragher* and *Ellerth* affirmed, govern Title VII. See *supra*, at 452-454. It is blind to the realities of the workplace, and it discounts the guidance of the EEOC, the agency Congress established to interpret, and superintend the enforcement of, Title VII. Under that guidance, the appropriate question is: Has the employer given the alleged harasser authority to take tangible employment actions or to control the conditions under which subordinates do their daily work? If the answer to either inquiry is yes, vicarious liability is in order, for the superior-subordinate working arrangement facilitating the harassment is of the employer's making.

A

Until today, our decisions have assumed that employees who direct subordinates' daily work are supervisors. In *Faragher*, the city of Boca Raton, Florida, employed Bill Terry and David Silverman to oversee the city's corps of ocean lifeguards. 524 U.S., at 780. Terry and Silverman "repeatedly subjected] *Faragher* and other female lifeguards to uninvited and offensive touching," and they regularly "ma[de] lewd remarks, and [spoke] of women in offensive terms." *Ibid*, (internal quotation marks omitted). Terry told a job applicant that "female lifeguards had sex with their male counterparts," and then "asked whether she would do the same." *Id.*, at 782. Silverman threatened to assign *Faragher* to toilet-cleaning duties for a year if she refused to date him. *Id.*, at 780. In words and conduct, Silverman and Terry made the beach a hostile place for women to work.

As Chief of Boca Raton's Marine Safety Division, Terry had authority to "hire new lifeguards (subject to the approval of higher management), to supervise all aspects of the lifeguards' work assignments, to engage in counseling, to deliver oral reprimands, and to make a record of any such discipline." *Id.*, at 781. Silverman's duties as a Marine Safety lieutenant included "making the lifeguards' daily assignments, and ... supervising their work and fitness training." *Ibid.* Both men "were granted virtually unchecked authority over their subordinates, directly controlling and supervising all aspects of *Faragher*'s day-to-day activities." *Id.*, at 808 (internal quotation marks and brackets omitted).

We may assume that Terry would fall within the definition of supervisor the Court adopts today. See *ante*, at 431-432.[1] But nothing in the *Faragher* record shows that Silverman would. Silverman had oversight and assignment responsibilities—he could punish lifeguards who would not date him with full-time toilet-cleaning duty—but there was no evidence that he had authority to take tangible employment actions. See *Faragher*, 524 U.S., at 780-781. Holding that Boca Raton was vicariously liable for Silverman's harassment, *id.*, at 808-809, the Court characterized him as Faragher's supervisor, see *id.*, at 780, and there was no dissent on that point, see *id.*, at 810 (Thomas, J., dissenting).

Subsequent decisions reinforced *Faragher*'s use of the term "supervisor" to encompass employees with authority to direct the daily work of their victims. In *Pennsylvania State Police v. Suders*, 542 U.S. 129,140 (2004), for example, the Court considered whether a constructive discharge occasioned by supervisor harassment ranks as a tangible employment action. The harassing employees lacked authority to discharge or demote the complainant, but they were "responsible for the day-to-day supervision" of the workplace and for overseeing employee shifts. *Suders v. Easton*, 325 F. 3d 432, 450, n. 11 (CA3 2003). Describing the harassing employees as the complainant's "supervisors," the Court proceeded to evaluate the complainant's constructive discharge claim under the *Ellerth* and *Faragher* framework. *Suders*, 542 U.S., at 134, 140-141.

It is true, as the Court says, *ante*, at 437-438, and n. 11, that *Faragher* and later cases did not squarely resolve whether an employee without power to take tangible employment actions may nonetheless qualify as a supervisor. But in laboring to establish that Silverman's supervisor status, undisputed in *Faragher*, is not dispositive here, the Court misses the forest for the trees. *Faragher* illustrates an all-too-plain reality: A supervisor with authority to control subordinates' daily work is no less aided in his harassment than is a supervisor with authority to fire, demote, or transfer. That Silverman could threaten Faragher with toilet-cleaning duties while Terry could orally reprimand her was inconsequential in *Faragher*, and properly so. What mattered was that both men took advantage of the power vested in them as agents of Boca Raton to facilitate their abuse. See 524 U.S., at 801 (Silverman and Terry "implicitly threaten[ed] to misuse their supervisory powers to deter any resistance or complaint."). And when, assisted by an agency relationship, in-charge superiors like Silverman perpetuate a discriminatory work environment, our decisions have appropriately held the employer vicariously liable, subject to the above-described affirmative defense. See *supra*, at 452-454.

B

Workplace realities fortify my conclusion that harassment by an employee with power to direct subordinates' day-to- day work activities should trigger vicarious employer liability. The following illustrations, none of them hypothetical, involve in-charge employees of the kind the Court today excludes from supervisory status.[2]

Yasharay Mack: Yasharay Mack, an African-American woman, worked for the Otis Elevator Company as an elevator mechanic's helper at the Metropolitan Life Building in New York City. James Connolly, the "mechanic in charge" and the senior employee at the site, targeted Mack for abuse. He commented frequently on her "fantastic ass," "luscious lips," and "beautiful eyes," and, using deplorable racial epithets, opined that minorities and women did not "belong in the business." Once, he pulled her on his lap, touched her buttocks, and tried to kiss her while others looked on. Connolly lacked authority to take tangible employment actions against mechanic's helpers, but he did assign their work, control their schedules, and direct the particulars of their workdays. When he became angry with Mack, for example, he denied her overtime hours. And when she complained about the mistreatment, he scoffed, "I get away with everything." See *Mack*, 326 F. 3d, at 120-121, 125-126 (internal quotation marks omitted).

Donna Rhodes: Donna Rhodes, a seasonal highway maintainer for the Illinois Department of Transportation, was responsible for plowing snow during winter months. Michael Poladian was a "Lead Lead Worker" and Matt Mara, a "Technician" at the maintenance yard where Rhodes worked. Both men assembled plow crews and managed the work assignments of employees in Rhodes's position, but neither had authority to hire, fire, promote, demote, transfer, or discipline employees. In her third season working at the yard, Rhodes was verbally assaulted with sex-based invectives and a pornographic image was taped to her locker. Poladian forced her to wash her truck in sub-zero temperatures, assigned her undesirable yard work instead of road crew work, and prohibited another employee from fixing the malfunctioning heating system in her truck. Conceding that Rhodes had been subjected to a sex-based hostile work environment, the Department of Transportation argued successfully in the District Court and Court of Appeals that Poladian and Mara were not Rhodes's supervisors because they lacked authority to take tangible employment actions against her. See *Rhodes v. Illinois Dept, of Transp.*, 359 F. 3d 498, 501-503, 506-507 (CA7 2004).

Clara Whitten: Clara Whitten worked at a discount retail store in Belton,

South Carolina. On Whitten's first day of work, the manager, Matt Green, told her to "give [him] what [he] want[ed]" in order to obtain approval for long weekends off from work. Later, fearing what might transpire, Whitten ignored Green's order to join him in an isolated storeroom. Angered, Green instructed Whitten to stay late and clean the store. He demanded that she work over the weekend despite her scheduled day off. Dismissing her as "dumb and stupid," Green threatened to make her life a "living hell." Green lacked authority to fire, promote, demote, or otherwise make decisions affecting Whitten's pocketbook. But he directed her activities, gave her tasks to accomplish, burdened her with undesirable work assignments, and controlled her schedule. He was usually the highest ranking employee in the store, and both Whitten and Green considered him the supervisor. See *Whitten*, 601 F. 3d, at 236, 244-247 (internal quotation marks omitted).

Monika Starke: CRST Van Expedited, Inc., an interstate transit company, ran a training program for newly hired truckdrivers requiring a 28-day on-the-road trip. Monika Starke participated in the program. Trainees like Starke were paired in a truck cabin with a single "lead driver" who lacked authority to hire, fire, promote, or demote, but who exercised control over the work environment for the duration of the trip. Lead drivers were responsible for providing instruction on CRST's driving method, assigning specific tasks, and scheduling rest stops. At the end of the trip, lead drivers evaluated trainees' performance with a nonbinding pass or fail recommendation that could lead to full driver status. Over the course of Starke's training trip, her first lead driver, Bob Smith, filled the cabin with vulgar sexual remarks, commenting on her breast size and comparing the gear stick to genitalia. A second lead driver, David Goodman, later forced her into unwanted sex with him, an outrage to which she submitted, believing it necessary to gain a passing grade. See *EEOC v. CRST Van Expedited, Inc.*, 679 F. 3d 657, 665-666, 684-685 (CA8 2012).

In each of these cases, a person vested with authority to control the conditions of a subordinate's daily work life used his position to aid his harassment. But in none of them would the Court's severely confined definition of supervisor yield vicarious liability for the employer. The senior elevator mechanic in charge, the Court today tells us, was Mack's co-worker, not her supervisor. So was the store manager who punished Whitten with long hours for refusing to give him what he wanted. So were the lead drivers who controlled all aspects of Starke's working environment, and the yard worker who kept other employees from helping Rhodes to control the heat in her truck.

As anyone with work experience would immediately grasp, James Connolly, Michael Poladian, Matt Mara, Matt Green, Bob Smith, and David Goodman wielded employer- conferred supervisory authority over their victims. Each man's discriminatory harassment derived force from, and was facilitated by, the control reins he held. *Cf. Burlington N. & S. F. R. Co. v. White*,

548 U.S. 53, 70-71 (2006) ("Common sense suggests that one good way to discourage an employee .. . from bringing discrimination charges would be to insist that she spend more time performing the more arduous duties and less time performing those that are easier or more agreeable."). Under any fair reading of Title VII, in each of the illustrative cases, the superior employee should have been classified a supervisor whose conduct would trigger vicarious liability.[3]

C

Within a year after the Court's decisions in *Faragher* and *Ellerth*, the EEOC defined "supervisor" to include any employee with "authority to undertake or recommend tangible employment decisions," or with "authority to direct [another] employee's daily work activities." EEOC Guidance 405:7654. That definition should garner "respect proportional to its 'power to persuade.'" *United States v. Mead Corp.*, 533 U.S. 218, 235 (2001) (quoting *Skidmore v. Swift & Co.*, 323 U.S. 134, 140 (1944)). See also *Crawford v. Metropolitan Government of Nashville and Davidson Cty.*, 555 U.S. 271, 276 (2009) (EEOC guidelines merited Skidmore deference); *Federal Express Corp. v. Holowecki*, 552 U.S. 389, 399-403 (2008) (same); *Meritor*, 477 U.S., at 65 (same).[4]

The EEOC's definition of supervisor reflects the agency's "informed judgment" and "body of experience" in enforcing Title VII. *Id.*, at 65 (internal quotation marks omitted). For 14 years, in enforcement actions and litigation, the EEOC has firmly adhered to its definition. See Brief for United States as Amicus Curiae 28 (citing numerous briefs in the Courts of Appeals setting forth the EEOC's understanding).

In developing its definition of supervisor, the EEOC paid close attention to the *Faragher* and *Ellerth* framework. An employer is vicariously liable only when the authority it has delegated enables actionable harassment, the EEOC recognized. EEOC Guidance 405:7654. For that reason, a supervisor's authority must be "of a sufficient magnitude so as to assist the harasser . . . in carrying out the harassment." *Ibid.* Determining whether an employee wields sufficient authority is not a mechanical inquiry, the EEOC explained; instead, specific facts about the employee's job function are critical. *Id.*, at 405:7653 to 405:7654. Thus, an employee with authority to increase another's workload or assign undesirable tasks may rank as a supervisor, for those powers can enable harassment. *Id.*, at 405:7654. On the other hand, an employee "who directs only a limited number of tasks or assignments" ordinarily would not qualify as a supervisor, for her harassing conduct is not likely to be aided materially by the agency relationship. *Id.*, at 405:7655.

In my view, the EEOC's definition, which the Court puts down as "a study in ambiguity," *ante*, at 442, has the ring of truth and, therefore, powerfully persuasive force. As a precondition to vicarious employer liability, the EEOC explained, the harassing supervisor must wield authority of sufficient magnitude to enable the harassment. In other words, the aided-in-accomplishment standard requires "something more than the employment relation itself." *Ellerth*, 524 U.S., at 760. Furthermore, as the EEOC perceived, in assessing an employee's qualification as a supervisor, context is often key. See *infra*, at 465-466. I would accord the agency's judgment due respect.

III

Exhibiting remarkable resistance to the thrust of our prior decisions, workplace realities, and the EEOC Guidance, the Court embraces a position that relieves scores of employers of responsibility for the behavior of the supervisors they employ. Trumpeting the virtues of simplicity and administrability, the Court restricts supervisor status to those with power to take tangible employment actions. In so restricting the definition of supervisor, the Court once again shuts from sight the "robust protection against workplace discrimination Congress intended Title VII to secure." *Ledbetter v. Goodyear Tire & Rubber Co.*, 550 U.S. 618, 660 (2007) (Ginsburg, J., dissenting).

A

The Court purports to rely on the *Ellerth* and *Faragher* framework to limit supervisor status to those capable of taking tangible employment actions. *Ante*, at 432, 439-440. That framework, we are told, presupposes "a sharp line between co-workers and supervisors." *Ante*, at 439. The definition of supervisor decreed today, the Court insists, is "clear," "readily applied," and "easily workable," *ante*, at 432, 441, when compared to the EEOC's vague standard, *ante*, at 442-443.

There is reason to doubt just how "clear" and "workable" the Court's definition is. A supervisor, the Court holds, is someone empowered to "take tangible employment actions against the victim, *i.e.*, to effect a 'significant change in employment status, such as hiring, firing, failing to promote, reassignment with significantly different responsibilities, or a decision causing a significant change in benefits.'" *Ante*, at 431 (quoting *Ellerth*, 524 U.S., at 761). Whether reassignment authority makes someone a supervisor might depend on whether the reassignment carries economic consequences. *Ante*, at 437-438, n. 9. The power to discipline other employees, when the discipline has economic consequences, might count, too. *Ibid.* So might the power to initiate or make recommendations about tangible employment actions. *Ante*, at 437, n. 8. And when an employer "concentrates all decisionmaking authority in a few individuals" who rely on information from "other workers who actually interact with the affected employee," the other workers may rank as supervisors (or maybe not; the Court does not commit one way or the other). *Ante*, at 446-447.

Someone in search of a bright line might well ask, what counts as "significantly different responsibilities"? Can any economic consequence make a reassignment or disciplinary action "significant," or is there a minimum threshold? How concentrated must the decisionmaking authority be to deem those not formally endowed with that authority nevertheless "supervisors"? The Court leaves these questions unanswered, and its liberal use of "mights" and "mays," *ante*, at 437-438, n. 9, 446-447, dims the light it casts.[5]

That the Court has adopted a standard, rather than a clear rule, is not surprising, for no crisp definition of supervisor could supply the unwavering line the Court desires. Supervisors, like the workplaces they manage, come in all shapes and sizes. Whether a pitching coach supervises his pitchers (can he demote them?), or an artistic director supervises her opera star (can she impose significantly different responsibilities?), or a law firm associate supervises the firm's paralegals (can she fire them?) are matters not susceptible to mechanical rules and on-off switches. One cannot know whether an employer has vested supervisory authority in an employee, and whether harassment is aided by that authority, without looking to the particular working relationship between the harasser and the victim. That is why *Faragher* and *Ellerth* crafted an employer liability standard embracive of all whose authority significantly aids in the creation and perpetuation of harassment.

The Court's focus on finding a definition of supervisor capable of instant application is at odds with the Court's ordinary emphasis on the importance of particular circumstances in Title VII cases. *See, e.g., Burlington Northern*, 548 U.S., at 69 ("[T]he significance of any given act of retaliation will often depend upon the particular circumstances."); *Harris*, 510 U.S., at 23 ("[W]hether an environment is 'hostile' or 'abusive' can be determined only by looking at all the circumstances.").[6] The question of supervisory status, no less than the question whether retaliation or harassment has occurred, "depends on a constellation of surrounding circumstances, expectations, and relationships." *Oncale*, 523 U.S., at 81-82. The EEOC Guidance so perceives.

B

As a consequence of the Court's truncated conception of supervisory authority, the *Faragher* and *Ellerth* framework has shifted in a decidedly employer-friendly direction. This realignment will leave many harassment victims without an effective remedy and undermine Title VII's capacity to prevent workplace harassment.

The negligence standard allowed by the Court, see *ante*, at 445-446, scarcely affords the protection the *Faragher* and *Ellerth* framework gave victims harassed by those in control of their lives at work. Recall that an employer is negligent with regard to harassment only if it knew or should have known of the conduct but failed to take appropriate corrective action. See 29 CFR § 1604.11(d); EEOC Guidance 405:7652 to 405:7653. It is not uncommon for employers to lack actual or constructive notice of a harassing employee's conduct. See Lindemann & Grossman 1378-1379. An employee may have a reputation as a harasser among those in his vicinity, but if no complaint makes its way up to management, the employer will escape liability under a negligence standard. *Id.*, at 1378.

Faragher is illustrative. After enduring unrelenting harassment, Faragher reported Terry's and Silverman's conduct informally to Robert Gordon, another immediate supervisor. 524 U.S., at 782-783. But the lifeguards were "completely isolated from the City's higher management," and it did not occur to Faragher to pursue the matter with higher ranking city officials distant from the beach. at 783, 808 (internal quotation marks omitted). Applying a negligence standard, the Eleventh Circuit held that, despite the pervasiveness of the harassment, and despite Gordon's awareness of it, Boca Raton lacked constructive notice and therefore escaped liability. *Id.*, at 784-785. Under the vicarious liability standard, however, Boca Raton could not make out the affirmative defense, for it had failed to disseminate a policy against sexual harassment. *Id.*, at 808-809.

On top of the substantive differences in the negligence and vicarious liability standards, harassment victims, under today's decision, are saddled with the burden of proving the employer's negligence whenever the harasser lacks the power to take tangible employment actions. *Faragher* and *Ellerth*, by contrast, placed the burden squarely on the employer to make out the affirmative defense. See *Suders*, 542 U.S., at 146 (citing *Ellerth*, 524 U.S., at 765; *Faragher*, 524 U.S., at 807). This allocation of the burden was both sensible and deliberate: An employer has superior access to evidence bearing on whether it acted reasonably to prevent or correct harassing behavior, and superior resources to marshal that evidence. See 542 U.S., at 146, n. 7 ("The employer is in the best position to know what remedial procedures it offers to employees and how those procedures operate.").

Faced with a steeper substantive and procedural hill to climb, victims like Yasharay Mack, Donna Rhodes, Clara Whitten, and Monika Starke likely will find it impossible to obtain redress. We can expect that, as a consequence of restricting the supervisor category to those formally empowered to take tangible employment actions, victims of workplace harassment with meritorious Title VII claims will find suit a hazardous endeavor.[7]

Inevitably, the Court's definition of supervisor will hinder efforts to stamp out discrimination in the workplace. Because supervisors are comparatively few, and employees are many, "the employer has a greater opportunity to guard against misconduct by supervisors than by common workers," and a greater incentive to "screen [supervisors], train them, and monitor their performance." *Faragher*, 524 U.S., at 803. Vicarious liability for employers serves this end. When employers know they will be answerable for the injuries a harassing jobsite boss inflicts, their incentive to provide preventative instruction is heightened. If vicarious liability is confined to supervisors formally empowered to take tangible employment actions, however, employers will have a diminished incentive to train those who control their subordinates' work activities and schedules, *i.e.*, the supervisors who "actually interact" with employees. *Ante*, at 447.

IV

I turn now to the case before us. Maetta Vance worked as substitute server and part-time catering assistant for Ball State University's Banquet and Catering Division. During the period in question, she alleged, Saundra Davis, a catering specialist, and other Ball State employees subjected her to a racially hostile work environment. Applying controlling Circuit precedent, the District Court and Seventh Circuit concluded that Davis was not Vance's supervisor, and reviewed Ball State's liability for her conduct under a negligence standard. 646 F. 3d 461, 470-471 (2011); App. to Pet. for Cert. 53a-55a, 59a-60a. Because I would hold that the Seventh Circuit erred in restricting supervisor status to employees formally empowered to take tangible employment actions, I would remand for application of the proper standard to Vance's claim. On this record, however, there is cause to anticipate that Davis would not qualify as Vance's supervisor.[8]

Supervisor status is based on "job function rather than job title," and depends on "specific facts" about the working relationship. EEOC Guidance 405:7654. See *supra*, at 462-463. Vance has adduced scant evidence that Davis controlled the conditions of her daily work. Vance stated in an affidavit that the general manager of the Catering Division, Bill Kimes, was charged with "overall supervision in the kitchen," including "reassigning] people to perform different tasks" and "controlling] the schedule." App. 431. The chef, Shannon Fultz, assigned tasks by preparing "prep lists" of daily duties. *Id.*, at 277-279, 427. There is no allegation that Davis had a hand in creating these prep lists, nor is there any indication that, in fact, Davis otherwise controlled the particulars of Vance's workday. Vance herself testified that she did not know whether Davis was her supervisor. *Id.*, at 198.

True, Davis' job description listed among her responsibilities "[l]ead[ing] and directing] kitchen part-time, substitute, and student employee helpers via demonstration, coaching, and overseeing their work." *Id.*, at 13. And another employee testified to believing that Davis was "a supervisor." *Id.*, at 386. But because the supervisor-status inquiry should focus on substance, not labels or paper descriptions, it is doubtful that this slim evidence would enable Vance to survive a motion for summary judgment. Nevertheless, I would leave it to the Seventh Circuit to decide, under the proper standard for supervisory status, what impact, if any, Davis' job description and the coworker's statement should have on the determination of Davis' status.[9]

V

Regrettably, the Court has seized upon Vance's thin case to narrow the definition of supervisor, and thereby manifestly limit Title VII's protections against workplace harassment. Not even Ball State, the defendant-employer in this case, has advanced the restrictive definition the Court adopts. See *supra*, at 455. Yet the Court, insistent on constructing artificial categories where context should be key, proceeds on an immoderate and unrestrained course to corral Title VII.

Congress has, in the recent past, intervened to correct this Court's wayward interpretations of Title VII. See Lilly Ledbetter Fair Pay Act of 2009,123 Stat. 5, superseding *Ledbetter v. Goodyear Tire & Rubber Co.*, 550 U.S. 618 (2007). See also Civil Rights Act of 1991,105 Stat. 1071, superseding in part *Lorance v. AT&T Technologies, Inc.*, 490 U.S. 900 (1989); *Martin v. Wilks*, 490 U.S. 755 (1989); *Wards Cove Packing Co. v. Atonio*, 490 U.S. 642 (1989); and *Price Waterhouse v. Hopkins*, 490 U.S. 228 (1989). The ball is once again in Congress' court to correct the error into which this

Court has fallen, and to restore the robust protections against workplace harassment the Court weakens today.

* * *

For the reasons stated, I would reverse the judgment of the Seventh Circuit and remand the case for application of the proper standard for determining who qualifies as a supervisor.

---

1. It is not altogether evident that Terry would qualify under the Court's test. His authority to hire was subject to approval by higher management, *Faragher v. Boca Raton*, 524 U.S. 775, 781 (1998), and there is scant indication that he possessed other powers on the Court's list. The Court observes that Terry was able to "recommen[d]" and "initiate] " tangible employment actions. *Ante*, at 437, n. 8 (internal quotation marks omitted). Nothing in the *Faragher* record, however, shows that Terry had authority to take such actions himself. *Faragher*'s complaint alleged that Terry said he would never promote a female lifeguard to the rank of lieutenant, 524 U.S., at 780, but that statement hardly suffices to establish that he had ultimate promotional authority. Had Boca Raton anticipated the position the Court today announces, the city might have urged classification of Terry as Faragher's superior, but not her "supervisor."

2. The illustrative cases reached the appellate level after grants of summary judgment in favor of the employer. Like the Courts of Appeals in each case, I recount the facts in the light most favorable to the employee, the nonmoving party.

3. The Court misses the point of the illustrations. See *ante*, at 447-448, and nn. 15-16. Even under a vicarious liability rule, the Court points out, employers might escape liability for reasons other than the harasser's status as supervisor. For example, Rhodes might have avoided summary judgment in favor of her employer; even so, it would have been open to the employer to raise and prove to a jury the *Faragher/Ellerth* affirmative defense, see *supra*, at 453. No doubt other barriers also might impede an employee from prevailing, for example, Whitten's and Starke's intervening bankruptcies, see *Whitten v. Fred's, Inc.*, No. 8:08-0218-HMH-BHH, 2010 WL 2757005 (D SC, July 12, 2010); *EEOC v. CRST Van Expedited, Inc.*, 679 F. 3d 657, 678, and n. 14 (CA8 2012), or Mack's withdrawal of her complaint for reasons not apparent from the record, see *ante*, at 448, n. 15. That, however, is no reason to restrict the definition of supervisor in a way that leaves out those genuinely in charge.

4. Respondents' *amici* maintain that the EEOC Guidance is ineligible for deference under *Skidmore v. Swift & Co.*, 323 U.S. 134 (1944), because it interprets *Faragher* and *Burlington Industries, Inc. v. Ellerth*, 524 U.S. 742 (1998), not the text of Title VII. See Brief for *Society for Human Resource Management et al.* 11-16. They are mistaken. The EEOC Guidance rests on the employer liability framework set forth in *Faragher* and *Ellerth*, but both the framework and EEOC Guidance construe the term "agent" in 42 U.S.C. §2000e(b).

5. Even the Seventh Circuit, whose definition of supervisor the Court adopts in large measure, has candidly acknowledged that, under its definition, supervisor status is not a clear and certain thing. See *Doe v. Oberweis Dairy*, 456 F. 3d 704, 717 (2006) ("The difficulty of classification in this case arises from the fact that Nayman, the shift supervisor, was in between the paradigmatic classes [of supervisor and co-worker]. He had supervisory responsibility in the sense of authority to direct the work of the [ice-cream] scoopers, and he was even authorized to issue disciplinary write-ups, but he had no authority to fire them. He was either an elevated coworker or a diminished supervisor.").

6. The Court worries that the EEOC's definition of supervisor will confound jurors who must first determine whether the harasser is a supervisor and second apply the correct employer liability standard. *Ante*, at 443-445, and nn. 13, 14. But the Court can point to no evidence that jury instructions on supervisor status in jurisdictions following the EEOC Guidance have in fact proved unworkable or confusing to jurors. Moreover, under the Court's definition of supervisor, jurors in many cases will be obliged to determine, as a threshold question, whether the alleged harasser possessed supervisory authority. See *supra*, at 464-465 and this page.

7. Nor is the Court's confinement of supervisor status needed to deter insubstantial claims. Under the EEOC Guidance, a plaintiff must meet the threshold requirement of actionable harassment and then show that her supervisor's authority was of "sufficient magnitude" to assist in the harassment. See EEOC Guidance 405:7652, 405:7654.

8. In addition to concluding that Davis was not Vance's supervisor, the District Court held that the conduct Vance alleged was "neither sufficiently severe nor pervasive to be considered objectively hostile for the purposes of Title VII." App. to Pet. for Cert. 66a. The Seventh Circuit declined to address this issue. See 646 F. 3d 461, 471 (2011). If the case were remanded, the Court of Appeals could resolve the hostile environment issue first, and then, if necessary, Davis' status as supervisor or coworker.

9. The Court agrees that Davis "would probably not qualify" as Vance's supervisor under the EEOC's definition. *Ante*, at 449. Then why, one might ask, does the Court nevertheless reach out to announce its restrictive standard in this case, one in which all parties, including the defendant-employer, accept the fitness for Title VII of the EEOC Guidance? See *supra*, at 455.

SHELBY COUNTY V. HOLDER

570 U.S. 529 (2013)

This case centers on the constitutionality of provisions of the Voting Rights Act of 1965 that require certain local and state governments to obtain preclearance from federal authorities before making any changes to their voting laws or practices, as well as the formulas used to determine which jurisdictions are subject to such preclearance requirements.

In a 5-4 decision authored by Chief Justice Roberts, the Court ruled these coverage formulas to be unconstitutional because they were based on now-obsolete 40 year old information, which rendered them an impermissible burden on the states. Consequently, the preclearance requirements are no longer be applicable until Congress enacts a new coverage formula.

Justice Ginsburg dissented, joined by Justices Breyer, Sotomayor, and Kagan.

SHELBY COUNTY V. HOLDER

I n the Court's view, the very success of §5 of the Voting Rights Act
demands its dormancy. Congress was of another mind. Recognizing that
large progress has been made, Congress determined, based on a voluminous record, that the scourge of discrimination was not yet extirpated. The
question this case presents is who decides whether, as currently operative, §5
remains justifiable,[1] this Court, or a Congress charged with the obligation to
enforce the post-Civil War Amendments "by appropriate legislation." With
overwhelming support in both Houses, Congress concluded that, for two
prime reasons, §5 should continue in force, unabated. First, continuance would
facilitate completion of the impressive gains thus far made; and second, continuance would guard against backsliding. Those assessments were well within
Congress' province to make and should elicit this Court's unstinting
approbation.

I

"[V]oting discrimination still exists; no one doubts that." *Ante,* at 536. But
the Court today terminates the remedy that proved to be best suited to block
that discrimination. The Voting Rights Act of 1965 (VRA or Act) has worked to
combat voting discrimination where other remedies had been tried and failed.
Particularly effective is the VRA's requirement of federal preclearance for all
changes to voting laws in the regions of the country with the most aggravated
records of rank discrimination against minority voting rights.

A century after the Fourteenth and Fifteenth Amendments guaranteed citizens the right to vote free of discrimination on the basis of race, the "blight of racial discrimination in voting" continued to "infec[t] the electoral process in parts of our country." *South Carolina v. Katzenbach*, 383 U.S. 301, 308 (1966). Early attempts to cope with this vile infection resembled battling the Hydra. Whenever one form of voting discrimination was identified and prohibited, others sprang up in its place. This Court repeatedly encountered the remarkable "variety and persistence" of laws disenfranchising minority citizens. *Id.*, at 311. To take just one example, the Court, in 1927, held unconstitutional a Texas law barring black voters from participating in primary elections, *Nixon v. Herndon*, 273 U.S. 536, 541; in 1944, the Court struck down a "reenacted" and slightly altered version of the same law, *Smith v. Allwright*, 321 U.S. 649, 658; and in 1953, the Court once again confronted an attempt by Texas to "circumvent[t] " the Fifteenth Amendment by adopting yet another variant of the all-white primary, *Terry v. Adams*, 345 U.S. 461, 469.

During this era, the Court recognized that discrimination against minority voters was a quintessential political problem requiring a political solution. As Justice Holmes explained: If "the great mass of the white population intends to keep the blacks from voting," "relief from [that] great political wrong, if done, as alleged, by the people of a State and the State itself, must be given by them or by the legislative and political department of the government of the United States." *Giles v. Harris*, 189 U.S. 475, 488 (1903).

Congress learned from experience that laws targeting particular electoral practices or enabling case-by-case litigation were inadequate to the task. In the Civil Rights Acts of 1957,1960, and 1964, Congress authorized and then expanded the power of "the Attorney General to seek injunctions against public and private interference with the right to vote on racial grounds." *Katzenbach*, 383 U.S., at 313. But circumstances reduced the ameliorative potential of these legislative Acts:

> "Voting suits are unusually onerous to prepare, sometimes requiring as many as 6,000 man-hours spent combing through registration records in preparation for trial. Litigation has been exceedingly slow, in part because of the ample opportunities for delay afforded voting officials and others involved in the proceedings. Even when favorable decisions have finally been obtained, some of the States affected have merely switched to discriminatory devices not covered by the federal decrees or have enacted difficult new tests designed to prolong the existing disparity between white and Negro registration. Alternatively, certain local officials have defied and evaded court orders or have simply closed their registration offices to freeze the voting rolls." *Id.*, at 314 (footnote omitted).

Patently, a new approach was needed.

Answering that need, the Voting Rights Act became one of the most consequential, efficacious, and amply justified exercises of federal legislative power in our Nation's history. Requiring federal preclearance of changes in voting laws in the covered jurisdictions—those States and localities where opposition to the Constitution's commands were most virulent—the VRA provided a fit solution for minority voters as well as for States. Under the preclearance regime established by §5 of the VRA, covered jurisdictions must submit proposed changes in voting laws or procedures to the Department of Justice (DOJ), which has 60 days to respond to the changes. 79 Stat. 439, codified at 42 U.S.C. § 1973c(a). A change will be approved unless DOJ finds it has "the purpose [or] . . . the effect of denying or abridging the right to vote on account of race or color." *Ibid.* In the alternative, the covered jurisdiction may seek approval by a three-judge District Court in the District of Columbia.

After a century's failure to fulfill the promise of the Fourteenth and Fifteenth Amendments, passage of the VRA finally led to signal improvement on this front. "The Justice Department estimated that in the five years after [the VRA's] passage, almost as many blacks registered [to vote] in Alabama, Mississippi, Georgia, Louisiana, North Carolina, and South Carolina as in the entire century before 1965." Davidson, The Voting Rights Act: A Brief History, in Controversies in Minority Voting 7, 21 (B. Grofman & C. Davidson eds. 1992). And in assessing the overall effects of the VRA in 2006, Congress found that "[significant progress has been made in eliminating first generation barriers experienced by minority voters, including increased numbers of registered minority voters, minority voter turnout, and minority representation in Congress, State legislatures, and local elected offices. This progress is the direct result of the Voting Rights Act of 1965." Fannie Lou Hamer, Rosa Parks, and Coretta Scott King Voting Rights Act Reauthorization and Amendments Act of 2006 (hereinafter 2006 Reauthorization), § 2(b)(1), 120 Stat. 577. On that matter of cause and effects there can be no genuine doubt.

Although the VRA wrought dramatic changes in the realization of minority voting rights, the Act, to date, surely has not eliminated all vestiges of discrimination against the exercise of the franchise by minority citizens. Jurisdictions covered by the preclearance requirement continued to submit, in large numbers, proposed changes to voting laws that the Attorney General declined to approve, auguring that barriers to minority voting would quickly resurface were the preclearance remedy eliminated. *City of Rome v. United States*, 446 U.S. 156, 181 (1980). Congress also found that as "registration and voting of minority citizens increas[ed], other measures may be resorted to which would dilute increasing minority voting strength." *Ibid,* (quoting H. R. Rep. No. 94-196, p. 10 (1975)). See also *Shaw v. Reno*, 509 U.S. 630,640 (1993) ("[I]t soon became apparent that guaranteeing equal access to the polls would not suffice to root out other racially discriminatory voting practices" such as voting dilution). Efforts to reduce the impact of minority votes, in contrast to direct attempts to block access to the ballot, are aptly described as "second-genera-tion barriers" to minority voting.

Second-generation barriers come in various forms. One of the blockages is racial gerrymandering, the redrawing of legislative districts in an "effort to segregate the races for purposes of voting." *Id.*, at 642. Another is adoption of a system of at-large voting in lieu of district-by-district voting in a city with a sizable black minority. By switching to at- large voting, the overall majority could control the election of each city council member, effectively eliminating the potency of the minority's votes. Grofman & Davidson, The Effect of Munic-ipal Election Structure on Black Representation in Eight Southern States, in Quiet Revolution in the

South 301, 319 (C. Davidson & B. Grofman eds. 1994) (hereinafter Quiet Revolution). A similar effect could be achieved if the city engaged in discrimi-natory annexation by incorporating majority-white areas into city limits, thereby decreasing the effect of VRA-occasioned increases in black voting. Whatever the device employed, this Court has long recognized that vote dilu-tion, when adopted with a discriminatory purpose, cuts down the right to vote as certainly as denial of access to the ballot. Shaw, 509 U.S., at 640-641; *Allen v. State Bd. of Elections*, 393 U.S. 544, 569 (1969); *Reynolds v. Sims*, 377 U.S. 533, 555 (1964). See also H. R. Rep. No. 109- 478, p. 6 (2006) (although "[discrimination today is more subtle than the visible methods used in 1965," "the effect and results are the same, namely a diminishing of the minority community's ability to fully participate in the electoral process and to elect their preferred candidates").

In response to evidence of these substituted barriers, Congress reauthorized the VRA for 5 years in 1970, for 7 years in 1975, and for 25 years in 1982. *Ante*, at 538-539. Each time, this Court upheld the reauthorization as a valid exercise of congressional power. *Ante*, at 539. As the 1982 reauthorization approached its 2007 expiration date, Congress again considered whether the VRA's preclearance mechanism remained an appropriate response to the problem of voting discrimination in covered jurisdictions.

Congress did not take this task lightly. Quite the opposite. The 109th Congress that took responsibility for the renewal started early and conscien-tiously. In October 2005, the House began extensive hearings, which continued into November and resumed in March 2006. S. Rep. No. 109- 295, p. 2 (2006). In April 2006, the Senate followed suit, with hearings of its own. *Ibid.* In May 2006, the bills that became the VRA's reauthorization were introduced in both Houses. *Ibid.* The House held further hearings of considerable length, as did the Senate, which continued to hold hearings into June and July. H. R. Rep. No. 109-478, at 5; S. Rep. No. 109-295, at 3-4. In mid-July, the House considered and rejected four amendments, then passed the reauthorization by a vote of 390 yeas to 33 nays. 152 Cong. Rec. 14303-14304 (2006); Persily, The

Promise and Pitfalls of the New Voting Rights Act, 117 Yale L. J. 174, 182-183 (2007) (hereinafter Persily). The bill was read and debated in the Senate, where it passed by a vote of 98 to 0. 152 Cong. Rec. 15325 (2006). President Bush signed it a week later, on July 27, 2006, recognizing the need for "further work . . . in the fight against injustice," and calling the reauthorization "an example of our continued commitment to a united America where every person is valued and treated with dignity and respect." 152 Cong. Rec. 16946-16947 (2006).

In the long course of the legislative process, Congress "amassed a sizable record." *Northwest Austin Municipal Util. Dist. No. One v. Holder*, 557 U.S. 193, 205 (2009). See also 679 F. 3d 848, 865-873 (CADC 2012) (describing the "extensive record" supporting Congress' determination that "serious and widespread intentional discrimination persisted in covered jurisdictions"). The House and Senate Judiciary Committees held 21 hearings, heard from scores of witnesses, and received a number of investigative reports and other written documentation of continuing discrimination in covered jurisdictions. In all, the legislative record Congress compiled filled more than 15,000 pages. H. R. Rep. No. 109-478, at 5, 11-12; S. Rep. No. 109-295, at 2-4, 15. The compilation presents countless "examples of flagrant racial discrimination" since the last reauthorization; Congress also brought to light systematic evidence that "intentional racial discrimination in voting remains so serious and widespread in covered jurisdictions that section 5 preclearance is still needed." 679 F. 3d, at 866.

After considering the full legislative record, Congress made the following findings: The VRA has directly caused significant progress in eliminating first-generation barriers to ballot access, leading to a marked increase in minority voter registration and turnout and the number of minority elected officials. 2006 Reauthorization § 2(b)(1). But despite this progress, "second generation barriers constructed to prevent minority voters from fully participating in the electoral process" continued to exist, as well as racially polarized voting in the covered jurisdictions, which increased the political vulnerability of racial and language minorities in those jurisdictions. §§2(b)(2)-(3), 120 Stat. 577. Extensive "[e]vidence of continued discrimination," Congress concluded, "clearly show[ed] the continued need for Federal oversight" in covered jurisdictions. §§2(b)(4)-(5), at 577-578. The overall record demonstrated to the federal lawmakers that, "without the continuation of the Voting Rights Act of 1965 protections, racial and language minority citizens will be deprived of the opportunity to exercise their right to vote, or will have their votes diluted, undermining the significant gains made by minorities in the last 40 years." § 2(b)(9), *id.*, at 578.

Based on these findings, Congress reauthorized preclearance for another 25 years, while also undertaking to reconsider the extension after 15 years to ensure that the provision was still necessary and effective. 42 U.S.C. §§

1973b(a)(7), (8) (2006 ed., Supp. V). The question before the Court is whether Congress had the authority under the Constitution to act as it did.

II

In answering this question, the Court does not write on a clean slate. It is well established that Congress' judgment regarding exercise of its power to enforce the Fourteenth and Fifteenth Amendments warrants substantial deference. The VRA addresses the combination of race discrimination and the right to vote, which is "preservative of all rights." *Yick Wo v. Hopkins*, 118 U.S. 356, 370 (1886). When confronting the most constitutionally invidious form of discrimination, and the most fundamental right in our democratic system, Congress' power to act is at its height.

The basis for this deference is firmly rooted in both constitutional text and precedent. The Fifteenth Amendment, which targets precisely and only racial discrimination in voting rights, states that, in this domain, "Congress shall have power to enforce this article by appropriate legislation."[2] In choosing this language, the Amendment's framers invoked Chief Justice Marshall's formulation of the scope of Congress' powers under the Necessary and Proper Clause:

> "Let the end be legitimate, let it be within the scope of the constitution, and *all means which are appropriate, which are plainly adapted to that end*, which are not prohibited, but consist with the letter and spirit of the constitution, are constitutional." *McCulloch v. Maryland*, 4 Wheat. 316, 421 (1819) (emphasis added).

It cannot tenably be maintained that the VRA, an Act of Congress adopted to shield the right to vote from racial discrimination, is inconsistent with the letter or spirit of the Fifteenth Amendment, or any provision of the Constitution read in light of the Civil War Amendments. Nowhere in today's opinion, or in *Northwest Austin*,[3] is there clear recognition of the transformative effect the Fifteenth Amendment aimed to achieve. Notably, "the Founders' first successful amendment told Congress that it could 'make no law' over a certain domain"; in contrast, the Civil War Amendments used "language [that] authorized transformative new federal statutes to uproot all vestiges of unfreedom and inequality" and provided "sweeping enforcement powers . . . to enact 'appropriate' legislation targeting state abuses." A. Amar, America's Constitution: A Biography 361, 363, 399 (2005). See also McConnell, Institutions and Interpretation: A Critique of *City of Boerne v. Flores*, 111 Harv. L. Rev. 153, 182 (1997) (quoting Civil War-era framer: "[T]he remedy for the violation of the fourteenth and fifteenth amendments was expressly not left to the courts. The remedy was legislative.").

The stated purpose of the Civil War Amendments was to arm Congress with the power and authority to protect all persons within the Nation from violations of their rights by the States. In exercising that power, then, Congress may use "all means which are appropriate, which are plainly adapted" to the constitutional ends declared by these Amendments. *McCulloch*, 4 Wheat., at 421. So when Congress acts to enforce the right to vote free from racial discrimination, we ask not whether Congress has chosen the means most wise, but whether Congress has rationally selected means appropriate to a legitimate end. "It is not for us to review the congressional resolution of [the need for its chosen remedy]. It is enough that we be able to perceive a basis upon which the Congress might resolve the conflict as it did." *Katzenbach v. Morgan*, 384 U.S. 641, 653 (1966).

Until today, in considering the constitutionality of the VRA, the Court has accorded Congress the full measure of respect its judgments in this domain should garner. *South Carolina v. Katzenbach* supplies the standard of review: "As against the reserved powers of the States, Congress may use any rational means to effectuate the constitutional prohibition of racial discrimination in voting." 383 U.S., at 324. Faced with subsequent reauthorizations of the VRA, the Court has reaffirmed this standard. *E.g., City of Rome*, 446 U.S., at 178. Today's Court does not purport to alter settled precedent establishing that the dispositive question is whether Congress has employed "rational means."

For three reasons, legislation reauthorizing an existing statute is especially likely to satisfy the minimal requirements of the rational-basis test. First, when reauthorization is at issue, Congress has already assembled a legislative record justifying the initial legislation. Congress is entitled to consider that pre-existing record as well as the record before it at the time of the vote on reauthorization. This is especially true where, as here, the Court has repeatedly affirmed the statute's constitutionality and Congress has adhered to the very model the Court has upheld. See *id.*, at 174 ("The appellants are asking us to do nothing less than overrule our decision in *South Carolina v. Katzenbach* . . . , in which we upheld the constitutionality of the Act."); *Lopez v. Monterey County*, 525 U.S. 266, 283 (1999) (similar).

Second, the very fact that reauthorization is necessary arises because Congress has built a temporal limitation into the Act. It has pledged to review, after a span of years (first 15, then 25) and in light of contemporary evidence, the continued need for the VRA. *Cf. Grutter v. Bollinger*, 539 U.S. 306, 343 (2003) (anticipating, but not guaranteeing, that, in 25 years, "the use of racial preferences [in higher education] will no longer be necessary").

Third, a reviewing court should expect the record supporting reauthorization to be less stark than the record originally made. Demand for a record of violations equivalent to the one earlier made would expose Congress to a catch-22. If the statute was working, there would be less evidence of discrimination, so opponents might argue that Congress should not be allowed to renew the statute. In contrast, if the statute was not working, there would be plenty of evidence of discrimination, but scant reason to renew a failed regulatory regime. See Persily 193-194.

This is not to suggest that congressional power in this area is limitless. It is this Court's responsibility to ensure that Congress has used appropriate means. The question meet for judicial review is whether the chosen means are "adapted to carry out the objects the amendments have in view." *Ex parte Virginia*, 100 U.S. 339, 346 (1880). The Court's role, then, is not to substitute its judgment for that of Congress, but to determine whether the legislative record sufficed to show that "Congress could rationally have determined that [its chosen] provisions were appropriate methods." *City of Rome*, 446 U.S., at 176-177.

In summary, the Constitution vests broad power in Congress to protect the right to vote, and in particular to combat racial discrimination in voting. This Court has repeatedly reaffirmed Congress' prerogative to use any rational means in exercise of its power in this area. And both precedent and logic dictate that the rational-means test should be easier to satisfy, and the burden on the statute's challenger should be higher, when what is at issue is the reauthorization of a remedy that the Court has previously affirmed, and that Congress found, from contemporary evidence, to be working to advance the Legislature's legitimate objective.

III

The 2006 reauthorization of the Voting Rights Act fully satisfies the standard stated in *McCulloch*, 4 Wheat., at 421: Congress may choose any means "appropriate" and "plainly adapted to" a legitimate constitutional end. As we shall see, it is implausible to suggest otherwise.

A

I begin with the evidence on which Congress based its decision to continue the preclearance remedy. The surest way to evaluate whether that remedy remains in order is to see if preclearance is still effectively preventing discriminatory changes to voting laws. See *City of Rome*, 446 U.S., at 181 (identifying "information on the number and types of submissions made by covered jurisdictions and the number and nature of objections interposed by the Attorney General" as a primary basis for upholding the 1975 reauthorization). On that score, the record before Congress was huge. In fact, Congress found there were more DOJ objections between 1982 and 2004 (626) than there were between 1965 and the 1982 reauthorization (490). 1 Voting Rights Act: Evidence of

Continued Need, Hearing before the Subcommittee on the Constitution of the House Committee on the Judiciary, 109th Cong., 2d Sess., 172 (2006) (hereinafter Evidence of Continued Need).

All told, between 1982 and 2006, DOJ objections blocked over 700 voting changes based on a determination that the changes were discriminatory. H. R. Rep. No. 109-478, at 21. Congress found that the majority of DOJ objections included findings of discriminatory intent, see 679 F. 3d, at 867, and that the changes blocked by preclearance were "calculated decisions to keep minority voters from fully participating in the political process," H. R. Rep. No. 109-478, at 21. On top of that, over the same time period DOJ and private plaintiffs succeeded in more than 100 actions to enforce the §5 preclearance requirements. 1 Evidence of Continued Need 186, 250.

In addition to blocking proposed voting changes through preclearance, DOJ may request more information from a jurisdiction proposing a change. In turn, the jurisdiction may modify or withdraw the proposed change. The number of such modifications or withdrawals provides an indication of how many discriminatory proposals are deterred without need for formal objection. Congress received evidence that more than 800 proposed changes were altered or withdrawn since the last reauthorization in 1982. H. R. Rep. No. 109- 478, at 40-41.[4] Congress also received empirical studies finding that DOJ's requests for more information had a significant effect on the degree to which covered jurisdictions "compl[ied] with their obligatio[n]" to protect minority voting rights. 2 Evidence of Continued Need 2555.

Congress also received evidence that litigation under §2 of the VRA was an inadequate substitute for preclearance in the covered jurisdictions. Litigation occurs only after the fact, when the illegal voting scheme has already been put in place and individuals have been elected pursuant to it, thereby gaining the advantages of incumbency. 1 at 97. An illegal scheme might be in place for several election cycles before a §2 plaintiff can gather sufficient evidence to challenge it. 1 Voting Rights Act: Section 5 of the Act— History, Scope, and Purpose: Hearing before the Subcommittee on the Constitution of the House Committee on the Judiciary, 109th Cong., 1st Sess., 92 (2005) (hereinafter Section 5 Hearing). And litigation places a heavy financial burden on minority voters. See *id.*, at 84. Congress also received evidence that preclearance lessened the litigation burden on covered jurisdictions themselves, because the preclearance process is far less costly than defending against a § 2 claim, and clearance by DOJ substantially reduces the likelihood that a § 2 claim will be mounted. Reauthorizing the Voting Rights Act's Temporary Provisions: Policy Perspectives and Views From the Field: Hearing before the Subcommittee on the Constitution, Civil Rights and Property Rights of the Senate Committee on the Judiciary, 109th Cong., 2d Sess., 13, 120-121 (2006). See also Brief for State of New York et al. as *Amici curiae* 8-9 (Section 5 "reduc[es] the likelihood that a jurisdiction will face costly and protracted Section 2 litigation.").

The number of discriminatory changes blocked or deterred by the preclearance requirement suggests that the state of voting rights in the covered jurisdictions would have been significantly different absent this remedy. Surveying the type of changes stopped by the preclearance procedure conveys a sense of the extent to which §5 continues to protect minority voting rights. Set out below are characteristic examples of changes blocked in the years leading up to the 2006 reauthorization:

- In 1995, Mississippi sought to reenact a dual voter registration system, "which was initially enacted in 1892 to disenfranchise Black voters," and for that reason, was struck down by a federal court in 1987. H. R. Rep. No. 109-478, at 39.
- Following the 2000 census, the city of Albany, Georgia, proposed a redistricting plan that DOJ found to be "designed with the purpose to limit and retrogress the increased black voting strength . . . in the city as a whole." *Id.*, at 37 (internal quotation marks omitted).
- In 2001, the mayor and all-white five-member Board of Aldermen of Kilmichael, Mississippi, abruptly canceled the town's election after "an unprecedented number" of African-American candidates announced they were running for office. DOJ required an election, and the town elected its first black mayor and three black aldermen. *Id.*, at 36-37.
- In 2006, this Court found that Texas' attempt to redraw a congressional district to reduce the strength of Latino voters bore "the mark of intentional discrimination that could give rise to an equal protection violation," and ordered the district redrawn in compliance with the VRA. *League of United Latin American Citizens v. Perry*, 548 U.S. 399, 440 (2006). In response, Texas sought to undermine this Court's order by curtailing early voting in the district, but was blocked by an action to enforce the §5 preclearance requirement. See Order in *League of United Latin American Citizens v. Texas*, No. 06-cv- 1046 (WD Tex., Dec. 5, 2006), Doc. 8.
- In 2003, after African-Americans won a majority of the seats on the school board for the first time in history, Charleston County, South Carolina, proposed an at-large voting mechanism for the board. The proposal, made without consulting any of the African-American members of the school board, was found to be an " 'exact replica' " of an earlier voting scheme that, a federal court had determined, violated the VRA. 811 F. Supp. 2d 424, 483 (DC 2011). See also S. Rep. No. 109-295, at 309. DOJ invoked §5 to block the proposal.

- In 1993, the city of Millen, Georgia, proposed to delay the election in a majority-black district by two years, leaving that district without representation on the city council while the neighboring majority-white district would have three representatives. 1 Section 5 Hearing 744. DOJ blocked the proposal. The county then sought to move a polling place from a predominantly black neighborhood in the city to an inaccessible location in a predominantly white neighborhood outside city limits. *Id.*, at 816.
- In 2004, Waller County, Texas, threatened to prosecute two black students after they announced their intention to run for office. The county then attempted to reduce the availability of early voting in that election at polling places near a historically black university. 679 F. 3d, at 865-866.
- In 1990, Dallas County, Alabama, whose county seat is the city of Selma, sought to purge its voter rolls of many black voters. DOJ rejected the purge as discriminatory, noting that it would have disqualified many citizens from voting "simply because they failed to pick up or return a voter update form, when there was no valid requirement that they do so." 1 Section 5 Hearing 356.

These examples, and scores more like them, fill the pages of the legislative record. The evidence was indeed sufficient to support Congress' conclusion that "racial discrimination in voting in covered jurisdictions [remained] serious and pervasive." 679 F. 3d, at 865.[5]

Congress further received evidence indicating that formal requests of the kind set out above represented only the tip of the iceberg. There was what one commentator described as an "avalanche of case studies of voting rights violations in the covered jurisdictions," ranging from "outright intimidation and violence against minority voters" to "more subtle forms of voting rights deprivations." Persily 202. This evidence gave Congress ever more reason to conclude that the time had not yet come for relaxed vigilance against the scourge of race discrimination in voting.

True, conditions in the South have impressively improved since passage of the Voting Rights Act. Congress noted this improvement and found that the VRA was the driving force behind it. 2006 Reauthorization § 2(b)(1). But Congress also found that voting discrimination had evolved into subtler second-generation barriers, and that eliminating preclearance would risk loss of the gains that had been made. §§ 2(b)(2), (9). Concerns of this order, the Court previously found, gave Congress adequate cause to reauthorize the VRA. *City of Rome*, 446 U.S., at 180-182 (congressional reauthorization of the preclearance requirement was justified based on "the number and nature of objections interposed by the Attorney General" since the prior reauthorization;

extension was "necessary to preserve the limited and fragile achievements of the Act and to promote further amelioration of voting discrimination" (internal quotation marks omitted)). Facing such evidence then, the Court expressly rejected the argument that disparities in voter turnout and number of elected officials were the only metrics capable of justifying reauthorization of the VRA. *Ibid.*

B

I turn next to the evidence on which Congress based its decision to reauthorize the coverage formula in § 4(b). Because Congress did not alter the coverage formula, the same jurisdictions previously subject to preclearance continue to be covered by this remedy. The evidence just described, of preclearance's continuing efficacy in blocking constitutional violations in the covered jurisdictions, itself grounded Congress' conclusion that the remedy should be retained for those jurisdictions.

There is no question, moreover, that the covered jurisdictions have a unique history of problems with racial discrimination in voting. *Ante*, at 545-546. Consideration of this long history, still in living memory, was altogether appropriate. The Court criticizes Congress for failing to recognize that "history did not end in 1965." *Ante*, at 552. But the Court ignores that "what's past is prologue." W. Shakespeare, The Tempest, act 2, sc. 1. And "[t]hose who cannot remember the past are condemned to repeat it." 1 G. Santayana, The Life of Reason 284 (1905). Congress was especially mindful of the need to reinforce the gains already made and to prevent backsliding. 2006 Reauthorization § 2(b)(9).

Of particular importance, even after 40 years and thousands of discriminatory changes blocked by preclearance, conditions in the covered jurisdictions demonstrated that the formula was still justified by "current needs." Northwest Austin, 557 U.S., at 203.

Congress learned of these conditions through a report, known as the Katz study, that looked at §2 suits between 1982 and 2004. To Examine the Impact and Effectiveness of the Voting Rights Act: Hearing before the Subcommittee on the Constitution of the House Committee on the Judiciary, 109th Cong., 1st Sess., 964-1124 (2005) (hereinafter Impact and Effectiveness). Because the private right of action authorized by §2 of the VRA applies nationwide, a comparison of §2 lawsuits in covered and noncovered jurisdictions provides an appropriate yardstick for measuring differences between covered and noncovered jurisdictions. If differences in the risk of voting discrimination between covered and noncovered jurisdictions had disappeared, one would expect that the rate of successful §2 lawsuits would be roughly the same in both areas.[6] The study's findings, however, indicated that racial discrimination in voting remains "concentrated in the jurisdictions singled out for preclearance." Northwest Austin, 557 U.S., at 203.

Although covered jurisdictions account for less than 25 percent of the country's population, the Katz study revealed that they accounted for 56 percent of successful § 2 litigation since 1982. Impact and Effectiveness 974. Controlling for population, there were nearly four times as many successful § 2 cases in covered jurisdictions as there were in noncovered jurisdictions. 679 F. 3d, at 874. The Katz study further found that §2 lawsuits are more likely to succeed when they are filed in covered jurisdictions than in noncovered jurisdictions. Impact and Effectiveness 974. From these findings—ignored by the Court—Congress reasonably concluded that the coverage formula continues to identify the jurisdictions of greatest concern.

The evidence before Congress, furthermore, indicated that voting in the covered jurisdictions was more racially polarized than elsewhere in the country. H. R. Rep. No. 109-478, at 34-35. While racially polarized voting alone does not signal a constitutional violation, it is a factor that increases the vulnerability of racial minorities to discriminatory changes in voting law. The reason is twofold. First, racial polarization means that racial minorities are at risk of being systematically outvoted and having their interests underrepresented in legislatures. Second, "when political preferences fall along racial lines, the natural inclinations of incumbents and ruling parties to entrench themselves have predictable racial effects. Under circumstances of severe racial polarization, efforts to gain political advantage translate into race-specific disadvantages." Ansolabehere, Persily, & Stewart, Regional Differences in Racial Polarization in the 2012 Presidential Election: Implications for the Constitutionality of Section 5 of the Voting Rights Act, 126 Harv. L. Rev. Forum 205, 209 (2013).

In other words, a governing political coalition has an incentive to prevent changes in the existing balance of voting power. When voting is racially polarized, efforts by the ruling party to pursue that incentive "will inevitably discriminate against a racial group." *Ibid.* Just as buildings in California have a greater need to be earthquake proofed, places where there is greater racial polarization in voting have a greater need for prophylactic measures to prevent purposeful race discrimination. This point was understood by Congress and is well recognized in the academic literature. See 2006 Reauthorization § 2(b)(3), 120 Stat. 577 ("The continued evidence of racially polarized voting in each of the jurisdictions covered by the [preclearance requirement] demonstrates that racial and language minorities remain politically vulnerable."); H. R. Rep. No. 109-478, at 35; Davidson, The Recent Evolution of Voting Rights Law Affecting Racial and Language Minorities, in Quiet Revolution 21, 22.

The case for retaining a coverage formula that met needs on the ground was therefore solid. Congress might have been charged with rigidity had it afforded covered jurisdictions no way out or ignored jurisdictions that needed superintendence. Congress, however, responded to this concern. Critical components of the congressional design are the statutory provisions allowing jurisdictions to "bail out" of preclearance, and for court-ordered "bail ins." See Northwest Austin, 557 U.S., at 199. The VRA permits a jurisdiction to bail out by showing that it has complied with the Act for ten years, and has engaged in efforts to eliminate intimidation and harassment of voters. 42 U.S.C. § 1973b(a) (2006 ed. and Supp. V). It also authorizes a court to subject a noncovered jurisdiction to federal preclearance upon finding that violations of the Fourteenth and Fifteenth Amendments have occurred there. § 1973a(c) (2006 ed.).

Congress was satisfied that the VRA's bailout mechanism provided an effective means of adjusting the VRA's coverage over time. H. R. Rep. No. 109-478, at 25 (the success of bailout "illustrates that: (1) covered status is neither permanent nor over-broad; and (2) covered status has been and continues to be within the control of the jurisdiction such that those jurisdictions that have a genuinely clean record and want to terminate coverage have the ability to do so"). Nearly 200 jurisdictions have successfully bailed out of the preclearance requirement, and DOJ has consented to every bailout application filed by an eligible jurisdiction since the current bailout procedure became effective in 1984. Brief for Federal Respondent 54. The bail-in mechanism has also worked. Several jurisdictions have been subject to federal preclearance by court orders, including the States of New Mexico and Arkansas. App. to Brief for Federal Respondent la-3a.

This experience exposes the inaccuracy of the Court's portrayal of the Act as static, unchanged since 1965. Congress designed the VRA to be a dynamic statute, capable of adjusting to changing conditions. True, many covered jurisdictions have not been able to bail out due to recent acts of noncompliance with the VRA, but that truth reinforces the congressional judgment that these jurisdictions were rightfully subject to preclearance, and ought to remain under that regime.

IV

Congress approached the 2006 reauthorization of the VRA with great care and seriousness. The same cannot be said of the Court's opinion today. The Court makes no genuine attempt to engage with the massive legislative record that Congress assembled. Instead, it relies on increases in voter registration and turnout as if that were the whole story. See *ante*, at 551. Without even identifying a standard of review, the Court dismissively brushes off arguments based on "data from the record," and declines to enter the "debat[e about] what [the] record shows." *Ante*, at 553. One would expect more from an opinion striking at the heart of the Nation's signal piece of civil-rights legislation.

I note the most disturbing lapses. First, by what right, given its usual restraint, does the Court even address Shelby County's facial challenge to the VRA? Second, the Court veers away from controlling precedent regarding the "equal sovereignty" doctrine without even acknowledging that it is doing so. Third, hardly showing the respect ordinarily paid when Congress acts to implement the Civil War Amendments, and as just stressed, the Court does not even deign to grapple with the legislative record.

A

Shelby County launched a purely facial challenge to the VRA's 2006 reauthorization. "A facial challenge to a legislative Act," the Court has other times said, "is, of course, the most difficult challenge to mount successfully, since the challenger must establish that no set of circumstances exists under which the Act would be val*id.*" *United States v. Salerno*, 481 U.S. 739, 745 (1987).

"[U]nder our constitutional system[,] courts are not roving commissions assigned to pass judgment on the validity of the Nation's laws." *Broadrick v. Oklahoma*, 413 U.S. 601, 610- 611 (1973). Instead, the "judicial Power" is limited to deciding particular "Cases" and "Controversies." U.S. Const., Art. Ill, §2. "Embedded in the traditional rules governing constitutional adjudication is the principle that a person to whom a statute may constitutionally be applied will not be heard to challenge that statute on the ground that it may conceivably be applied unconstitutionally to others, in other situations not before the Court." *Broadrick*, 413 U.S., at 610. Yet the Court's opinion in this case contains not a word explaining why Congress lacks the power to subject to preclearance the particular plaintiff that initiated this lawsuit— Shelby County, Alabama. The reason for the Court's silence is apparent, for as applied to Shelby County, the VRA's preclearance requirement is hardly contestable.

Alabama is home to Selma, site of the "Bloody Sunday" beatings of civil-rights demonstrators that served as the catalyst for the VRA's enactment. Following those events, Martin Luther King, Jr., led a march from Selma to Montgomery, Alabama's capital, where he called for passage of the VRA. If the Act passed, he foresaw, progress could be made even in Alabama, but there had to be a steadfast national commitment to see the task through to completion. In King's words, "the arc of the moral universe is long, but it bends toward justice." G. May, Bending Toward Justice: The Voting Rights Act and the Transformation of American Democracy 144 (2013).

History has proved King right. Although circumstances in Alabama have changed, serious concerns remain. Between 1982 and 2005, Alabama had one of the highest rates of successful § 2 suits, second only to its VRA-covered neighbor Mississippi. 679 F. 3d, at 897 (Williams, J., dissenting). In other words, even while subject to the restraining effect of §5, Alabama was found to have "deni[ed] or abridge[d]" voting rights "on account of race or color" more frequently than nearly all other States in the Union. 42 U.S.C. § 1973(a). This fact prompted the dissenting judge below to concede that "a more narrowly tailored coverage formula" capturing Alabama and a handful of other jurisdictions with an established track record of racial discrimination in voting "might be defensible." 679 F. 3d, at 897 (opinion of Williams, J.). That is an understatement. Alabama's sorry history of §2 violations alone provides sufficient justification for Congress' determination in 2006 that the State should remain subject to §5's preclearance requirement.[7]

A few examples suffice to demonstrate that, at least in Alabama, the "current burdens" imposed by §5's preclearance requirement are "justified by current needs." Northwest Austin, 557 U.S., at 203. In the interim between the VRA's 1982 and 2006 reauthorizations, this Court twice confronted purposeful racial discrimination in Alabama. In *Pleasant Grove v. United States*, 479 U.S. 462 (1987), the Court held that Pleasant Grove—a city in Jefferson County, Shelby County's neighbor—engaged in purposeful discrimination by annexing all-white areas while rejecting the annexation request of an adjacent black neighborhood. The city had "shown unambiguous opposition to racial integration, both before and after the passage of the federal civil rights laws," and its strategic annexations appeared to be an attempt "to provide for the growth of a monolithic white voting block" for "the impermissible purpose of minimizing future black voting strength." at 465, 471-472.

Two years before Pleasant Grove, the Court in *Hunter v. Underwood*, 471 U.S. 222 (1985), struck down a provision of the Alabama Constitution that prohibited individuals convicted of misdemeanor offenses "involving moral turpitude" from voting. *Id.*, at 223 (internal quotation marks omitted). The provision violated the Fourteenth Amendment's Equal Protection Clause, the Court unanimously concluded, because "its original enactment was motivated by a desire to discriminate against blacks on account of race[,] and the [provision] continues to this day to have that effect." *Id.*, at 233.

Pleasant Grove and *Hunter* were not anomalies. In 1986, a Federal District Judge concluded that the at-large election systems in several Alabama counties violated § 2. *Dillard v. Crenshaw Cty.*, 640 F. Supp. 1347,1354-1363 (MD Ala. 1986). Summarizing its findings, the court stated that "[f]rom the late 1800's through the present, [Alabama] has consistently erected barriers to keep black persons from full and equal participation in the social, economic, and political life of the state." *Id.*, at 1360.

The *Dillard* litigation ultimately expanded to include 183 cities, counties, and school boards employing discriminatory at-large election systems. *Dillard v. Baldwin Cty. Bd. of Ed.*, 686 F. Supp. 1459, 1461 (MD Ala. 1988). One of those defendants was Shelby County, which eventually signed a consent decree to resolve the claims against it. See *Dillard v. Crenshaw Cty.*, 748 F. Supp. 819 (MD Ala. 1990).

Although the *Dillard* litigation resulted in overhauls of numerous electoral systems tainted by racial discrimination, concerns about backsliding persist. In 2008, for example, the city of Calera, located in Shelby County, requested preclearance of a redistricting plan that "would have eliminated the city's sole majority-black district, which had been created pursuant to the consent decree in *Dillard*" 811 F. Supp. 2d, at 443. Although DOJ objected to the plan, Calera forged ahead with elections based on the unprecleared voting changes, resulting in the defeat of the incumbent African- American councilman who represented the former majority- black district. *Ibid.* The city's defiance required DOJ to bring a §5 enforcement action that ultimately yielded appropriate redress, including restoration of the majority-black district. *Ibid.*] Brief for Respondent-Intervenor Cunningham et al. 20.

A recent Federal Bureau of Investigation (FBI) investigation provides a further window into the persistence of racial discrimination in state politics. See *United States v. McGregor*, 824 F. Supp. 2d 1339, 1344-1348 (MD Ala. 2011). Recording devices worn by state legislators cooperating with the FBI's investigation captured conversations between members of the state legislature and their political allies. The recorded conversations are shocking. Members of the State Senate derisively refer to African-Americans as "Aborigines" and talk openly of their aim to quash a particular gambling-related referendum because the referendum, if placed on the ballot, might increase African-American voter turnout. *Id.*, at 1345-1346 (internal quotation marks omitted). See also *id.*, at 1345 (legislators and their allies expressed concern that if the referendum were placed on the ballot, " '[e]very black, every illiterate' would be 'bused [to the polls] on HUD financed buses'"). These conversations occurred not in the 1870's, or even in the 1960's, they took place in 2010. *Id.*, at 1344-1345. The District Judge presiding over the criminal trial at which the recorded conversations were introduced commented that the "recordings represent compelling evidence that political exclusion through racism remains a real and enduring problem" in Alabama. *Id.*, at 1347. Racist sentiments, the judge observed, "remain regrettably entrenched in the high echelons of state government." *Ibid.*

These recent episodes forcefully demonstrate that §5's preclearance requirement is constitutional as applied to Alabama and its political subdivisions.[8] And under our case law, that conclusion should suffice to resolve this case. See *United States v. Raines*, 362 U.S. 17, 24-25 (1960) ("[I]f the complaint here called for an application of the statute clearly constitutional under the Fifteenth Amendment, that should have been an end to the question of constitutionality."). See also *Nevada Dept. of Human Resources v. Hibbs*, 538 U.S. 721, 743 (2003) (Scalia, J., dissenting) (where, as here, a state or local government raises a facial challenge to a federal statute on the ground that it exceeds Congress' enforcement powers under the Civil War Amendments, the challenge fails if the opposing party is able to show that the statute "could constitutionally be applied to some jurisdictions").

This Court has consistently rejected constitutional challenges to legislation enacted pursuant to Congress' enforcement powers under the Civil War Amendments upon finding that the legislation was constitutional as applied to the particular set of circumstances before the Court. See *United States v. Georgia*, 546 U.S. 151, 159 (2006) (Title II of the Americans with Disabilities Act of 1990 (ADA) validly abrogates state sovereign immunity "insofar as [it] creates a private cause of action . . . for conduct that actually violates the Fourteenth Amendment"); *Tennessee v. Lane*, 541 U.S. 509, 530-534 (2004) (Title II of the ADA is constitutional "as it applies to the class of cases implicating the fundamental right of access to the courts"); *Raines*, 362 U.S., at 24-26 (federal statute proscribing deprivations of the right to vote based on race was constitutional as applied to the state officials before the Court, even if it could not constitutionally be applied to other parties). A similar approach is warranted here.[9]

The VRA's exceptionally broad severability provision makes it particularly inappropriate for the Court to allow Shelby County to mount a facial challenge to §§ 4(b) and 5 of the VRA, even though application of those provisions to the county falls well within the bounds of Congress' legislative authority. The severability provision states:

> "If any provision of [this Act] or the application thereof to any person or circumstances is held invalid, the remainder of [the Act] and the application of the provision to other persons not similarly situated or to other circumstances shall not be affected thereby." 42 U.S.C. §1973p.

In other words, even if the VRA could not constitutionally be applied to certain States—*e.g.*, Arizona and Alaska, see *ante*, at 542—§1973p calls for those unconstitutional applications to be severed, leaving the Act in place for jurisdictions as to which its application does not transgress constitutional limits.

Nevertheless, the Court suggests that limiting the jurisdictional scope of the VRA in an appropriate case would be to "try our hand at updating the statute." *Ante*, at 554. Just last Term, however, the Court rejected this very argument when addressing a materially identical severability provision, explaining that such a provision is "Congress' explicit textual instruction to leave unaffected the remainder of [the Act]" if any particular "application is unconstitutional." *National Federation of Independent Business v. Sebelius*, 567 U.S. 519, 586 (2012) (plurality opinion) (internal quotation marks omitted); *id.*, at 645-646 (GINSBURG, J., concurring in part, concurring in judgment in part, and dissenting in part) (agreeing with the plurality's severability analysis). See also *Raines*, 362 U.S., at 23 (a statute capable of some constitutional applications may nonetheless be susceptible to a facial challenge only in "that rarest of cases where this Court can justifiably think itself able confidently to discern that Congress would not have desired its legislation to stand at all unless it could validly stand in its every application"). Leaping to resolve Shelby County's facial challenge without considering whether application of the VRA to Shelby County is constitutional, or even addressing the VRA's severability provision, the Court's opinion can hardly be described as an exemplar of restrained and moderate decisionmaking. Quite the opposite. Hubris is a fit word for today's demolition of the VRA.

B

The Court stops any application of §5 by holding that §4(b)'s coverage formula is unconstitutional. It pins this result, in large measure, to "the fundamental principle of equal sovereignty." *Ante,* at 542, 544-545, 556. In Katzenbach, however, the Court held, in no uncertain terms, that the principle " *applies only to the terms upon which States are admitted to the Union,* and not to the remedies for local evils which have subsequently appeared." 383 U.S., at 328-329 (emphasis added).

Katzenbach, the Court acknowledges, "rejected the notion that the [equal sovereignty] principle operate[s] as a bar on differential treatment outside [the] context [of the admission of new States]." *Ante,* at 544 (citing 383 U.S., at 328-329; emphasis deleted). But the Court clouds that once clear understanding by citing dictum from *Northwest Austin* to convey that the principle of equal sovereignty "remains highly pertinent in assessing subsequent disparate treatment of States." *Ante,* at 544 (citing 557 U.S., at 203). See also *ante,* at 556 (relying on *Northwest Austin's,* "emphasis on [the] significance" of the equal-sovereignty principle). If the Court is suggesting that dictum in *Northwest Austin* silently overruled *Katzenbach's* limitation of the equal-sovereignty doctrine to "the admission of new States," the suggestion is untenable. *Northwest Austin* cited *Katzenbach's* holding in the course of declining to decide whether the VRA was constitutional or even what standard of review applied to the question. 557 U.S., at 203-204. In today's decision, the Court ratchets up what was pure dictum in *Northwest Austin,* attributing breadth to the equal-sovereignty principle in flat contradiction of *Katzenbach.* The Court does so with nary an explanation of why it finds *Katzenbach* wrong, let alone any discussion of whether stare decisis nonetheless counsels adherence to *Katzenbach's* ruling on the limited "significance" of the equal-sovereignty principle.

Today's unprecedented extension of the equal-sovereignty principle outside its proper domain—the admission of new States—is capable of much mischief. Federal statutes that treat States disparately are hardly novelties. *See, e.g.,* 28 U.S.C. §3704(a)(l) (no State may operate or permit a sports- related gambling scheme, unless that State conducted such a scheme "at any time during the period beginning January 1, 1976, and ending August 31, 1990"); 26 U.S.C. §142(Z) (Environmental Protection Agency required to locate green building project in a State meeting specified population criteria); 42 U.S.C. §3796bb(b) (at least 50 percent of rural drug enforcement assistance funding must be allocated to States with "a population density of fifty-two or fewer persons per square mile or a State in which the largest county has fewer than one hundred and fifty thousand people, based on the decennial census of 1990 through fiscal year 1997"); §§13925, 13971 (similar population criteria for funding to combat rural domestic violence); § 10136(c)(6) (specifying rules applicable to Nevada's Yucca Mountain nuclear waste site, and providing that "[n]o State, other than the State of Nevada, may receive financial assistance under this subsection after December 22, 1987"). Do such provisions remain safe given the Court's expansion of equal sovereignty's sway?

Of gravest concern, Congress relied on our pathmarking *Katzenbach* decision in each reauthorization of the VRA. It had every reason to believe that the Act's limited geographical scope would weigh in favor of, not against, the Act's constitutionality. *See, e.g., United States v. Morrison*, 529 U.S. 598, 626-627 (2000) (confining preclearance regime to States with a record of discrimination bolstered the VRA's constitutionality). Congress could hardly have foreseen that the VRA's limited geographic reach would render the Act constitutionally suspect. See Persily 195 ("[S]upporters of the Act sought to develop an evidentiary record for the principal purpose of explaining why the covered jurisdictions should remain covered, rather than justifying the coverage of certain jurisdictions but not others.").

In the Court's conception, it appears, defenders of the VRA could not prevail upon showing what the record overwhelmingly bears out, *i.e.*, that there is a need for continuing the preclearance regime in covered States. In addition, the defenders would have to disprove the existence of a comparable need elsewhere. See Tr. of Oral Arg. 61-62 (suggesting that proof of egregious episodes of racial discrimination in covered jurisdictions would not suffice to carry the day for the VRA, unless such episodes are shown to be absent elsewhere). I am aware of no precedent for imposing such a double burden on defenders of legislation.

C

The Court has time and again declined to upset legislation of this genre unless there was no or almost no evidence of unconstitutional action by States. See, *e.g., City of Boerne v. Flores*, 521 U.S. 507, 530 (1997) (legislative record "mention[ed] no episodes [of the kind the legislation aimed to check] occurring in the past 40 years"). No such claim can be made about the congressional record for the 2006 VRA reauthorization. Given a record replete with examples of denial or abridgment of a paramount federal right, the Court should have left the matter where it belongs: in Congress' bailiwick.

Instead, the Court strikes §4(b)'s coverage provision because, in its view, the provision is not based on "current conditions." *Ante,* at 550. It discounts, however, that one such condition was the preclearance remedy in place in the covered jurisdictions, a remedy Congress designed both to catch discrimination before it causes harm, and to guard against return to old ways. 2006 Reauthorization §§ 2(b)(3), (9). Volumes of evidence supported Congress' determination that the prospect of retrogression was real. Throwing out preclearance when it has worked and is continuing to work to stop discriminatory changes is like throwing away your umbrella in a rainstorm because you are not getting wet.

But, the Court insists, the coverage formula is no good; it is based on "decades-old data and eradicated practices." *Ante,* at 551. Even if the legislative record shows, as engaging with it would reveal, that the formula accurately identifies the jurisdictions with the worst conditions of voting discrimination, that is of no moment, as the Court sees it. Congress, the Court decrees, must "star[t] from scratch." *Ante,* at 556. I do not see why that should be so.

Congress' chore was different in 1965 than it was in 2006. In 1965, there were a "small number of States . . . which in most instances were familiar to Congress by name," on which Congress fixed its attention. *Katzenbach,* 383 U.S., at 328. In drafting the coverage formula, "Congress began work with reliable evidence of actual voting discrimination in a great majority of the States" it sought to target. at 329. "The formula [Congress] eventually evolved to describe these areas" also captured a few States that had not been the subject of congressional factfinding. *Ibid.* Nevertheless, the Court upheld the formula in its entirety, finding it fair "to infer a significant danger of the evil" in all places the formula covered. *Ibid.*

The situation Congress faced in 2006, when it took up reauthorization of the coverage formula, was not the same. By then, the formula had been in effect for many years, and all of the jurisdictions covered by it were "familiar to Congress by name." *Id.,* at 328. The question before Congress: Was there still a sufficient basis to support continued application of the preclearance remedy in each of those already-identified places? There was at that point no chance that the formula might inadvertently sweep in new areas that were not the subject of congressional findings. And Congress could determine from the record whether the jurisdictions captured by the coverage formula still belonged under the preclearance regime. If they did, there was no need to alter the formula. That is why the Court, in addressing prior reauthorizations of the VRA, did not question the continuing "relevance" of the formula.

Consider once again the components of the record before Congress in 2006. The coverage provision identified a known list of places with an undisputed history of serious problems with racial discrimination in voting. Recent evidence relating to Alabama and its counties was there for all to see. Multiple Supreme Court decisions had upheld the coverage provision, most recently in 1999. There was extensive evidence that, due to the preclearance mechanism, conditions in the covered jurisdictions had notably improved. And there was evidence that preclearance was still having a substantial real-world effect, having stopped hundreds of discriminatory voting changes in the covered jurisdictions since the last reauthorization. In addition, there was evidence that racial polarization in voting was higher in covered jurisdictions than elsewhere, increasing the vulnerability of minority citizens in those jurisdictions. And countless witnesses, reports, and case studies documented continuing problems with voting discrimination in those jurisdictions. In light of this record, Congress had more than a reasonable basis to conclude that the existing coverage formula was not out of sync with conditions on the ground in covered areas. And certainly Shelby County was no candidate for release through the mechanism Congress provided. See *supra*, at 581, 583-584.

The Court holds §4(b) invalid on the ground that it is "irrational to base coverage on the use of voting tests 40 years ago, when such tests have been illegal since that time." *Ante*, at 556. But the Court disregards what Congress set about to do in enacting the VRA. That extraordinary legislation scarcely stopped at the particular tests and devices that happened to exist in 1965. The grand aim of the Act is to secure to all in our polity equal citizenship stature, a voice in our democracy undiluted by race. As the record for the 2006 reauthorization makes abundantly clear, second- generation barriers to minority voting rights have emerged in the covered jurisdictions as attempted substitutes for the first-generation barriers that originally triggered preclearance in those jurisdictions. See *supra*, at 563-564, 566, 573-575.

The sad irony of today's decision lies in its utter failure to grasp why the VRA has proved effective. The Court appears to believe that the VRA's success in eliminating the specific devices extant in 1965 means that preclearance is no longer needed. *Ante*, at 552-553, 554, 556. With that belief, and the argument derived from it, history repeats itself. The same assumption—that the problem could be solved when particular methods of voting discrimination are identified and eliminated—was indulged and proved wrong repeatedly prior to the VRA's enactment. Unlike prior statutes, which singled out particular tests or devices, the VRA is grounded in Congress' recognition of the "variety and persistence" of measures designed to impair minority voting rights. *Katzenbach*, 383 U.S., at 311; *supra*, at 560. In truth, the evolution of voting discrimination into more subtle second-generation barriers is powerful evidence that a remedy as effective as preclearance remains vital to protect minority voting rights and prevent backsliding.

Beyond question, the VRA is no ordinary legislation. It is extraordinary because Congress embarked on a mission long delayed and of extraordinary importance: to realize the purpose and promise of the Fifteenth Amendment. For a half century, a concerted effort has been made to end racial discrimination in voting. Thanks to the VRA, progress once the subject of a dream has been achieved and continues to be made.

The record supporting the 2006 reauthorization of the VRA is also extraordinary. It was described by the Chairman of the House Judiciary Committee as "one of the most extensive considerations of any piece of legislation that the United States Congress has dealt with in the 2714 years" he had served in the House. 152 Cong. Rec. 14230 (2006) (statement of Rep. Sensenbrenner). After exhaustive evidence gathering and deliberative process, Congress reauthorized the VRA, including the coverage provision, with overwhelming bipartisan support. It was the judgment of Congress that "40 years has not been a sufficient amount of time to eliminate the vestiges of discrimination following nearly 100 years of disregard for the dictates of the 15th amendment and to ensure that the right of all citizens to vote is protected as guaranteed by the Constitution." 2006 Reauthorization §2(b)(7), 120 Stat. 578. That determination of the body empowered to enforce the Civil War Amendments "by appropriate legislation" merits this Court's utmost respect. In my judgment, the Court errs egregiously by overriding Congress' decision.

* * *

For the reasons stated, I would affirm the judgment of the Court of Appeals.

---

1. The Court purports to declare unconstitutional only the coverage formula set out in §4(b). See *ante*, at 557. But without that formula, §5 is immobilized.

2. The Constitution uses the words "right to vote" in five separate places: the Fourteenth, Fifteenth, Nineteenth, Twenty-Fourth, and Twenty-Sixth Amendments. Each of these Amendments contains the same broad empowerment of Congress to enact "appropriate legislation" to enforce the protected right. The implication is unmistakable: Under our constitutional structure, Congress holds the lead rein in making the right to vote equally real for all U.S. citizens. These Amendments are in line with the special role assigned to Congress in protecting the integrity of the democratic process in federal elections. U.S. Const., Art. I, §4 ("[T]he Congress may at any time by Law make or alter" regulations concerning the "Times, Places and Manner of holding Elections for Senators and Representatives."); *Arizona v. Inter Tribal Council of Ariz., Inc., ante,* at 8.

3. Acknowledging the existence of "serious constitutional questions," see *ante*, at 555 (internal quotation marks omitted), does not suggest how those questions should be answered.

4. This number includes only changes actually proposed. Congress also received evidence that many covered jurisdictions engaged in an "informal consultation process" with DOJ before formally submitting a proposal, so that the deterrent effect of preclearance was far broader than the formal submissions alone suggest. The Continuing Need for Section 5 Pre- Clearance:

Hearing before the Senate Committee on the Judiciary, 109th Cong., 2d Sess., 53-54 (2006). All agree that an unsupported assertion about "deterrence" would not be sufficient to justify keeping a remedy in place in perpetuity. See *ante*, at 550. But it was certainly reasonable for Congress to consider the testimony of witnesses who had worked with officials in covered jurisdictions and observed a real-world deterrent effect.

5. For an illustration postdating the 2006 reauthorization, see *South Carolina v. United States*, 898 F. Supp. 2d 30 (DC 2012), which involved a South Carolina voter-identification law enacted in 2011. Concerned that the law would burden minority voters, DOJ brought a §5 enforcement action to block the law's implementation. In the course of the litigation, South Carolina officials agreed to binding interpretations that made it "far easier than some might have expected or feared" for South Carolina citizens to vote. *Id.*, at 37. A three-judge panel precleared the law after adopting both interpretations as an express "condition of preclearance." *Id.*, at 37-38. Two of the judges commented that the case demonstrated "the continuing utility of Section 5 of the Voting Rights Act in deterring problematic, and hence encouraging non-discriminatory, changes in state and local voting laws." *Id.*, at 54 (Bates, J., concurring).

6. Because preclearance occurs only in covered jurisdictions and can be expected to stop the most obviously objectionable measures, one would expect a lower rate of successful §2 lawsuits in those jurisdictions if the risk of voting discrimination there were the same as elsewhere in the country.

7. This lawsuit was filed by Shelby County, a political subdivision of Alabama, rather than by the State itself. Nevertheless, it is appropriate to judge Shelby County's constitutional challenge in light of instances of discrimination statewide because Shelby County is subject to §5's preclearance requirement by virtue of *Alabama's* designation as a covered jurisdiction under §4(b) of the VRA. See *ante*, at 540. In any event, Shelby County's recent record of employing an at-large electoral system tainted by intentional racial discrimination is by itself sufficient to justify subjecting the county to §5's preclearance mandate. See *infra*, at 583-584.

8. Congress continued preclearance over Alabama, including Shelby County, after considering evidence of current barriers there to minority voting clout. Shelby County, thus, is no "redhead" caught up in an arbitrary scheme. See *ante*, at 554.

9. The Court does not contest that Alabama's history of racial discrimination provides a sufficient basis for Congress to require Alabama and its political subdivisions to preclear electoral changes. Nevertheless, the Court asserts that Shelby County may prevail on its facial challenge to §4's coverage formula because it is subject to §5's preclearance requirement by virtue of that formula. See *ante*, at 554-555 ("The county was selected [for preclearance] based on th[e coverage] formula."). This misses the reality that Congress decided to subject Alabama to preclearance based on evidence of continuing constitutional violations in that State. See *supra*, at 585, n. 8.

BURWELL V. HOBBY LOBBY STORES

573 U.S. 682 (2014)

This case is about the right of closely held for-profit corporations to be exempt from certain regulations that their owners believe violate their personal religious beliefs. The owners of Hobby Lobby stated that their right to religious freedom was violated by the Affordable Car Act's mandate that they provide to all employees health insurance that included coverage of contraceptives. The owners of Hobby Lobby contended that paying for others' use of birth control violated their religious beliefs.

In a 5-4 decision written by Justice Alito, the Court held that the Religious Freedom Restoration Act applied to closely held for-profit corporations and protected the religious freedom and conscious rights of the owners of such corporations. These companies would be exempt from regulations that violated their owners' conscience, provided there was a less restrictive means of furthering the state's regulatory interest available.

Justice Ginsburg dissented, joined in part by Justices Sotomayor, Breyer, and Kagan.

BURWELL V. HOBBY LOBBY STORES

I n a decision of startling breadth, the Court holds that commercial
enterprises, including corporations, along with partnerships and sole
proprietorships, can opt out of any law (saving only tax laws) they judge
incompatible with their sincerely held religious beliefs. See *ante*, at 705-736.
Compelling governmental interests in uniform compliance with the law, and
disadvantages that religion-based opt-outs impose on others, hold no sway, the
Court decides, at least when there is a "less restrictive alternative." *Ante*, at 734.
And such an alternative, the Court suggests, there always will be whenever, in
lieu of tolling an enterprise claiming a religion-based exemption, the government, *i.e.*, the general public, can pick up the tab. See *ante*, at 728-731.[1]

The Court does not pretend that the First Amendment's Free Exercise
Clause demands religion-based accommodations so extreme, for our decisions
leave no doubt on that score. *See infra*, at 744-746. Instead, the Court holds that
Congress, in the Religious Freedom Restoration Act of 1993 (RFRA or Act), 42
U.S.C. §2000bb et seq., dictated the extraordinary religion-based exemptions
today's decision endorses. In the Court's view, RFRA demands accommodation of a for-profit corporation's religious beliefs no matter the impact that
accommodation may have on third parties who do not share the corporation
owners' religious faith—in these cases, thousands of women employed by
Hobby Lobby and Conestoga or dependents of persons those corporations
employ. Persuaded that Congress enacted RFRA to serve a far less radical
purpose, and mindful of the havoc the Court's judgment can introduce, I
dissent.

I

"The ability of women to participate equally in the economic and social life of the Nation has been facilitated by their ability to control their reproductive lives." *Planned Parenthood of Southeastern Pa. v. Casey*, 505 U.S. 833, 856 (1992). Congress acted on that understanding when, as part of a nationwide insurance program intended to be comprehensive, it called for coverage of preventive care responsive to women's needs. Carrying out Congress' direction, the Department of Health and Human Services (HHS), in consultation with public health experts, promulgated regulations requiring group health plans to cover all forms of contraception approved by the Food and Drug Administration (FDA). The genesis of this coverage should enlighten the Court's resolution of these cases.

A

The Affordable Care Act (ACA), in its initial form, specified three categories of preventive care that health plans must cover at no added cost to the plan participant or beneficiary.[2] Particular services were to be recommended by the U.S. Preventive Services Task Force, an independent panel of experts. The scheme had a large gap, however; it left out preventive services that "many women's health advocates and medical professionals believe are critically important." 155 Cong. Rec. 28841 (2009) (statement of Sen. Boxer). To correct this oversight, Senator Barbara Mikulski introduced the Women's Health Amendment, which added to the ACA's minimum coverage requirements a new category of preventive services specific to women's health.

Women paid significantly more than men for preventive care, the amendment's proponents noted; in fact, cost barriers operated to block many women from obtaining needed care at all. *See, e.g., id.*, at 29070 (statement of Sen. Feinstein) ("Women of childbearing age spend 68 percent more in out-of-pocket health care costs than men."); at 29302 (statement of Sen. Mikulski) ("copayments are [often] so high that [women] avoid getting [preventive and screening services] in the first place"). And increased access to contraceptive services, the sponsors comprehended, would yield important public health gains. *See, e.g., id.*, at 29768 (statement of Sen. Durbin) ("This bill will expand health insurance coverage to the vast majority of [the 17 million women of reproductive age in the United States who are uninsured] . . . . This expanded access will reduce unintended pregnancies.").

As altered by the Women's Health Amendment's passage, the ACA requires new insurance plans to include coverage without cost sharing of "such additional preventive care and screenings . . . as provided for in comprehensive guidelines supported by the Health Resources and Services Administration [(HRSA)]," a unit of HHS. 42 U.S.C. §300gg- 13(a)(4). Thus charged, the HRSA developed recommendations in consultation with the Institute of Medicine (IOM). See 77 Fed. Reg. 8725-8726 (2012).[3] The IOM convened a group of independent experts, including "specialists in disease prevention [and] women's health"; those experts prepared a report evaluating the efficacy of a number of preventive services. IOM, Clinical Preventive Services for Women: Closing the Gaps 2 (2011) (hereinafter IOM Report). Consistent with the findings of "[n]umerous health professional associations" and other organizations, the IOM experts determined that preventive coverage should include the "full range" of FDA-approved contraceptive methods. *Id.*, at 10. See also *id.*, at 102-110.

In making that recommendation, the IOM's report expressed concerns similar to those voiced by congressional proponents of the Women's Health Amendment. The report noted the disproportionate burden women carried for comprehensive health services and the adverse health consequences of excluding contraception from preventive care available to employees without cost sharing. *See, e.g., id.*, at 19 ("[W]omen are consistently more likely than men to report a wide range of cost-related barriers to receiving . . . medical tests and treatments and to filling prescriptions for themselves and their families."); *id.*, at 103-104, 107 (pregnancy may be contraindicated for women with certain medical conditions, for example, some congenital heart diseases, pulmonary hypertension, and Marfan syndrome, and contraceptives may be used to reduce risk of endometrial cancer, among other serious medical conditions); *id.*, at 103 (women with unintended pregnancies are more likely to experience depression and anxiety, and their children face "increased odds of preterm birth and low birth weight").

In line with the IOM's suggestions, the HRSA adopted guidelines recommending coverage of "[a]ll [FDA-]approved contraceptive methods, sterilization procedures, and patient education and counseling for all women with reproductive capacity."[4] Thereafter, HHS, the Department of Labor, and the Department of Treasury promulgated regulations requiring group health plans to include coverage of the contraceptive services recommended in the HRSA guidelines, subject to certain exceptions, described *infra*, at 763-764.[5] This opinion refers to these regulations as the contraceptive coverage requirement.

B

While the Women's Health Amendment succeeded, a countermove proved unavailing. The Senate voted down the so-called "conscience amendment," which would have enabled any employer or insurance provider to deny coverage based on its asserted "religious beliefs or moral convictions." 158 Cong. Rec. 1415 (2012); see *id.*, at 2622-2634 (debate and vote).[6] That amendment, Senator Mikulski observed, would have "pu[t] the personal opinion of employers and insurers over the practice of medicine." *Id.*, at 2450. Rejecting the "conscience amendment," Congress left health care decisions—including the choice among contraceptive methods— in the hands of women, with the aid of their health care providers.

II

Any First Amendment Free Exercise Clause claim Hobby Lobby or Conestoga[7] might assert is foreclosed by this Court's decision in *Employment Div., Dept, of Human Resources of Ore. v. Smith*, 494 U.S. 872 (1990). In *Smith*, two members of the Native American Church were dismissed from their jobs and denied unemployment benefits because they ingested peyote at, and as an essential element of, a religious ceremony. Oregon law forbade the consumption of peyote, and this Court, relying on that prohibition, rejected the employees' claim that the denial of unemployment benefits violated their free exercise rights. The First Amendment is not offended, *Smith* held, when "prohibiting the exercise of religion . . . is not the object of [governmental regulation] but merely the incidental effect of a generally applicable and otherwise valid provision." *Id.*, at 878; see *id.*, at 878-879 ("an individual's religious beliefs [do not] excuse him from compliance with an otherwise valid law prohibiting conduct that the State is free to regulate"). The ACA's contraceptive coverage requirement applies generally, it is "otherwise valid," it trains on women's well-being, not on the exercise of religion, and any effect it has on such exercise is incidental.

Even if *Smith* did not control, the Free Exercise Clause would not require the exemption Hobby Lobby and Conestoga seek. Accommodations to religious beliefs or observances, the Court has clarified, must not significantly impinge on the interests of third parties.[8]

The exemption sought by Hobby Lobby and Conestoga would override significant interests of the corporations' employees and covered dependents. It would deny legions of women who do not hold their employers' beliefs access to contraceptive coverage that the ACA would otherwise secure. See *Catholic Charities of Sacramento, Inc. v. Superior Court*, 32 Cal. 4th 527, 565, 85 P. 3d 67, 93 (2004) ("We are unaware of any decision in which . . . [the U.S. Supreme Court] has exempted a religious objector from the operation of a neutral, generally applicable law despite the recognition that the requested exemption would detrimentally affect the rights of third parties."). In sum, with respect to free exercise claims no less than free speech claims, " '[y]our right to swing your arms ends just where the other man's nose begins.'" Chafee, Freedom of Speech in War Time, 32 Harv. L. Rev. 932, 957 (1919).

III

A

Lacking a tenable claim under the Free Exercise Clause, Hobby Lobby and Conestoga rely on RFRA, a statute instructing that " [g]overnment shall not substantially burden a person's exercise of religion even if the burden results from a rule of general applicability" unless the government shows that applica- tion of the burden is "the least restrictive means" to further a "compelling governmental interest." 42 U.S.C. § 2000bb-l(a), (b)(2). In RFRA, Congress "adopt[ed] a statutory rule comparable to the constitutional rule rejected in *Smith.*" *Gonzales v. O Centro Beneficente União do Vegetal*, 546 U.S. 418, 424 (2006).

RFRA's purpose is specific and written into the statute itself. The Act was crafted to "restore the compelling interest test as set forth in *Sherbert v. Verner*, 374 U.S. 398 (1963) and *Wisconsin v. Yoder*, 406 U.S. 205 (1972) and to guarantee its application in all cases where free exercise of religion is substantially burdened." § 2000bb(b)(l).[9] See also § 2000bb(a)(5) ("[T]he compelling interest test as set forth in prior Federal court rulings is a workable test for striking sensible balances between religious liberty and competing prior governmental interests."); *ante*, at 736 (agreeing that the pre-*Smith* compelling interest test is "workable" and "strike [s] sensible balances").

The legislative history is correspondingly emphatic on RFRA's aim. *See, e.g.*, S. Rep. No. 103-111, p. 12 (1993) (hereinafter Senate Report) (RFRA's purpose was "only to overturn the Supreme Court's decision in *Smith*," not to "unsettle other areas of the law."); 139 Cong. Rec. 26178 (1993) (statement of Sen. Kennedy) (RFRA was "designed to restore the compelling interest test for deciding free exercise claims."). In line with this restorative purpose, Congress expected courts considering RFRA claims to "look to free exercise cases decided prior to *Smith* for guidance." Senate Report 8. See also H. R. Rep. No. 103-88, pp. 6-7 (1993) (hereinafter House Report) (same). In short, the Act rein- states the law as it was prior to *Smith*, without "creating] . .. new rights for any religious practice or for any potential litigant." 139 Cong. Rec. 26178 (statement of Sen. Kennedy). Given the Act's moderate purpose, it is hardly surprising that RFRA's enactment in 1993 provoked little controversy. See Brief for Senator Murray et al. as *Amici Curiae* 8 (hereinafter Senators Brief) (RFRA was approved by a 97-to-3 vote in the Senate and a voice vote in the House of Representatives).

B

Despite these authoritative indications, the Court sees RFRA as a bold initiative departing from, rather than restoring, pre-*Smith* jurisprudence. See *ante*, at 695, n. 3, 696, 706, 714-716. To support its conception of RFRA as a measure detached from this Court's decisions, one that sets a new course, the Court points first to the Religious Land Use and Institutionalized Persons Act of 2000 (RLUIPA), 42 U.S.C. §2000cc et seq., which altered RFRA's definition of the term "exercise of religion." RFRA, as originally enacted, defined that term to mean "the exercise of religion under the First Amendment to the Constitution." § 2000bb- 2(4) (1994 ed.). See *ante*, at 695-696. As amended by RLUIPA, RFRA's definition now includes "any exercise of religion, whether or not compelled by, or central to, a system of religious belief." §2000bb-2(4) (2012 ed.) (cross-referencing § 2000cc-5). That definitional change, according to the Court, reflects "an obvious effort to effect a complete separation from First Amendment case law." *Ante*, at 696.

The Court's reading is not plausible. RLUIPA's alteration clarifies that courts should not question the centrality of a particular religious exercise. But the amendment in no way suggests that Congress meant to expand the class of entities qualified to mount religious accommodation claims, nor does it relieve courts of the obligation to inquire whether a government action substantially burdens a religious exercise. See *Rasul v. Myers*, 563 F. 3d 527, 535 (CADC 2009) (Brown, J., concurring) ("There is no doubt that RLUIPA's drafters, in changing the definition of 'exercise of religion,' wanted to broaden the scope of the kinds of practices protected by RFRA, not increase the universe of individuals protected by RFRA."); H. R. Rep. No. 106-219, p. 30 (1999). See also *Gilardi v. United States Dept, of Health and Human Servs.*, 733 F. 3d 1208, 1211 (CADC 2013) (RFRA, as amended, "provides us with no helpful definition of 'exercise of religion.' "); *Henderson v. Kennedy*, 265 F. 3d 1072, 1073 (CADC 2001) ("The [RLUIPA] amendments did not alter RFRA's basic prohibition that the '[government shall not substantially burden a person's exercise of religion.' ").[10]

Next, the Court highlights RFRA's requirement that the government, if its action substantially burdens a person's religious observance, must demonstrate that it chose the least restrictive means for furthering a compelling interest. "[B]y imposing a least-restrictive-means test," the Court suggests, RFRA "went beyond what was required by our pre-*Smith* decisions." *Ante*, at 706, n. 18 (citing *City of Boerne v. Flores*, 521 U.S. 507 (1997)). See also *ante*, at 695, n. 3. But as RFRA's statements of purpose and legislative history make clear, Congress intended only to restore, not to scrap or alter, the balancing test as this Court had applied it pre-*Smith*. See *supra*, at 746-747. See also Senate Report 9 (RFRA's "compelling interest test generally should not be construed more stringently or more leniently than it was prior to *Smith*.'")', House Report 7 (same).

The Congress that passed RFRA correctly read this Court's pre-*Smith* case law as including within the "compelling interest test" a "least restrictive means" requirement. *See, e.g.,* Senate Report 5 ("Where [a substantial] burden is placed upon the free exercise of religion, the Court ruled [in *Sherbert*], the

Government must demonstrate that it is the least restrictive means to achieve a compelling governmental interest."). And the view that the pre-*Smith* test included a "least restrictive means" requirement had been aired in testimony before the Senate Judiciary Committee by experts on religious freedom. *See, e.g.,* Hearing on S. 2969 before the Senate Committee on the Judiciary, 102d Cong., 2d Sess., 78-79 (1993) (statement of Prof. Douglas Laycock).

Our decision in *City of Boerne*, it is true, states that the least restrictive means requirement "was not used in the pr e-*Smith* jurisprudence RFRA purported to codify." See *ante*, at 695, n. 3, 706, n. 18. As just indicated, however, that statement does not accurately convey the Court's pre-

Smith jurisprudence. See *Sherbert v. Verner*, 374 U.S. 398, 407 (1963) ("[I]t would plainly be incumbent upon the [government] to demonstrate that no alternative forms of regulation would combat [the problem] without infringing First Amendment rights."); *Thomas v. Review Bd. of Ind. Employment Security Div.*, 450 U.S. 707, 718 (1981) ("The state may justify an inroad on religious liberty by showing that it is the least restrictive means of achieving some compelling state interest."). See also Berg, The New Attacks on Religious Freedom Legislation and Why They Are Wrong, 21 Cardozo L. Rev. 415, 424 (1999) ("In Boerne, the Court erroneously said that the least restrictive means test 'was not used in the pre-*Smith* jurisprudence.'").[11]

C

With RFRA's restorative purpose in mind, I turn to the Act's application to the instant lawsuits. That task, in view of the positions taken by the Court, requires consideration of several questions, each potentially dispositive of Hobby Lobby's and Conestoga's claims: Do for-profit corporations rank among "person[s]" who "exercise . . . religion"? Assuming that they do, does the contraceptive coverage requirement "substantially burden" their religious exercise? If so, is the requirement "in furtherance of a compelling government interest"? And last, does the requirement represent the least restrictive means for furthering that interest?

Misguided by its errant premise that RFRA moved beyond the pre-*Smith* case law, the Court falters at each step of its analysis.

1

RFRA's compelling interest test, as noted, see *supra*, at 746, applies to government actions that "substantially burden *a person's exercise of religion*." 42 U.S.C. §2000bb- 1(a) (emphasis added). This reference, the Court submits, incorporates the definition of "person" found in the Dictionary Act, 1 U.S.C. § 1, which extends to "corporations, companies, associations, firms, partnerships, societies, and joint stock companies, as well as individuals." See *ante*, at 707- 709. The Dictionary Act's definition, however, controls only where "context" does not "indicat[e] otherwise." §1. Here, context does so indicate. RFRA speaks of "a person's *exercise of religion.*" 42 U.S.C. §2000bb-l(a) (emphasis added). See also §§2000bb-2(4), 2000cc-5(7)(a).[12] Whether a corporation qualifies as a "person" capable of exercising religion is an inquiry one cannot answer without reference to the "full body" of pre-*Smith* "free-exercise caselaw." *Gilardi*, 733 F. 3d, at 1212. There is in that case law no support for the notion that free exercise rights pertain to for- profit corporations.

Until this litigation, no decision of this Court recognized a for-profit corporation's qualification for a religious exemption from a generally applicable law, whether under the Free Exercise Clause or RFRA.[13] The absence of such precedent is just what one would expect, for the exercise of religion is characteristic of natural persons, not artificial legal entities. As Chief Justice Marshall observed nearly two centuries ago, a corporation is "an artificial being, invisible, intangible, and existing only in contemplation of law." *Trustees of Dartmouth College v. Woodward*, 4 Wheat. 518, 636 (1819). Corporations, Justice Stevens more recently reminded, "have no consciences, no beliefs, no feelings, no thoughts, no desires." *Citizens United v. Federal Election Common*, 558 U.S. 310, 466 (2010) (opinion concurring in part and dissenting in part).

The First Amendment's free exercise protections, the Court has indeed recognized, shelter churches and other nonprofit religion-based organizations.[14] "For many individuals, religious activity derives meaning in large measure from participation in a larger religious community," and "furtherance of the autonomy of religious organizations often furthers individual religious freedom as well." *Corporation of Presiding Bishop of Church of Jesus Christ of Latter-day Saints v. Amos*, 483 U.S. 327, 342 (1987) (Brennan, J., concurring in judgment). The Court's "special solicitude to the rights of religious organizations," *Hosanna-Tabor Evangelical Lutheran Church and School v. EEOC*, 565 U.S. 171,189 (2012), however, is just that. No such solicitude is traditional for commercial organizations.[15] Indeed, until today, religious exemptions had never been extended to any entity operating in "the commercial, profit-making world." *Amos*, 483 U.S., at 337.[16]

The reason why is hardly obscure. Religious organizations exist to foster the interests of persons subscribing to the same religious faith. Not so of for-profit corporations. Workers who sustain the operations of those corporations commonly are not drawn from one religious community. Indeed, by law, no religion-based criterion can restrict the work force of for-profit corporations. See 42 U.S.C. §§2000e(b), 2000e-l(a), 2000e-2(a); *cf. Trans World Airlines, Inc. v. Hardison*, 432 U.S. 63, 80-81 (1977) (Title VII requires reasonable accommodation of an employee's religious exercise, but such accommodation must not come "at the expense of othe[r] [employees]"). The distinction between a community made up of believers in the same religion and one embracing persons of diverse beliefs, clear as it is, constantly escapes the Court's attention.[17] One can only wonder why the Court shuts this key difference from sight.

Reading RFRA, as the Court does, to require extension of religion-based exemptions to for-profit corporations surely is not grounded in the pr e-*Smith* precedent Congress sought to preserve. Had Congress intended RFRA to initiate a change so huge, a clarion statement to that effect likely would have been made in the legislation. See *Whitman v. American Trucking Assns.*, Inc., 531 U.S. 457, 468 (2001) (Congress does not "hide elephants in mouseholes"). The text of RFRA makes no such statement and the legislative history does not so much as mention for-profit corporations. See *Hobby Lobby Stores, Inc. v. Sebelius*, 723 F. 3d 1114, 1169 (CA10 2013) (Briscoe, C. J., concurring in part and dissenting in part) (legislative record lacks "any suggestion that Congress foresaw, let alone intended, that RFRA would cover for-profit corporations"). See also Senators Brief 10-13 (none of the cases cited in House or Senate Judiciary Committee Reports accompanying RFRA, or mentioned during floor speeches, recognized the free exercise rights of for-profit corporations).

The Court notes that for-profit corporations may support charitable causes and use their funds for religious ends, and therefore questions the distinction between such corporations and religious nonprofit organizations. See *ante*, at 709-713. See also *ante*, at 738 (Kennedy, J., concurring) (criticizing the Government for "distinguishing between different religious believers—burdening one while accommodating the other—when it may treat both equally by offering both of them the same accommodation").[18] Again, the Court forgets that religious organizations exist to serve a community of believers. For-profit corporations do not fit that bill. Moreover, history is not on the Court's side. Recognition of the discrete characters of "ecclesiastical and lay" corporations dates back to Blackstone, see 1 W. Blackstone, Commentaries on the Laws of England 458 (1765), and was reiterated by this Court centuries before the enactment of the Internal Revenue Code, see *Terrett v. Taylor*, 9 Cranch 43, 49 (1815) (describing religious corporations); *Trustees of Dartmouth College*, 4 Wheat., at 645 (discussing "eleemosynary" corporations, including those "created for the promotion of religion"). To reiterate, "for-profit corporations are different from religious non-profits in that they use labor to make a profit, rather than to perpetuate [the] religious valued] [shared by a community of believers]." *Gilardi*, 733 F. 3d, at 1242 (Edwards, J., concurring in part and dissenting in part) (emphasis deleted).

Citing *Braunfeld v. Brown*, 366 U.S. 599 (1961), the Court questions why, if "a sole proprietorship that seeks to make a profit may assert a free-exercise claim, [Hobby Lobby and Conestoga] can't . . . do the same?" *Ante*, at 710 (footnote omitted). See also *ante*, at 705-706. But even accepting, *arguendo*, the premise that unincorporated business enterprises may gain religious accommodations under the Free Exercise Clause, the Court's conclusion is unsound. In a sole proprietorship, the business and its owner are one and the same. By incorporating a business, however, an individual separates herself from the entity and escapes personal responsibility for the entity's obligations. One might ask why the separation should hold only when it serves the interest of those who control the corporation. In any event, Braunfeld is hardly impressive authority for the entitlement Hobby Lobby and Conestoga seek. The free exercise claim asserted there was promptly rejected on the merits.

The Court's determination that RFRA extends to for- profit corporations is bound to have untoward effects. Although the Court attempts to cabin its language to closely held corporations, its logic extends to corporations of any size, public or private.[19] Little doubt that RFRA claims will proliferate, for the Court's expansive notion of corporate personhood—combined with its other errors in construing RFRA—invites for-profit entities to seek religion-based exemptions from regulations they deem offensive to their faith.

2

Even if Hobby Lobby and Conestoga were deemed RFRA "person[s]," to gain an exemption, they must demonstrate that the contraceptive coverage requirement "substantially burden[s] [their] exercise of religion." 42 U.S.C. §2000bb- 1(a). Congress no doubt meant the modifier "substantially" to carry weight. In the original draft of RFRA, the word "burden" appeared unmodified. The word "substantially" was inserted pursuant to a clarifying amendment offered by Senators Kennedy and Hatch. See 139 Cong. Rec. 26180. In proposing the amendment, Senator Kennedy stated that RFRA, in accord with the Court's pre-*Smith* case law, "does not require the Government to justify every action that has some effect on religious exercise." *Ibid.*

The Court barely pauses to inquire whether any burden imposed by the contraceptive coverage requirement is substantial. Instead, it rests on the Greens' and Hahns' "belie[f] that providing the coverage demanded by the HHS regulations is connected to the destruction of an embryo in a way that is sufficient to make it immoral for them to provide the coverage." *Ante*, at 724.[20] I agree with the Court that the Green and Hahn families' religious convictions regarding contraception are sincerely held. See *Thomas*, 450 U.S., at 715 (courts are not to question where an individual "dr[aws] the line" in defining which practices run afoul of her religious beliefs). See also 42 U.S.C. §§2000bb-l(a), 2000bb-2(4), 2000cc-5(7)(A).[21] But those beliefs, however deeply held, do not suffice to sustain a RFRA claim. RFRA, properly understood, distinguishes between "factual allegations that [plaintiffs'] beliefs are sincere and of a religious nature," which a court must accept as true, and the "legal conclusion . . .

that [plaintiffs'] religious exercise is substantially burdened," an inquiry the court must undertake. *Kaemmerling v. Lappin*, 553 F. 3d 669, 679 (CADC 2008).

That distinction is a facet of the pre-*Smith* jurisprudence RFRA incorporates. *Bowen v. Roy*, 476 U.S. 693 (1986), is instructive. There, the Court rejected a free exercise challenge to the Government's use of a Native American child's Social Security number for purposes of administering benefit programs. Without questioning the sincerity of the father's religious belief that "use of [his daughter's Social Security] number may harm [her] spirit," the Court concluded that the Government's internal uses of that number "place[d] [no] restriction on what [the father] may believe or what he may do." *Id.*, at 699. Recognizing that the father's "religious views may not accept" the position that the challenged uses concerned only the Government's internal affairs, the Court explained that "for the adjudication of a constitutional claim, the Constitution, rather than an individual's religion, must supply the frame of reference." *Id.*, at 700-701, n. 6. See also *Hernandez v. Commissioner*, 490 U.S. 680, 699 (1989) (distinguishing between, on the one hand, "question[s] [of] the centrality of particular beliefs or practices to a faith, or the validity of particular litigants' interpretations of those creeds," and, on the other, "whether the alleged burden imposed [by the challenged government action] is a substantial one"). Inattentive to this guidance, today's decision elides entirely the distinction between the sincerity of a challenger's religious belief and the substantiality of the burden placed on the challenger.

Undertaking the inquiry that the Court forgoes, I would conclude that the connection between the families' religious objections and the contraceptive coverage requirement is too attenuated to rank as substantial. The requirement carries no command that Hobby Lobby or Conestoga purchase or provide the contraceptives they And objectionable. Instead, it calls on the companies covered by the requirement to direct money into undifferentiated funds that finance a wide variety of benefits under comprehensive health plans. Those plans, in order to comply with the ACA, see *supra*, at 741-744, must offer contraceptive coverage without cost sharing, just as they must cover an array of other preventive services.

Importantly, the decisions whether to claim benefits under the plans are made not by Hobby Lobby or Conestoga, but by the covered employees and dependents, in consultation with their health care providers. Should an employee of Hobby Lobby or Conestoga share the religious beliefs of the Greens and Hahns, she is of course under no compulsion to use the contraceptives in question. But "[n]o individual decision by an employee and her physician—be it to use contraception, treat an infection, or have a hip replaced—is in any meaningful sense [her employer's] decision or action." *Grote v. Sebelius*, 708 F. 3d 850, 865 (CA7 2013) (Rovner, J., dissenting). It is doubtful that Congress, when it specified that burdens must be "substantia[l]," had in mind a linkage thus interrupted by independent decisionmakers (the woman and her health counselor) standing between the challenged government action and the religious exercise claimed to be infringed. Any decision to use contraceptives made by a woman covered under Hobby Lobby's or Conestoga's plan will not be propelled by the Government, it will be the woman's autonomous choice, informed by the physician she consults.

3

Even if one were to conclude that Hobby Lobby and Conestoga meet the substantial burden requirement, the Government has shown that the contraceptive coverage for which the ACA provides furthers compelling interests in public health and women's well-being. Those interests are concrete, specific, and demonstrated by a wealth of empirical evidence. To recapitulate, the mandated contraception coverage enables women to avoid the health problems unintended pregnancies may visit on them and their children. See IOM Report 102-107. The coverage helps safeguard the health of women for whom pregnancy may be hazardous, even life threatening. See Brief for American College of Obstetricians and Gynecologists et al. as *Amici curiae* 14-15. And the mandate secures benefits wholly unrelated to pregnancy, preventing certain cancers, menstrual disorders, and pelvic pain. Brief for Ovarian Cancer National Alliance et al. as *Amici curiae* 4, 6-7, 15-16; 78 Fed. Reg. 39872 (2013); IOM Report 107.

That Hobby Lobby and Conestoga resist coverage for only 4 of the 20 FDA-approved contraceptives does not lessen these compelling interests. Notably, the corporations exclude intrauterine devices (IUDs), devices significantly more effective and significantly more expensive than other contraceptive methods. See *id.*, at 105.[22] Moreover, the Court's reasoning appears to permit commercial enterprises like Hobby Lobby and Conestoga to exclude from their group health plans all forms of contraceptives. See Tr. of Oral Arg. 38-39 (counsel for Hobby Lobby acknowledged that his "argument . . . would apply just as well if the employer said 'no contraceptives'" (internal quotation marks added)).

Perhaps the gravity of the interests at stake has led the Court to assume, for purposes of its RFRA analysis, that the compelling interest criterion is met in these cases. See *ante*, at 728.[23] It bears note in this regard that the cost of an IUD is nearly equivalent to a month's full-time pay for workers earning the minimum wage, Brief for Guttmacher Institute et al. as *Amici curiae* 16; that almost one-third of women would change their contraceptive method if costs were not a factor, Frost & Darroch, Factors Associated With Contraceptive Choice and Inconsistent Method Use, United States, 2004, 40 Perspectives on Sexual & Reproductive Health 94, 98 (2008); and that only one-fourth of women who request an IUD actually have one inserted after finding out how expensive it would be, Gariepy, Simon, Patel, Creinin, & Schwarz, The Impact of Out-of-Pocket Expense on IUD Utilization Among Women With Private Insurance, 84 Contraception e39, e40 (2011). See also Eisenberg, McNicholas, & Peipert, Cost as a Barrier to Long-Acting Reversible Contraceptive (LARC) Use in Adolescents, 52 J. Adolescent Health S60 (2013) (recent study found that women who face out-of-pocket IUD costs in excess of $50 were "11-times less likely to obtain an IUD than women who had to pay less than $50"); Postleth-waite, Trussed, Zoolakis, Shabear, & Petitti, A Comparison of Contraceptive Procurement Pre- and Post-Benefit Change, 76 Contraception 360, 361-362 (2007) (when one health system eliminated patient cost sharing for IUDs, use of this form of contraception more than doubled).

Stepping back from its assumption that compelling interests support the contraceptive coverage requirement, the Court notes that small employers and grandfathered plans are not subject to the requirement. If there is a compelling interest in contraceptive coverage, the Court suggests, Congress would not have created these exclusions. See *ante,* at 726-728.

Federal statutes often include exemptions for small employers, and such provisions have never been held to undermine the interests served by these statutes. *See, e.g.,* Family and Medical Leave Act of 1993, 29 U.S.C. §2611(4)(A) (i) (applicable to employers with 50 or more employees); Age Discrimination in Employment Act of 1967, 29 U.S.C. § 630(b) (originally exempting employers with fewer than 50 employees, 81 Stat. 605, the statute now governs employers with 20 or more employees); Americans With Disabilities Act of 1990, 42 U.S.C. § 12111(5)(A) (applicable to employers with 15 or more employees); Title VII, 42 U.S.C. § 2000e(b) (originally exempting employers with fewer than 25 employees, see *Arbaugh v. Y & H Corp.,* 546 U.S. 500, 505, n. 2 (2006), the statute now governs employers with 15 or more employees).

The ACA's grandfathering provision, 42 U.S.C. § 18011, allows a phasing-in period for compliance with a number of the ACA's requirements (not just the contraceptive coverage or other preventive services provisions). Once specified changes are made, grandfathered status ceases. See 45 CFR § 147.140(g). Hobby Lobby's own situation is illustrative. By the time this litigation commenced, Hobby Lobby did not have grandfathered status. Asked why by the District Court, Hobby Lobby's counsel explained that the "grandfathering require-ments mean that you can't make a whole menu of changes to your plan that involve things like the amount of co-pays, the amount of co-insurance, deductibles, that sort of thing." App. in No. 13-354, pp. 39-40. Counsel acknowledged that, "just because of economic realities, our plan has to shift over time. I mean, insurance plans, as everyone knows, shif[t] over time." at 40.[24] The percentage of employees in grandfathered plans is steadily declining, having dropped from 56% in 2011 to 48% in 2012 to 36% in 2013. Kaiser Family

Foundation & Health Research & Educ. Trust, Employer Benefits 2013 Annual Survey 7, 196. In short, far from ranking as a categorical exemption, the grandfathering provision is "temporary, intended to be a means for gradually transitioning employers into mandatory coverage." *Gilardi*, 733 F. 3d, at 1241 (Edwards, J., concurring in part and dissenting in part).

The Court ultimately acknowledges a critical point: RFRA's application "must take adequate account of the burdens a requested accommodation may impose on non-beneficiaries." *Ante*, at 729, n. 37 (quoting *Cutter v. Wilkinson*, 544 U.S. 709, 720 (2005); emphasis added). No tradition, and no prior decision under RFRA, allows a religion-based exemption when the accommodation would be harmful to others— here, the very persons the contraceptive coverage requirement was designed to protect. *Cf. supra*, at 745-746; *Prince v. Massachusetts*, 321 U.S. 158, 177 (1944) (Jackson, J., dissenting) ("[The] limitations which of necessity bound religious freedom . . . begin to operate whenever activities begin to affect or collide with liberties of others or of the public.").

4

After assuming the existence of compelling government interests, the Court holds that the contraceptive coverage requirement fails to satisfy RFRA's least restrictive means test. But the Government has shown that there is no less restrictive, equally effective means that would both (1) satisfy the challengers' religious objections to providing insurance coverage for certain contraceptives (which they believe cause abortions); and (2) carry out the objective of the ACA's contraceptive coverage requirement, to ensure that women employees receive, at no cost to them, the preventive care needed to safeguard their health and well-being. A "least restrictive means" cannot require employees to relinquish benefits accorded them by federal law in order to ensure that their commercial employers can adhere unreservedly to their religious tenets. See *supra*, at 745-746, 764.[25]

Then let the government pay (rather than the employees who do not share their employer's faith), the Court suggests. "The most straightforward [alternative]," the Court asserts, "would be for the Government to assume the cost of providing . . . contraceptives . . . to any women who are unable to obtain them under their health-insurance policies due to their employers' religious objections." *Ante*, at 728. The ACA, however, requires coverage of preventive services through the existing employer-based system of health insurance "so that [employees] face minimal logistical and administrative obstacles." 78 Fed. Reg. 39888. Impeding women's receipt of benefits "by requiring them to take steps to learn about, and to sign up for, a new [government funded and administered] health benefit" was scarcely what Congress contemplated. *Ibid*. Moreover, Title X of the Public Health Service Act, 42 U.S.C. §300 et seq., "is the nation's only dedicated source of federal funding for safety net family planning services." Brief for National Health Law Program et al. as *Amici curiae* 23. "Safety net programs like Title X are not designed to absorb the unmet needs of. . . insured individuals." *Id.*, at 24. Note, too, that Congress declined to write into law the preferential treatment Hobby Lobby and Conestoga describe as a less restrictive alternative. See *supra*, at 744.

And where is the stopping point to the "let the government pay" alternative? Suppose an employer's sincerely held religious belief is offended by health coverage of vaccines, or paying the minimum wage, see *Tony and Susan Alamo Foundation v. Secretary of Labor*, 471 U.S. 290, 303 (1985), or according women equal pay for substantially similar work, see *Dole v. Shenandoah Baptist Church*, 899 F. 2d 1389, 1392 (CA4 1990)? Does it rank as a less restrictive alternative to require the government to provide the money or benefit to which the employer has a religion-based objection?[26] Because the Court cannot easily answer that question, it proposes something else: extension to commercial enterprises of the accommodation already afforded to nonprofit religion-based organizations. See *ante*, at 692-693, 698-699, 730-732. "At a minimum," according to the Court, such an approach would not "impinge on [Hobby Lobby's and Conestoga's] religious belief." *Ante*, at 731. I have already discussed the "special solicitude" generally accorded nonprofit religion-based organizations that exist to serve a community of believers, solicitude never before accorded to commercial enterprises comprising employees of diverse faiths. See *supra*, at 752-755.

Ultimately, the Court hedges on its proposal to align for- profit enterprises with nonprofit religion-based organizations. "We do not decide today whether [the] approach [the opinion advances] complies with RFRA for purposes of all religious claims." *Ante*, at 731. Counsel for Hobby Lobby was similarly noncommittal. Asked at oral argument whether the Court-proposed alternative was acceptable,[27] counsel responded: "We haven't been offered that accommodation, so we haven't had to decide what kind of objection, if any, we would make to that." Tr. of Oral Arg. 86-87.

Conestoga suggests that, if its employees had to acquire and pay for the contraceptives (to which the corporation objects) on their own, a tax credit would qualify as a less restrictive alternative. See Brief for Petitioners in No. 13- 356, p. 64. A tax credit, of course, is one variety of "let the government pay." In addition to departing from the existing employer-based system of health insurance, Conestoga's alternative would require a woman to reach into her own pocket in the first instance, and it would do nothing for the woman too poor to be aided by a tax credit.

In sum, in view of what Congress sought to accomplish, *i.e.*, comprehensive preventive care for women furnished through employer-based health plans, none of the proffered alternatives would satisfactorily serve the compelling interests to which Congress responded.

IV

Among the pathmarking pre-*Smith* decisions RFRA preserved is *United States v. Lee*, 455 U.S. 252 (1982). Lee, a sole proprietor engaged in farming and carpentry, was a member of the Old Order Amish. He sincerely believed that withholding Social Security taxes from his employees or paying the employer's share of such taxes would violate the Amish faith. This Court held that, although the obligations imposed by the Social Security system conflicted with Lee's religious beliefs, the burden was not unconstitutional. *Id.*, at 260-261. See also *id.*, at 258 (recognizing the important governmental interest in providing a "nationwide . . . comprehensive insurance system with a variety of benefits available to all participants, with costs shared by employers and employees").[28] The Government urges that Lee should control the challenges brought by Hobby Lobby and Conestoga. See Brief for Respondents in No. 13-356, p. 18. In contrast, today's Court dismisses Lee as a tax case. See *ante*, at 733- 734. Indeed, it was a tax case and the Court in Lee homed in on "[t]he difficulty in attempting to accommodate religious beliefs in the area of taxation." 455 U.S., at 259.

But the Lee Court made two key points one cannot confine to tax cases. "When followers of a particular sect enter into commercial activity as a matter of choice," the Court observed, "the limits they accept on their own conduct as a matter of conscience and faith are not to be superimposed on statutory schemes which are binding on others in that activity." *Id.*, at 261. The statutory scheme of employer-based comprehensive health coverage involved in these cases is surely binding on others engaged in the same trade or business as the corporate challengers here, Hobby Lobby and Conestoga. Further, the Court recognized in that allowing a religion-based exemption to a commercial employer would "operat[e] to impose the employer's religious faith on the employees." *Ibid.*[29] No doubt the Greens and Hahns and all who share their beliefs may decline to acquire for themselves the contraceptives in question. But that choice may not be imposed on employees who hold other beliefs. Working for Hobby Lobby or Conestoga, in other words, should not deprive employees of the preventive care available to workers at the shop next door,[30] at least in the absence of directions from the Legislature or Administration to do so.

Why should decisions of this order be made by Congress or the regulatory authority, and not this Court? Hobby Lobby and Conestoga surely do not stand alone as commercial enterprises seeking exemptions from generally applicable laws on the basis of their religious beliefs. See, *e.g., Newman v. Piggie*

Park Enterprises, Inc., 256 F. Supp. 941, 945 (SC 1966) (owner of restaurant chain refused to serve black patrons based on his religious beliefs opposing racial integration), aff'd in relevant part and rev'd in part on other grounds, 377 F. 2d 433 (CA4 1967), aff'd and modified on other grounds, 390 U.S. 400 (1968); *In re State ex rel. McClure*, 370 N. W. 2d 844, 847 (Minn. 1985) (born-again Christians who owned closely held, for-profit health clubs believed that the Bible proscribed hiring or retaining an "individua[l] living with but not married to a person of the opposite sex," "a young, single woman working without her father's consent or a married woman working without her husband's consent," and any person "antagonistic to the Bible," including "fornicators and homo-sexuals" (internal quotation marks omitted)), appeal dism'd, 478 U.S. 1015 (1986); *Elane Photography, LLC v. Willock*, 2013-NMSC-040, 309 P. 3d 53 (for-profit photography business owned by a husband and wife refused to photo-graph a lesbian couple's commitment ceremony based on the religious beliefs of the company's owners), cert, denied, 572 U.S. 1046 (2014). Would RFRA require exemptions in cases of this ilk? And if not, how does the Court divine which religious beliefs are worthy of accommodation, and which are not? Isn't the Court disarmed from making such a judgment given its recognition that "courts must not presume to determine . . . the plausibility of a religious claim"? *Ante*, at 724.

Would the exemption the Court holds RFRA demands for employers with religiously grounded objections to the use of certain contraceptives extend to employers with religiously grounded objections to blood transfusions (Jeho-vah's Witnesses); antidepressants (Scientologists); medications derived from pigs, including anesthesia, intravenous fluids, and pills coated with gelatin (certain Muslims, Jews, and Hindus); and vaccinations (Christian Scientists, among others)?[31] According to counsel for Hobby Lobby, "each one of these cases . . . would have to be evaluated on its own . . . applying] the compelling interest-least restrictive alternative test." Tr. of Oral Arg. 6. Not much help there for the lower courts bound by today's decision.

The Court, however, sees nothing to worry about. Today's cases, the Court concludes, are "concerned solely with the contraceptive mandate. Our decision should not be understood to hold that an insurance-coverage mandate must necessarily fall if it conflicts with an employer's religious beliefs. Other coverage requirements, such as immunizations, may be supported by different interests (for example, the need to combat the spread of infectious diseases) and may involve different arguments about the least restrictive means of providing them." *Ante*, at 733. But the Court has assumed, for RFRA purposes, that the interest in women's health and well-being is compelling and has come up with no means adequate to serve that interest, the one motivating Congress to adopt the Women's Health Amendment.

There is an overriding interest, I believe, in keeping the courts "out of the business of evaluating the relative merits of differing religious claims," Lee, 455 U.S., at 263, n. 2 (Stevens, J., concurring in judgment), or the sincerity with which an asserted religious belief is held. Indeed, approving some religious claims while deeming others unworthy of accommodation could be "perceived as favoring one religion over another," the very "risk the Establishment Clause was designed to preclude." *Ibid.* The Court, I fear, has ventured into a minefield, *cf. Spencer v. World Vision, Inc.,* 633 F. 3d 723, 730 (CA9 2011) (O'Scannlain, J., concurring), by its immoderate reading of RFRA. I would confine religious exemptions under that Act to organizations formed "for a religious purpose," "engage[d] primarily in carrying out that religious purpose," and not "engaged . . . substantially in the exchange of goods or services for money beyond nominal amounts." See *id.,* at 748 (Kleinfeld, J., concurring).

* * *

For the reasons stated, I would reverse the judgment of the Court of Appeals for the Tenth Circuit and affirm the judgment of the Court of Appeals for the Third Circuit.

---

1. The Court insists it has held none of these things, for another less restrictive alternative is at hand: extending an existing accommodation, currently limited to religious nonprofit organizations, to encompass commercial enterprises. See *ante,* at 692-693. With that accommodation extended, the Court asserts, "women would still be entitled to all [Food and Drug Administration]-approved contraceptives without cost sharing." *Ante,* at 693. In the end, however, the Court is not so sure. In stark contrast to the Court's initial emphasis on this accommodation, it ultimately declines to decide whether the highlighted accommodation is even lawful. See *ante,* at 731 ("We do not decide today whether an approach of this type complies with RFRA . . . .").
2. See 42 U.S.C. § 300gg-13(a)(1)-(3) (group health plans must provide coverage, without cost sharing, for (1) certain "evidence-based items or services" recommended by the U.S. Preventive Services Task Force; (2) immunizations recommended by an advisory committee of the Centers for Disease Control and Prevention; and (3) "with respect to infants, children, and adolescents, evidence-informed preventive care and screenings provided for in the comprehensive guidelines supported by the Health Resources and Services Administration").
3. The IOM is an arm of the National Academy of Sciences, an organization Congress established "for the explicit purpose of furnishing advice to the Government." *Public Citizen v. Department of Justice,* 491 U.S. 440, 460, n. 11 (1989) (internal quotation marks omitted).
4. HRSA, HHS, Women's Preventive Services Guidelines, available at http://www.hrsa.gov/womensguidelines/ (all Internet materials as visited June 27,2014, and available in Clerk of Court's case file), reprinted in App. to Brief for Petitioners in No. 13-354, pp. 43a-44a. See also 77 Fed. Reg. 8725-8726 (2012).
5. 45 CFR § 147.130(a)(1)(iv) (2013) (HHS); 29 CFR § 2590.715-2713(a) (1)(iv) (2013) (Labor); 26 CFR § 54.9815-2713(a)(1)(iv) (2013) (Treasury).
6. Separating moral convictions from religious beliefs would be of questionable legitimacy. See *Welsh v. United States,* 398 U.S. 333, 357-358 (1970) (Harlan, J., concurring in result).
7. As the Court explains, see *ante,* at 700-705, these cases arise from two separate lawsuits, one filed by Hobby Lobby, its affiliated business (Mardel), and the family that operates these businesses (the Greens); the other filed by Conestoga and the family that owns and controls that business (the Hahns). Unless otherwise specified, this opinion refers to the respective groups of plaintiffs as Hobby Lobby and Conestoga.

8. See *Wisconsin v. Yoder*, 406 U.S. 205, 230 (1972) ("This case, of course, is not one in which any harm to the physical or mental health of the child or to the public safety, peace, order, or welfare has been demonstrated or may be properly inferred."); *Estate of Thornton v. Caldor, Inc.*, 472 U.S. 703 (1985) (invalidating state statute requiring employers to accommodate an employee's Sabbath observance where that statute failed to take into account the burden such an accommodation would impose on the employer or other employees). Notably, in construing the Religious Land Use and Institutionalized Persons Act of 2000 (RLUIPA), 42 U.S.C. § 2000cc et seq., the Court has cautioned that "adequate account" must be taken of "the burdens a requested accommodation may impose on nonbeneficiaries." *Cutter v. Wilkinson*, 544 U.S. 709, 720 (2005); see *id.*, at 722 ("an accommodation must be measured so that it does not override other significant interests"). A balanced approach is all the more in order when the Free Exercise Clause itself is at stake, not a statute designed to promote accommodation to religious beliefs and practices.

9. Under *Sherbert* and *Yoder*, the Court "requir[ed] the government to justify any substantial burden on religiously motivated conduct by a compelling state interest and by means narrowly tailored to achieve that interest." *Employment Div., Dept of Human Resources of Ore. v. Smith*, 494 U.S. 872, 894 (1990) (O'Connor, J., concurring in judgment).

10. RLUIPA, the Court notes, includes a provision directing that "[t]his chapter [*i.e.*, RLUIPA] shall be construed in favor of a broad protection of religious exercise, to the maximum extent permitted by the terms of [the Act] and the Constitution." 42 U.S.C. § 2000cc-3(g); see *ante*, at 695-696, 714. RFRA incorporates RLUIPA's definition of "exercise of religion," as RLUIPA does, but contains no omnibus rule of construction governing the statute in its entirety.

11. The Court points out that I joined the majority opinion in *City of Boerne* and did not then question the statement that "least restrictive means . . . was not used [pre-*Smith*]." *Ante*, at 706, n. 18. Concerning that observation, I remind my colleagues of Justice Jackson's sage comment: "I see no reason why I should be consciously wrong today because I was unconsciously wrong yesterday." *Massachusetts v. United States*, 333 U.S. 611, 639-640 (1948) (dissenting opinion).

12. As earlier explained, see *supra*, at 748, RLUIPA's amendment of the definition of "exercise of religion" does not bear the weight the Court places on it. Moreover, it is passing strange to attribute to RLUIPA any purpose to cover entities other than "religious assembl[ies] or institution[s]." 42 U.S.C. § 2000cc(a)(1). But *cf. ante*, at 714. That law applies to land-use regulation. §2000cc(a)(1). To permit commercial enterprises to challenge zoning and other land-use regulations under RLUIPA would "dramatically expand the statute's reach" and deeply intrude on local prerogatives, contrary to Congress' intent. Brief for National League of Cities et al. as *Amici Curiae* 26.

13. The Court regards *Gallagher v. Crown Kosher Super Market of Mass., Inc.*, 366 U.S. 617 (1961), as "suggest[ing] . . . that for-profit corporations possess [free-exercise] rights." *Ante*, at 714. See also *ante*, at 709, n. 21. The suggestion is barely there. True, one of the five challengers to the Sunday closing law assailed in Gallagher was a corporation owned by four Orthodox Jews. The other challengers were human individuals, not artificial, law-created entities, so there was no need to determine whether the corporation could institute the litigation. Accordingly, the plurality stated it could pretermit the question "whether appellees ha[d] standing" because *Braunfeld v. Brown*, 366 U.S. 599 (1961), which upheld a similar closing law, was fatal to their claim on the merits. Id, at 631.

14. *See, e.g., Hosanna-Tabor Evangelical Lutheran Church and School v. EEOC*, 565 U.S. 171 (2012); *Gonzales v. O Centro Espirita Beneficente União do Vegetal*, 546 U.S. 418 (2006); Church of *Lukumi Babalu Aye, Inc. v. Hialeah*, 508 U.S. 520 (1993); *Jimmy Swaggart Ministries v. Board of Equalization of Cal.*, 493 U.S. 378 (1990).

15. Typically, Congress has accorded to organizations religious in character religion-based exemptions from statutes of general application. *E.g.*, 42 U.S.C. § 2000e-1(a) (Title VII exemption from prohibition against employment discrimination based on religion for "a religious corporation, association, educational institution, or society with respect to the employment of individuals of a particular religion to perform work connected with the carrying on . . . of its activities"); 42 U.S.C. § 12113(d)(1) (parallel exemption in Americans With Disabilities Act of 1990). It can scarcely be maintained that RFRA enlarges these exemptions to allow Hobby Lobby and Conestoga to hire only persons who share the religious beliefs of the Greens or Hahns. Nor does the Court suggest otherwise. *Cf. ante*, at 716-717.

The Court does identify two statutory exemptions it reads to cover for-profit corporations, 42 U.S.C. §§ 300a-7(b)(2) and 238n(a), and infers from them that "Congress speaks with specificity when it intends a religious accommodation not to extend to for-profit corporations," *ante*, at 717. The Court's inference is unwarranted. The exemptions the Court cites cover certain medical personnel who object to performing or assisting with abortions. *Cf. ante*, at 716, n. 27 ("the protection provided by §238n(a) differs significantly from the protection provided by RFRA"). Notably, the Court does not assert that these exemptions have in fact been afforded to for-profit corporations. See §238n(c) ("health care entity" covered by exemption is a term defined to include "an individual physician, a postgraduate physician training program, and a participant in a program of training in the health professions"); Tozzi, Whither Free Exercise: *Employment Division v. Smith* and the Rebirth of State Constitutional Free Exercise Clause Jurisprudence? 48 J. Catholic Legal Studies 269, 296, n. 133 (2009) ("Catholic physicians, but not necessarily hospitals, . . . may be able to invoke [§238n(a)] . . . ."); *cf.* S. 137, 113th Cong., 1st Sess., 2-3 (2013) (as introduced) (Abortion Non-Discrimination Act of 2013, which would amend the definition of "health care entity" in §238n to include "hospitals]," "health insurance plan[s]," and other health care facilities). These provisions are revealing in a way that detracts from one of the Court's main arguments. They show that Congress is not content to rest on the Dictionary Act when it wishes to ensure that particular entities are among those eligible for a religious accommodation.

Moreover, the exemption codified in §238n(a) was not enacted until three years after RFRA's passage. See Omnibus Consolidated Rescissions and Appropriations Act of 1996, §515, 110 Stat. 1321-245. If, as the Court believes, RFRA opened all statutory schemes to religion-based challenges by for-profit corporations, there would be no need for a statute- specific, post-RFRA exemption of this sort.

16. That is not to say that a category of plaintiffs, such as resident aliens, may bring RFRA claims only if this Court expressly "addressed their [free-exercise] rights before *Smith*" *Ante*, at 716. Continuing with the Court's example, resident aliens, unlike corporations, are flesh-and-blood individuals who plainly count as persons sheltered by the First Amendment, see *United States v. Verdugo-Urquidez*, 494 U.S. 259, 271 (1990) (citing *Bridges v. Wixon*, 326 U.S. 135, 148 (1945)), and *a fortiori*, RFRA.

17. I part ways with Justice Kennedy on the context relevant here. He sees it as the employers exercise [of] their religious beliefs within the context of their own closely held, for-profit corporations." *Ante*, at 737 (concurring opinion). See also *ante*, at 733 (opinion of the Court) (similarly concentrating on religious faith of employers without reference to the different beliefs and liberty interests of employees). I see as the relevant context the employers' asserted right to exercise religion within a nationwide program designed to protect against health hazards employees who do not subscribe to their employers' religious beliefs.

18. According to the Court, the Government "concedes" that "nonprofit corporation[s]" are protected by RFRA. *Ante*, at 708. See also *ante*, at 709, 712,718. That is not an accurate description of the Government's position, which encompasses only "churches," "religious institutions," and "religious non-profits." Brief for Respondents in No. 13-356, p. 28 (emphasis added). See also Reply Brief in No. 13-354, p. 8 ("RFRA incorporates the longstanding and common-sense distinction between religious organizations, which sometimes have been accorded accommodations under generally applicable laws in recognition of their accepted religious character, and for- profit corporations organized to do business in the commercial world.").

19. The Court does not even begin to explain how one might go about ascertaining the religious scruples of a corporation where shares are sold to the public. No need to speculate on that, the Court says, for "it seems unlikely" that large corporations "will often assert RFRA claims." *Ante*, at 717. Perhaps so, but as Hobby Lobby's case demonstrates, such claims are indeed pursued by large corporations, employing thousands of persons of different faiths, whose ownership is not diffuse. "Closely held" is not synonymous with "small." Hobby Lobby is hardly the only enterprise of sizable scale that is family owned or closely held. For example, the family-owned candy giant Mars, Inc., takes in $33 billion in revenues and has some 72,000 employees, and closely held Cargill, Inc., takes in more than $136 billion in revenues and employs some 140,000 persons. See Forbes, America's Largest Private Companies 2013, available at http://www.forbes.com/largest-private-companies/.

Nor does the Court offer any instruction on how to resolve the disputes that may crop up among corporate owners over religious values and accommodations. The Court is satisfied that "[s]tate corporate law provides a ready means for resolving any conflicts," *ante*, at 718, but the authorities cited in support of that proposition are hardly helpful. See Del. Code Ann., Tit. 8, § 351 (2011) (certificates of incorporation may specify how the business is managed); 1 J. Cox & T.

Hazen, Treatise on the Law of Corporations § 3:2 (3d ed. 2010) (section entitled "Selecting the state of incorporation"); 3 *id.*, §14:11, p. 48 (observing that "[d]espite the frequency of dissension and deadlock in close corporations, in some states neither legislatures nor courts have provided satisfactory solutions"). And even if a dispute settlement mechanism is in place, how is the arbiter of a religion-based intracorporate controversy to resolve the disagreement, given this Court's instruction that "courts have no business addressing [whether an asserted religious belief] is reasonable," *ante*, at 724?

20. The Court dismisses the argument, advanced by some amici, that the $2,000-per-employee tax charged to certain employers that fail to provide health insurance is less than the average cost of offering health insurance, noting that the Government has not provided the statistics that could support such an argument. See *ante*, at 720-722. The Court overlooks, however, that it is not the Government's obligation to prove that an asserted burden is insubstantial. Instead, it is incumbent upon plaintiffs to demonstrate, in support of a RFRA claim, the substantiality of the alleged burden.

21. The Court levels a criticism that is as wrongheaded as can be. In no way does the dissent "tell the plaintiffs that their beliefs are flawed." *Ante*, at 724. Right or wrong in this domain is a judgment no Member of this Court, or any civil court, is authorized or equipped to make. What the Court must decide is not "the plausibility of a religious claim," *ibid.* (internal quotation marks omitted), but whether accommodating that claim risks depriving others of rights accorded them by the laws of the United States. See *supra*, at 745-746; *infra*, at 765-766.

22. IUDs, which are among the most reliable forms of contraception, generally cost women more than $1,000 when the expenses of the office visit and insertion procedure are taken into account. See Eisenberg, McNicholas, & Peipert, Cost as a Barrier to Long-Acting Reversible Contraceptive (LARC) Use in Adolescents, 52 J. Adolescent Health S59, S60 (2013). See also Winner et al., Effectiveness of Long-Acting Reversible Contraception, 366 New Eng. J. Medicine 1998, 1999 (2012).

23. Although the Court's opinion makes this assumption grudgingly, see *ante*, at 726-728, one Member of the majority recognizes, without reservation, that "the [contraceptive coverage] mandate serves the Government's compelling interest in providing insurance coverage that is necessary to protect the health of female employees." *Ante*, at 737 (opinion of Kennedy, J.).

24. Hobby Lobby's *amicus* National Religious Broadcasters similarly states that, "[g]iven the nature of employers' needs to meet changing economic and staffing circumstances, and to adjust insurance coverage accordingly, the actual benefit of the 'grandfather' exclusion is de minimis and transitory at best." Brief for National Religious Broadcasters in No. 13-354, p. 28.

25. As the Court made clear in *Cutter*, the government's license to grant religion-based exemptions from generally applicable laws is constrained by the Establishment Clause. 544 U.S., at 720-722. "[W]e are a cosmopolitan nation made up of people of almost every conceivable religious preference," *Braunfeld*, 366 U.S., at 606, a "rich mosaic of religious faiths," *Town of Greece v. Galloway*, 572 U.S. 565, 628 (2014) (Kagan, J., dissenting). Consequently, one person's right to free exercise must be kept in harmony with the rights of her fellow citizens, and "some religious practices [must] yield to the common good." *United States v. Lee*, 455 U.S. 252, 259 (1982).

26. *Cf. Ashcroft v. American Civil Liberties Union*, 542 U.S. 656, 666 (2004) (in context of First Amendment Speech Clause challenge to a content-based speech restriction, courts must determine "whether the challenged regulation is the least restrictive means among available, effective alternatives" (emphasis added)).

27. On brief, Hobby Lobby and Conestoga barely addressed the extension solution, which would bracket commercial enterprises with nonprofit religion-based organizations for religious accommodations purposes. The hesitation is understandable, for challenges to the adequacy of the accommodation accorded religious nonprofit organizations are currently judice. See, e.g., *Little Sisters of the Poor Home for the Aged v. Sebelius*, 6 F. Supp. 3d 1225 (Colo. 2013), injunction pending appeal granted, 571 U.S. 1171 (2014). At another point in today's decision, the Court refuses to consider an argument neither "raised below [nor] advanced in this Court by any party," giving Hobby Lobby and Conestoga "[no] opportunity to respond to [that] novel claim." *Ante*, at 721. Yet the Court is content to decide these cases (and these cases only) on the ground that HHS could make an accommodation never suggested in the parties' presentations. RFRA cannot sensibly be read to "requir[e] the government to ... refute each and every conceivable alternative regulation," *United States v. Wilgus*, 638 F. 3d 1274, 1289 (CA10 2011), especially where the alternative on which the Court seizes was not pressed by any challenger.

214 | THE ESSENTIAL RUTH BADER GINSBURG

28. As a sole proprietor, Lee was subject to personal liability for violating the law of general application he opposed. His claim to a religion-based exemption would have been even thinner had he conducted his business as a corporation, thus avoiding personal liability.

29. Congress amended the Social Security Act in response to The amended statute permits Amish sole proprietors and partnerships (but not Amish-owned corporations) to obtain an exemption from the obligation to pay Social Security taxes only for employees who are co-religionists and who likewise seek an exemption and agree to give up their Social Security benefits. See 26 U.S.C. § 3127(a)(2), (b)(1). Thus, employers with sincere religious beliefs have no right to a religion-based exemption that would deprive employees of Social Security benefits without the employee's consent—an exemption analogous to the one Hobby Lobby and Conestoga seek here.

30. Cf. *Tony and Susan Alamo Foundation v. Secretary of Labor*, 471 U.S. 290, 299 (1985) (disallowing religion-based exemption that "would undoubtedly give [the commercial enterprise seeking the exemption] and similar organizations an advantage over their competitors").

31. Religious objections to immunization programs are not hypothetical. See *Phillips v. New York*, 27 F. Supp. 3d 310 (EDNY 2014) (dismissing free exercise challenges to New York's vaccination practices); Liberty Counsel, Compulsory Vaccinations Threaten Religious Freedom (2007), available at http://www.lc.org/media/9980/attachments/memo_ vaccination.pdf.